# *Hearing and Reading, Telling and Writing*

## A Charlotte Mason Language Arts Handbook

by
Sonya Shafer

Hearing and Reading, Telling and Writing: A Charlotte Mason Language Arts Handbook
© 2010, Sonya Shafer

All rights reserved. No part of this work may be reproduced or distributed in any form by any means—graphic, electronic, or mechanical, including photocopying, recording, taping, or storing in information storage and retrieval systems—without written permission from the publisher.

Cover Photo: Ruth Shafer
Cover Design: Ruth Shafer and John Shafer

Published by
Simply Charlotte Mason, LLC
P.O. Box 892
Grayson, Georgia 30017-0892

ISBN 978-1-61634-094-0

SimplyCharlotteMason.com

# Contents

Hearing and Reading, Telling and Writing . . . . . . . . . . . . . . . . . . . . . . . . . . . . . 5
Introduction . . . . . . . . . . . . . . . . . . . . . . . . . . . . . . . . . . . . . . . . . . . . . . . . . . . . 7

## *Part 1: Language Arts Simplified*

Chapter 1: Language Arts . . . . . . . . . . . . . . . . . . . . . . . . . . . . . . . . . . . . . . . . . 11
Chapter 2: Charlotte Mason's Language Arts Program . . . . . . . . . . . . . . . . . 15

## *Part 2: Integrated Methods*

Chapter 3: Good Literature . . . . . . . . . . . . . . . . . . . . . . . . . . . . . . . . . . . . . . 19
Chapter 4: Vocabulary . . . . . . . . . . . . . . . . . . . . . . . . . . . . . . . . . . . . . . . . . . 25
Chapter 5: Reading for Instruction . . . . . . . . . . . . . . . . . . . . . . . . . . . . . . . . 29
Chapter 6: Narration . . . . . . . . . . . . . . . . . . . . . . . . . . . . . . . . . . . . . . . . . . . 43
Chapter 7: Composition . . . . . . . . . . . . . . . . . . . . . . . . . . . . . . . . . . . . . . . . 63
Chapter 8: Reading Aloud . . . . . . . . . . . . . . . . . . . . . . . . . . . . . . . . . . . . . . . 73

## *Part 3: Language Arts Lessons*

Chapter 9: Beginning Reading . . . . . . . . . . . . . . . . . . . . . . . . . . . . . . . . . . . 79
Chapter 10: Copywork and Transcription . . . . . . . . . . . . . . . . . . . . . . . . . . 91
Chapter 11: Dictation . . . . . . . . . . . . . . . . . . . . . . . . . . . . . . . . . . . . . . . . . . 99
Chapter 12: Poetry and Shakespeare . . . . . . . . . . . . . . . . . . . . . . . . . . . . . . 107
Chapter 13: Recitation and Memorization . . . . . . . . . . . . . . . . . . . . . . . . . 119
Chapter 14: English Grammar . . . . . . . . . . . . . . . . . . . . . . . . . . . . . . . . . . 129

## *Appendix*

Proofreading and Reference Skills . . . . . . . . . . . . . . . . . . . . . . . . . . . . . . . . 137
Written Narration/Composition Samples . . . . . . . . . . . . . . . . . . . . . . . . . . 139
Poetry Narration Samples . . . . . . . . . . . . . . . . . . . . . . . . . . . . . . . . . . . . . . 159
Narration Questions that Charlotte Used . . . . . . . . . . . . . . . . . . . . . . . . . . 173
Narration Ideas . . . . . . . . . . . . . . . . . . . . . . . . . . . . . . . . . . . . . . . . . . . . . . 175
Two Mothers' Conversation about Teaching Reading . . . . . . . . . . . . . . . . . 179
A Beginning Reading Lesson Plan . . . . . . . . . . . . . . . . . . . . . . . . . . . . . . . . 183
English Grammar Lessons . . . . . . . . . . . . . . . . . . . . . . . . . . . . . . . . . . . . . . 187

# Hearing and Reading, Telling and Writing

"Our 'find' is that children have a natural aptitude for literary expression which they enjoy in hearing or reading and employ in telling or writing" (Vol. 6, p. 90).

# *Introduction*

In my years of helping other Charlotte Mason homeschoolers, probably the one topic that comes up most often is language arts. I receive questions from "How do you do language arts the Charlotte Mason way?" to "What about composition?" to "How do you teach spelling and vocabulary?" to "Can you recommend a living English grammar book?"

This handbook is the answer to those questions and more. In these pages you will find that Charlotte's approach to language arts is simple, saves time, and uses common sense methods.

It is my hope that having Charlotte's methods and ideas gathered into one place, along with her own words, will provide you with a quick go-to resource that will boost your confidence and reassure you that you have "this language arts thing" covered.

Blessings on you as you encourage your children in hearing and reading, telling and writing.

Excerpts from Charlotte Mason's books are surrounded by quotation marks and accompanied by a reference to which book in the series the excerpt came from.

Vol. 1: Home Education
Vol. 2: Parents and Children
Vol. 3: School Education
Vol. 4: Ourselves
Vol. 5: Formation of Character
Vol. 6: A Philosophy of Education

# Part 1

# Language Arts Simplified

# Chapter 1
## Language Arts

Don't let the fancy term throw you: "language arts." Back in Charlotte Mason's day that term didn't exist. It's simply an educational label that was invented along the way. In fact, let's take the term apart for a moment and think about what it means.

"Art" is a way of communicating an idea, whether it is done through music, paint, sculpture, or dance. The goal of "art" is to communicate an idea.

Now add the word "language" to that concept. The goal of "language arts" is to be able to use a language proficiently in order to communicate an idea.

That's it. Nothing scary or intimidating. Just learning how to communicate ideas through language. You've been teaching language arts to your children naturally since they were born.

## The Parts of Language Arts

Since we want our children to be proficient at communicating ideas through language, we want to make sure we cover all the ways language occurs. So language arts include the four main components of

- Listening,
- Reading,
- Speaking, and
- Writing.

Everything that relates to listening, speaking, reading, and writing in your selected language can be considered part of your language arts program.

Teachers through the years have tried to break down that big goal of "communicating ideas through language" into individual skills to work on (as teachers are apt to do). Most language arts programs will include these specific skills.

| | |
|---|---|
| Alphabet | Listening Skills |
| Phonics/Beginning Reading | Parts of Speech |
| Rhyming Words | Sentence Structure |
| Handwriting | Punctuation |
| Reading Comprehension | Capitalization |
| Writing Composition | Public Speaking |
| Vocabulary | Proofreading |
| Spelling | Grammar |

Reference skills (alphabetizing; using a dictionary, etc.)
Word study (homonyms, synonyms, prefixes, suffixes)

### Notes

*For most of you reading this book, that selected language will be English. So we will work from that viewpoint throughout the rest of this book. If your selected language is other than English, you can apply the same principles to your selected language.*

*Of all the skills listed, the only two I have not found specifically mentioned in Charlotte Mason's writings are proofreading and reference skills. However, Charlotte's principles easily apply to those skills. See page 137 for those ideas.*

# Language Arts

> *Notes*
>
> *Use this chart for reassurance whenever you get concerned that you've left out a specific skill.*

Most traditional language arts programs cover those skills as fifteen or more separate subjects. Charlotte Mason used about half that many subjects and still covered all the skills in an interesting and living way that kept the students' attention and encouraged them to love learning.

What's more, her methods gave balanced coverage to the four main language arts categories: listening, reading, speaking, and writing.

## Language Arts and CM Methods

Are you curious how Charlotte covered the fifteen-plus skills in half as many subjects? Here is a chart of how the various language arts skills are covered in Charlotte Mason methods.

| Language Art | Subject or Skill | CM Method |
| --- | --- | --- |
| Writing | Handwriting | Copywork |
| | Composition | Written narration; Poetry |
| | Spelling | Copywork; Dictation |
| | Punctuation Capitalization | Copywork; Dictation; Grammar |
| | Parts of speech; Sentence structure | Grammar; Dictation |
| | Vocabulary | Copywork; Written narration; Dictation |
| Reading | How to read (alphabet, phonics, sight words, etc.) | Beginning reading |
| | Reading comprehension | Narration (both oral and written); Reading for Instruction; Poetry |
| | Vocabulary | Copywork; Dictation; Narration; Reading for Instruction; Poetry |
| Speaking | Public speaking | Oral narration; Recitation |
| | Sentence structure | Grammar; Narration; Recitation |
| | Vocabulary | Narration; Recitation |
| Listening | Comprehension | Narration; Dictation; Recitation; Reading for Instruction; Poetry |
| | Rhyming words | Beginning reading; Poetry |

Or looking at it from the other perspective, the chart on page 13 lists the Charlotte Mason methods and the language arts skills that each one teaches.

# Language Arts

| CM Method | Subject or Skill | Language Art |
|---|---|---|
| Copywork | Handwriting; Punctuation; Capitalization; Vocabulary; Spelling | Writing<br>Reading |
| Narration | Reading comprehension; Listening comprehension; Public speaking (oral narration); Composition (written narration); Vocabulary; Sentence structure | Reading<br>Writing<br>Speaking<br>Listening |
| Prepared Dictation | Vocabulary; Spelling; Sentence structure; Punctuation; Capitalization; Listening comprehension | Writing<br>Reading<br>Listening |
| Grammar | Punctuation; Capitalization; Parts of speech; Sentence structure | Writing<br>Speaking |
| Beginning Reading | Rhyming words; How to read (alphabet, phonics, sight words, etc.) | Reading<br>Listening |
| Reading for Instruction | Reading comprehension; Vocabulary | Reading<br>Listening |
| Recitation | Public speaking; Vocabulary; Sentence structure; Listening comprehension | Speaking<br>Listening |
| Poetry | Rhyming words; Composition; Reading comprehension; Listening comprehension; Vocabulary | Listening<br>Speaking<br>Reading<br>Writing |

*Use this chart to remind yourself how rich Charlotte's methods are.*

One of Charlotte's main strategies was to integrate language arts studies into other subjects, rather than pulling them out as separate skills. So as the students were doing History, for example, they were also practicing listening, reading, speaking, and writing, because Charlotte used the methods of Reading for Instruction and Narration for History.

This strategy of integrating language arts has three great benefits.

• It encourages consistency. When the same expectations are carried across all subjects, consistency is strengthened. A student will progress in his language arts skills if he is expected to use them just as much in his History lesson as in a separate, say, Reading Comprehension lesson.

• It saves time and money. By using Charlotte's methods of integrating language arts, you can cover the fifteen-plus skills in half as many subjects, and you don't

## Notes

have to purchase separate materials for all the skills.

• It maintains the student's interest. Integrating language arts into other subjects means that your child will be working with living books and material he is already interested in. Plus, he will gain a sense of competency as he practices language arts in "real" settings, rather than in isolated exercises or lists.

Charlotte believed that children are much more capable of dealing with language than most adults give them credit for. And her methods communicated that idea to each child.

# Chapter 2
# Charlotte Mason's Language Arts Program

A Charlotte Mason language arts program is not complicated. Here is the simple breakdown grade by grade. Notice which methods are integrated into other subjects that you are teaching anyway, and which methods are designed for specific language arts lessons. You will find what Charlotte said, including the practical how-to's for each section of the chart, in the rest of this book.

| Grade 1 | 2 | 3 | 4 | 5 | 6 | 7 | 8 | 9 | 10 | 11 | 12 |
|---|---|---|---|---|---|---|---|---|---|---|---|
| **Integrated into Regular Subjects** (like History, Geography, Bible, Science, Literature, etc.) ||||||||||||
| **Basic Principles for all Grades:** Good literature, not twaddle; Vocabulary naturally through context ||||||||||||
| **Reading for Instruction:** Students this age have their lesson books read to them. ||| **Reading for Instruction:** Students this age read their lesson books for themselves. |||||||||
| **Oral Narration:** Naturally includes reading comprehension; preparation and practice for composition. ||||||||||||
| | | | **Written Narration:** Naturally includes reading comprehension; basis for composition guidance. |||||||||
| | | | Practice Reading Aloud ||||||||| 
| **Specific Language Arts Lessons** ||||||||||||
| **Beginning Reading:** Includes rhymes, phonics, and sight words; practice reading aloud. ||||||||||||
| **Copywork and Transcription:** Naturally includes capitalization, punctuation, beginning spelling awareness. ||| **Dictation:** Includes capitalization, punctuation, spelling; reinforces good writing style and English grammar |||||||||
| **Poetry:** Includes rhymes, memorization, and recitation. ||||||||||||
| | | | Shakespeare ||||||||| 
| | | | English Grammar |||||||||

# Part 2

# Integrated Methods

# Chapter 3
# Good Literature

*Notes*

*Good literature is a basic principle that should be integrated into regular subjects.*

"My favorite subject is history."

Jennie was floored. Did those words just come out of her daughter's mouth?

Jennie's mind flipped back to the day she decided to homeschool. She had a few concerns, but a big one was that she didn't know much about history or geography. In fact, she barely remembered anything from her school years in those two subjects. "How can I teach my children something I don't know myself?" she had asked her husband.

"You will learn right along with them," he had replied.

Fast forward to the day she heard about the Charlotte Mason Method and started using the best living books she could find in order to teach history and geography and literature and several other subjects.

*That's what made the difference,* she thought. *I didn't learn much at all from the textbooks we used when I was in school, but these wonderful living books have taught my children—and me—a lot. Much more than just history, in fact. Their language skills, vocabulary, writing skills, and reading comprehension have all been shaped by the best writings of the best minds.*

Jennie caught her daughter's eye and smiled. *We have come a long way and had a very pleasant trip!*

## Charlotte's Thoughts on Good Literature

### General Guidelines for All Grades
### 1. Give your child the best books you can find, not twaddle.

"For the children? They must grow up upon the best. There must never be a period in their lives when they are allowed to read or listen to twaddle or reading-made-easy. There is never a time when they are unequal to worthy thoughts, well put; inspiring tales, well told. Let Blake's 'Songs of Innocence' represent their standard in poetry; De Foe and Stevenson, in prose; and we shall train a race of readers who will demand *literature*—that is, the fit and beautiful expression of inspiring ideas and pictures of life" (Vol. 2, p. 263).

*Twaddle is talking down to a child and assuming he cannot understand.*

"The subject of 'Children's Literature' has been well threshed out, and only one thing remains to be said,—children have no natural appetite for twaddle, and a special literature for children is probably far less necessary than the book-sellers would have us suppose. Out of any list of 'the hundred best books,' I believe that seventy-five would be well within the range of children of eight or nine. They would delight in *Rasselas*, *Eöthen* would fascinate them as much as *Robinson Crusoe*, the *Faëry Queen*, with its allegory and knightly adventures and sense of free moving in woodland scenery, would exactly fall in with their humour. What they want is to be brought into touch with living thought of the best, and their intellectual life feeds upon it with little meddling on our part" (Vol. 3, p. 122).

**"For the children? They must grow up upon the best."**

## Good Literature

### Notes

"How injurious then is our habit of depreciating children; we water their books down and drain them of literary flavour, because we wrongly suppose that children cannot understand what we understand ourselves" (Vol. 6, p. 304).

**2. Good literature should help your child see the scenes in his imagination and "meet" the people in the story line.**

"Observe, there is a poor place close at hand, where pictures are painted for you and where people are introduced; but you cannot see the pictures with your eyes shut, and the people do not live and act in your thoughts; there is as much difference between this region outside and that within the Kingdom of Literature as there is between a panorama and the real, beautiful country it is intended to portray. It is a horrible waste of time to wander about in this outside region, yet many people spend a large part of their lives there, and never once get within sight of the beauties and delights within the Kingdom of Literature" (Vol. 4, Book 1, p. 40).

**3. Good literature gives a sense of delight in the words alone and how they are used.**

"There is another test, besides the two of scenes that you see and people that you know, which distinguishes Literature from the barren land on its borders; and if he is to apply this test, Intellect must keep his Beauty Sense always by his side. Read over, and see if you find a difference of flavour, shall I say, between the two passages that follow. Try if the first gives you a sense of delight in the words alone, without any thought of the meaning of them, if the very words seem to sing to you;—

> 'That time of year thou mayst in me behold
>     When yellow leaves, or none, or few, do hang
> Upon those boughs which shake against the cold,
>     Bare, ruined choirs, where late the sweet birds sang.'

"Now read the next passage;—

> 'Household Deities!
> Then only shall be happiness on earth
> When man shall feel your sacred power and love
> Your tranquil joys.'

Can you perceive that, though the second passage is true, thoughtful, and well expressed, it just misses a certain charm in the wording which makes words go home to our heart with living power? If you cannot see any difference in value between these two passages, perhaps you will do so some day" (Vol. 4, Book 1, pp. 40, 41).

**4. Good literature contains fitting words, all necessary to convey the precise meaning, that give a sense of fresh, musical delight.**

"The thing is, to keep your eye upon words and wait to feel their force and beauty; and, when words are so fit that no other words can be put in their places, so few that none can be left out without spoiling the sense, and so fresh and musical that they delight you, then you may be sure that you are reading Literature, whether in prose or poetry. A great deal of delightful literature can be recognised only by this test" (Vol. 4, Book 1, p. 41).

---

"When words are so fit that no other words can be put in their places, so few that none can be left out without spoiling the sense, and so fresh and musical that they delight you, then you may be sure that you are reading Literature."

### 5. The goal of literary studies is to give a living picture of a time period or concept, not just detailed facts.

"The object of children's literary studies is not to give them precise information as to who wrote what in the reign of whom?—but to give them a sense of the spaciousness of the days, not only of great Elizabeth, but of all those times of which poets, historians and the makers of tales, have left us living pictures" (Vol. 6, p. 184).

"Are we teaching geography? The child discovers with the explorer, journeys with the traveller, receives impressions new and vivid from some other mind which is immediately receiving these impressions; not after they have been made stale and dull by a process of filtering through many intermediate minds, and have found at last their way into a little text-book. Is he learning history? his concern is not with strings of names and of dates, nor with nice little reading-made-easy stories, brought down, as we mistakenly say, to the level of his comprehension; we recognise that his power of comprehension is at least equal to our own, and that it is only his ignorance of the attendant circumstances we have to deal with as luminously as we can.

"Books must be Living.—We recognise that history for him is, to live in the lives of those strong personalities which at any given time impress themselves most upon their age and country. This is not the sort of thing to be got out of nice little history books for children, whether 'Little Arthur's,' or somebody's 'Outlines.' We take the child to the living sources of history—a child of seven is fully able to comprehend *Plutarch*, in Plutarch's own words (translated), without any diluting and with little explanation. Give him living thought in this kind, and you make possible the co-operation of the living Teacher. The child's progress is by leaps and bounds, and you wonder why" (Vol. 2, p. 278).

### 6. The Bible is just as valuable as literature from ancient Greece or Rome—more so, since it reveals God to man.

"But it is singular that so few educationalists recognise that the Bible is not a single book, but a classic literature of wonderful beauty and interest; that, apart from its Divine sanctions and religious teaching, from all that we understand by 'Revelation,' the Bible, as a mere instrument of education, is, at the very least, as valuable as the classics of Greece or Rome. Here is poetry, the rhythm of which soothes even the jaded brain past taking pleasure in any other. Here is history, based on such broad, clear lines, such dealing of slow and sure and even-handed justice to the nations, such stories of national sins and national repentances, that the student realises, as from no other history, the solidarity of the race, the brotherhood, and, if we may call it so, the individuality of the nations. Here is philosophy which, of all the philosophies which have been propounded, is alone adequate to the interpretation of human life. We say not a word here of that which is the *raison d'être* of the Bible, its teaching of religion, its revelation of God to man; but to urge only one point more, all the literatures of the world put together utterly fail to give us a system of ethics, in precept and example, motive and sanction, complete as that to which we have been born as our common inheritance in the Bible" (Vol. 2, p. 104).

---

**Notes**

Raison d'être *means "reason for being."*

"Books must be Living."

## Good Literature

### Grades 1–6

*7. Your child should have read some literature by the time he is twelve.*

"In Language, by twelve, they should have a fair knowledge of English grammar, and should have read some literature" (Vol. 3, p. 235).

### Grades 7–12

*8. Don't introduce critical and analytic studies until your child has been thoroughly furnished with the ideas of great literature and has begun of his own accord to compare and examine critically.*

"This invective discovers a mistake in our educational methods. From the time a child is able to parse an English sentence till he can read Thucydides, his instruction is entirely critical and analytic. Does he read 'The Tempest,' the entrancing whole is not allowed to sink into, and become a part of him, because he is vexed about the 'vexed Bermoothes' and the like. His attention is occupied with linguistic criticism, not especially useful, and, from one point of view, harmful to him because it is distracting. It is as though one listened to 'Lycidas,' beautifully read, subject to the impertinence of continual interruptions in the way of question and explanation. We miss the general principle that critical studies are out of place until the mind is so 'throughly furnished' with ideas that, of its own accord, it compares and examines critically" (Vol. 5, pp. 293, 294).

## Questions to Ask on Good Literature

### General Guidelines for All Grades

- Am I seeking to give my child the best books I can find, not twaddle?
- Do the books I am using help my child see the scenes in his imagination and "meet" the people in the story line?
- Do the books I am using with my child give a sense of delight in how the words are used?
- Do the books I am using contain fitting words, few and precise, that give a sense of fresh delight?
- Do the books I am using give a living picture of the time period or concept, not just detailed facts?
- Do I consider the Bible to be the most valuable literature, since it reveals God to man?

### Grades 1–6

- Do I have plans for my child to read some literature before he is twelve?

### Grades 7–12

- Am I delaying critical analysis of literature until my child has been thoroughly furnished with the ideas of great literature first and has begun to analyze them on his own?

---

**Notes**

"All the literatures of the world put together utterly fail to give us a system of ethics, in precept and example, motive and sanction, complete as that to which we have been born as our common inheritance in the Bible."

## More Quotes on Good Literature

"Literature adds to reality, it does not simply describe it. It enriches the necessary competencies that daily life requires and provides; and in this respect, it irrigates the deserts that our lives have already become."—C. S. Lewis

"Literature is my Utopia. Here I am not disenfranchised. No barrier of the senses shuts me out from the sweet, gracious discourses of my book friends. They talk to me without embarrassment or awkwardness."—Helen Keller

"The things I want to know are in books; my best friend is the man who'll get me a book I ain't read."—Abraham Lincoln

"The man who does not read good books is no better than the man who can't."— Mark Twain

> *Notes*
>
> "The thing is, to keep your eye upon words and wait to feel their force and beauty."

# Chapter 4
# *Vocabulary*

"Have you noticed Gracie's new phrase lately?" Luke asked his mom.

Linda thought for a moment. "Oh, yes. She told me yesterday that she 'assumed' her toy dog couldn't feel her petting it. Is that what you mean?"

"Yes," grinned Luke. "She's 'assumed' several more things since then."

"It seems like she's using the word correctly," Linda replied.

"Every time," said Luke. "I just wondered whether you taught it to her."

Linda laughed. "No, not me. She must have picked it up from hearing us say it in conversations or read it aloud. You used to do that all the time when you were little."

"Actually, Mom, I still do," Luke admitted. "Just yesterday at soccer practice, I was the only guy on the team who knew what 'gregious' means. I have no idea where I learned it; must have been in a book I read."

## Charlotte's Thoughts on Vocabulary

### *General Guidelines for All Grades*

**1. Use everyday situations to increase your child's vocabulary.**

" 'Find out all you can about that cottage at the foot of the hill; but do not pry about too much.' Soon they are back, and there is a crowd of excited faces, and a hubbub of tongues, and random observations are shot breathlessly into the mother's ear. 'There are bee-hives.' 'We saw a lot of bees going into one.' 'There is a long garden.' 'Yes, and there are sunflowers in it.' 'And hen-and-chicken daisies and pansies.' 'And there's a great deal of a pretty blue flower with rough leaves, mother; what do you suppose it is?' 'Borage for the bees, most likely; they are very fond of it.' 'Oh, and there are apple and pear and plum trees on one side; there's a little path up the middle, you know.' 'On which hand side are the fruit trees?' 'The right—no, the left; let me see, which is my thimble-hand? Yes, it is the right-hand side.' 'And there are potatoes and cabbages, and mint and things on the other side.' 'Where are the flowers, then?' 'Oh, they are just the borders, running down each side of the path.' 'But we have not told mother about the wonderful apple tree; I should think there are a million apples on it, all ripe and rosy!' 'A *million*, Fanny?' 'Well, a great many, mother; I don't know how many.' And so on, indefinitely; the mother getting by degrees a complete description of the cottage and its garden.

"This is all play to the children, but the mother is doing invaluable work; she is training their powers of observation and expression, increasing their vocabulary and their range of ideas by giving them the name and the uses of an object at the right moment,—when they ask, 'What is it?' and 'What is it for?' " (Vol. 1, pp. 46, 47).

---

**Notes**

*Vocabulary through context is a basic principle that should be integrated into regular subjects.*

"She is training their powers of observation and expression, increasing their vocabulary and their range of ideas by giving them the name and the uses of an object at the right moment."

*Vocabulary*

## Notes

**Pari passu** *means "hand-in-hand."*

*A Form is somewhat similar to a Grade.*

"A child unconsciously gets the meaning of a new word from the context, if not the first time he meets with it, then the second or the third."

*2. As your child learns more about some thing, he will naturally desire the vocabulary to express his knowledge.*

"Set him face to face with a *thing*, and he is twenty times as quick as you are in knowing all about it; knowledge of things flies to the mind of a child as steel filings to magnet. And, *pari passu* with his knowledge of things, his vocabulary grows; for it is a law of the mind that what we know, we struggle to express. This fact accounts for many of the apparently aimless questions of children; they are in quest, not of knowledge, but of *words* to express the knowledge they have" (Vol. 1, pp. 67, 68).

*3. Do not pester your child to define words as he is reading.*

"When a child is reading, he should not be teased with questions as to the meaning of what he has read, the signification of this word or that; what is annoying to older people is equally annoying to children. Besides, it is not of the least consequence that they should be able to give the meaning of every word they read. A knowledge of meanings, that is, an ample and correct vocabulary, is only arrived at in one way—by the habit of reading" (Vol. 1, p. 228).

*4. Children discover the meanings of words from the context of what they are reading.*

"A child unconsciously gets the meaning of a new word from the context, if not the first time he meets with it, then the second or the third: but he is on the look-out, and will find out for himself the sense of any expression he does not understand" (Vol. 1, p. 228).

"A child's intercourse must always be with good books, the best that we can find. Of course, we have always known that this is the right thing for children in cultivated homes, but what about those in whose dwellings books are little known? One of the wise teachers in Gloucestershire notes that a recognition of two things is necessary in dealing with this problem. First, that,—

" 'To explain the meaning of words destroys interest in the story and annoys the child. Second, that in many instances it is unnecessary. Although a child's dictionary knowledge of words is lacking it does not follow that the meaning of a sentence or paragraph is unknown to him . . . . neither is the correct employment of the words beyond him in writing or narrating. Two examples of this power to sense the meaning were observed last term. There is a particular boy in Form IIB who has not hitherto been looked upon as possessing high intelligence. Classified by age he ought to be two Forms higher. Last term in taking the story of Romulus and Remus, I found that in power of narrating and degree of understanding (that is, of 'sensing' a paragraph and either translating it into his vocabulary or in using the words read to him) he stood above the others and also above the majority in the next higher Form' " (Vol. 6, p. 51).

*5. Most children do not need formal vocabulary lessons; they pick up new words easily in the course of their reading and discussions.*

"*Punch* has hit off the state of the case. 'Come and see the puff-puff, dear.' 'Do you mean the *locomotive*, grandmamma?' As a matter of fact, the child of four and five has a wider, more exact vocabulary in everyday use than that employed by his elders and betters, and is constantly adding to this vocabulary with surprising quickness; *ergo*, to give a child of this class a vocabulary is no part of direct education. Again, we know that nothing escapes the keen scrutiny of the little people. It is not their perceptive powers we have to train, but the habit of methodical observation and accurate record" (Vol. 2, p. 226).

### 6. Definitions or explanations can be given if your child asks for them.

"We depreciate children in another way. We are convinced that they cannot understand a literary vocabulary so we explain and paraphrase to our own heart's content but not to theirs. Educated mothers know that their children can read anything and do not offer explanations unless they are asked for them" (Vol. 6, p. 75).

"No explanation will really help him, and explanations of words and phrases spoil the text and should not be attempted unless children ask, What does so and so mean?" (Vol. 6, p. 192).

### 7. If your child has a limited vocabulary, due to a language delay or some other extenuating reason, you can increase his vocabulary little by little by teaching him to add adjectives and prepositional phrases to his statements.

"Because the children that he had to deal with had a limited vocabulary, and untrained observing powers, Pestalozzi taught them to see and then to say: 'I see a hole in the carpet. I see a small hole in the carpet. I see a small round hole in the carpet. I see a small round hole with a black edge in the carpet,' and so on; and such training may be good for such children" (Vol. 2, p. 226).

### 8. An education based on living books and narration results in a copious vocabulary.

"Children, I think, all children, so taught express themselves in forcible and fluent English and use a copious vocabulary" (Vol. 6, p. 28).

"I would have children taught *to read* before they learn the mechanical arts of reading and writing; and they learn delightfully; they give perfect attention to paragraph or page read to them and are able to relate the matter point by point, *in their own words*; but they demand classical English and cannot learn to read in this sense upon anything less. They begin their 'schooling' in 'letters' at six, and begin at the same time to learn mechanical reading and writing. A child does not lose by spending a couple of years in acquiring these because he is meanwhile 'reading' the Bible, history, geography, tales, with close attention and a remarkable power of reproduction, or rather, of translation into his own language; he is acquiring a copious vocabulary and the habit of consecutive speech. In a word, he is an educated child from the first, and his power of dealing with books, with several books in the course of a morning's 'school,' increases with his age" (Vol. 6, p. 30).

"Our 'find' is that children have a natural aptitude for literary expression which they enjoy in hearing or reading and employ in telling or writing. We might have guessed this long ago. All those speeches and sayings of untamed warriors and savage potentates which the historians have preserved for us, critics have declined as showing too much cultivated rhetoric to have been possible for any but highly

### Notes

**Punch** *was a British magazine.*

**Ergo** *means "therefore."*

*Children ages six to eight "read" their books by listening to the teacher read to them.*

"Educated mothers know that their children can read anything and do not offer explanations unless they are asked for them."

educated persons. But the time is coming when we shall perceive that only minds like those of children are capable of producing thoughts so fresh and so finely expressed. This natural aptitude for literature, or, shall we say, rhetoric, which overcomes the disabilities of a poor vocabulary without effort, should direct the manner of instruction we give, ruling out the talky-talky of the oral lesson and the lecture; ruling out, equally, compilations and text-books; and placing books in the hands of children and only those which are more or less literary in character that is, which have the terseness and vividness proper to literary work. The natural desire for knowledge does the rest and the children feed and grow" (Vol. 6, pp. 90, 91).

"I have no doubt that some of my readers are interested in the work we are doing in Elementary schools,—a work the more astonishing because children who have little vocabulary to begin with, no trace of literary background, show themselves able to hear or read a work of literary value and after a single reading to narrate pages with spirit and accuracy, not hedging at the longest names nor muddling complicated statements" (Vol. 6, p. 268).

## Questions to Ask about Vocabulary

### General Guidelines for All Grades

- Am I trying to use everyday situations to increase my child's vocabulary naturally?
- Do I understand that just because my child may not know a particular word, he probably still knows the concept?
- Am I being careful not to ask my child to define words as he is reading?
- Am I confident that my child will discover the meaning of words from the context of what he reads and hears?
- Do I define or explain words when my child asks me to?
- For language delayed children: Am I encouraging my child to gradually increase his vocabulary by adding adjectives and prepositional phrases to his statements a little at a time?
- Do I understand how using living books and narration can encourage a copious vocabulary?

## Other Quotes about Vocabulary

"We don't just borrow words; on occasion, English has pursued other languages down alleyways to beat them unconscious and rifle their pockets for new vocabulary."—Booker T. Washington

"A vocabulary of truth and simplicity will be of service throughout your life."—Winston Churchill

"He is acquiring a copious vocabulary and the habit of consecutive speech."

# Chapter 5
# *Reading for Instruction*

"What are you mumbling about over there?" David asked from his recliner.

"I'm sorry. Was I disturbing your newspaper?" Lynn replied. "I'm trying out a sort of educational challenge."

David folded his newspaper in his lap. "What kind of challenge?"

"Well, I'm testing a method that is supposed to help you remember what you read," explained Lynn. "I just read a chapter in this book, and now I'm trying to recall what it said, in order, and explain it to myself, along with my own thoughts on the matter. It's not as easy as it sounds."

"I wouldn't think it would be that difficult."

Lynn's eyes sparkled. "You are welcome to try too, you know. Tell me all the points in the last newspaper article you read and what you think about them."

David was silent for a few moments. "How about if we use your book for this first test? We can use my newspaper tomorrow as a follow up."

"That's fine," Lynn chuckled. "Actually, this is only the first part of the test. I'm going over this chapter in my head now before bed, then I'm supposed to see how much I remember tomorrow. That will be the real test, I think."

"You said this was an educational challenge. Does that mean it ties in to the kids' homeschooling somehow?" asked David.

"The children will have to do the same thing with their school books," Lynn explained. "They'll read a passage one time and then narrate it to me in their own words. Then I'll also test their long-term retention by asking them to narrate certain parts after about twelve weeks."

"I get it." David nodded and set the newspaper on the side table. "Okay, tell me your narration now, and then I'll have something to compare it to when you tell me all you can remember tomorrow. This ought to be interesting."

## Charlotte's Thoughts on Reading for Instruction

### *General Guidelines for All Grades*

*1. A habit of reading for instruction is different from a love of reading.*

"We all know that desultory reading is delightful and incidentally profitable but is not *education* whose concern is *knowledge*. That is, the mind of the desultory reader only rarely makes the act of appropriation which is necessary before the matter we read becomes personal knowledge. We must read in order to know or we do not know by reading" (Vol. 6, p. 13).

"Sir Philip Magnus, in a recent address on Headwork and Handwork in Elementary Schools, says some things worth pondering. Perhaps he gives his workshop too big a place in the school of the future, but certainly he puts his finger on the weak point in the work of both elementary and secondary schools—the

---

**Notes**

*Reading for instruction is a basic principle that should be integrated into regular subjects.*

*Reading for instruction means reading with the mind fully engaged so as to learn something.*

"We must read in order to know or we do not know by reading."

## Notes

'getting by heart scraps of knowledge, fragments of so-called science.' And we are with him in the emphasis he lays upon *reading and writing*; it is through these that even school 'studies' shall become 'for delight.' Writing, of course, comes of reading, and nobody can write well who does not read much. Sir Philip Magnus says, speaking of the schools of the future:—'We shall no longer require children to learn by constant repetition, scraps of history, geography, and grammar, nor try to teach them fragments of so-called science. The daily hours devoted to these tasks will be applicable to the creation of mental aptitudes, and will be utilised in showing the children how to obtain knowledge for themselves. . . . In future the main function of education will be to train our hands and our sense organs and intellectual faculties, so that we may be placed in a position of advantage for seeking knowledge. . . . The scope of the lessons will be enlarged. Children will be taught to read in order that they may desire to read, and to write that they may be able to write. . . . It will be the teacher's aim to create in his pupils a desire for knowledge, and consequently a love of reading, and to cultivate in them, by a proper selection of lessons, the pleasure which reading may be made to yield. The main feature of the reading lesson will be to show the use of books, how they may be consulted to ascertain what other people have said or done, and how they may be read for the pleasure they afford. The storing of the memory with facts is no part of elementary school work. . . . It is not enough that a child should learn how to write, he must know *what* to write. He must learn to describe clearly what he has heard or seen, to transfer to written language his sense-impressions, and to express concisely his own thoughts.'

"We should like to add a word to Sir Philip Magnus's conception, emphasising the *habit* of reading as a chief acquirement of school life. It is only those who have read who do read" (Vol. 3, pp. 232–234).

### 2. Reading for instruction is foundational to learning.

"There is only one way of learning, and the intelligent persons who can talk well on many subjects and the expert in one learn in the one way, that is, *they read to know*" (Vol. 6, p. 14).

"People are naturally divided into those who read and think and those who do not read or think; and the business of schools is to see that all their scholars shall belong to the former class; it is worth while to remember that thinking is inseparable from reading which is concerned with the content of a passage and not merely with the printed matter" (Vol. 6, p. 31).

"But the mind was a deceiver ever. Every teacher knows how a class will occupy itself diligently by the hour and accomplish nothing, even though the boys think they have been reading. We all know how ill we could stand an examination on the daily papers over which we pore. Details fail us, we can say,—'Did you see such and such an article?' but are not able to outline its contents. We try to remedy this vagueness in children by making them take down, and get up, notes of a given lesson: but we accomplish little. The mind appears to have an outer court into which matter can be taken and again expelled without ever having entered the inner place where personality dwells. Here we have the secret of learning by rote, a purely mechanical exercise of which no satisfactory account has been given, but which leaves the patient, or pupil, unaffected. Most teachers know the dreariness of piles of exercises into which no stray note of personality has escaped. Now there is a natural provision against this mere skimming of the ground by the educational plough. Give children the sort of knowledge that they are fitted to assimilate, served in a literary medium, and they will pay great attention" (Vol. 6, p. 257).

**3. Reading for instruction is not a separate subject. Lesson books in geography, history, science, and literature should give your child practice in reading for instruction.**

"Geography, English history, French history, and tales should afford exercise in careful reading" (Vol. 3, p. 307).

"Most schools give from eleven in the lowest to eight hours in the highest Forms to 'English' that is, from twenty to sixteen consecutive readings a week might be afforded in a wide selection of books,—literature, history, economics, etc.,—books read with the concentrated attention which makes a single reading suffice" (Vol. 6, p. 86)

"Their reading should be carefully ordered, for the most part in historical sequence; they should read to *know*, whether it be *Robinson Crusoe* or Huxley's *Physiography*" (Vol. 6, p. 341).

**4. To encourage reading for instruction, make sure your child's lesson books (and other books) are interesting, on level for his intelligence, and written with literary power, not twaddle.**

"A child has not begun his education until he has acquired the habit of reading to himself, with interest and pleasure, books fully on a level with his intelligence. I am speaking now of his lesson-books, which are all too apt to be written in a style of insufferable twaddle, probably because they are written by persons who have never chanced to meet a child. All who know children know that they do not talk twaddle and do not like it, and prefer that which appeals to their understanding. Their lesson-books should offer matter for their reading, whether aloud or to themselves; therefore they should be written with literary power. As for the matter of these books, let us remember that children can take in ideas and principles, whether the latter be moral or mechanical, as quickly and clearly as we do ourselves (perhaps more so); but detailed processes, lists and summaries, blunt the edge of a child's delicate mind" (Vol. 1, p. 229).

"This is what we have established in many thousands of cases, even in those of dull and backward children, that any person can understand any book of the right calibre (a question to be determined mainly by the age of the young reader); that the book must be in literary form; that children and young persons require no elucidation of what they read; that their attention does not flag while so engaged; that they master a few pages at a single reading so thoroughly that they can 'tell it back' at the time or months later whether it be the *Pilgrim's Progress* or one of Bacon's Essays or Shakespeare's plays" (Vol. 6, pp. 291, 292).

"It would, of course, be a foolish waste of time to give this sort of careful reading to a novel that has neither literary nor moral worth, and therefore it is well to confine

---

**Notes**

*See page 19 for more on selecting good books. You can also check out the free CM Bookfinder and SCM Curriculum Guide for suggestions at SimplyCharlotteMason.com.*

"A child has not begun his education until he has acquired the habit of reading to himself, with interest and pleasure, books fully on a level with his intelligence."

# Reading for Instruction

## Notes

*Charlotte was referring to Dobbin and Amelia in* Vanity Fair.

ourselves to the best—to novels that we can read over many times, each time with increased pleasure. The superficial way in which people read is illustrated by the fact that ninety-nine out of a hundred run away with the notion that Thackeray presents us with Amelia as an ideal woman; while few extract the solemn moral of the tale—that a man cannot give to a woman more than she is worth; and that Dobbin, the faithful Dobbin, found his life at last, not in Amelia, but in his books and his daughter. It is well that we should choose our authors with judgment, as we choose our friends, and then wait upon them respectfully to hear what they have to say to us" (Vol. 4, Book 2, p. 73).

"In the same way, we must be just in what we think about books. Trashy books are not worth the trouble of thinking about, and therefore they are not worth reading; but a book that is worth reading, whether it be a novel or a homily, contains the best thought of the writer, and we can only get at his meaning by serious thinking.

"As a fact, the books which make us think, the poems which we ponder, the lives of men which we consider, are of more use to us than volumes of good counsel. We read what boys call 'good books,' thinking how good they are, and how good we are to read them! Then it all goes, because the writer has put what he had to say so plainly that we have not had to think for ourselves; and it seems to be a law in the things of life and mind that we do not get anything for our own unless we work for it. It is a case of lightly come, lightly go. That is why we are told of our Lord that 'without a parable spake He not unto them.' He told the people stories which they might allow to pass lightly through their minds as an interest of the moment, or which they might think upon, form opinions upon, and find in them a guide to the meaning of their lives" (Vol. 4, Book 1, pp. 183, 184).

### 5. Students who have the habit of reading with absolute attention can cover more ground in fewer hours.

"Given absolute attention, and we can do much with four hundred hours a year (1,600 hours in our four years' course) but only if we go to work with a certainty that the young students crave knowledge of what we call the 'humanities,' that they read with absolute attention and that, having read, they *know*" (Vol. 6, p. 124).

### 6. Your child may not take naturally to getting instruction from good classical literature, because it requires more effort than what is commonly required in schools.

"They must be educated up to it. Some children, by right of descent, take to books as ducks to the water; but delight in a fine thought, well set, does not come by nature. Moreover, it is not the sort of thing that the training of the schools commonly aims at; to turn out men and women with enough exact knowledge for the occasions of life, and with wits on the alert for chances of promotion, that is what most schools pretend to, and, indeed, do, accomplish. The contention of scholars is, that a classical education does more, turns out men with intellects cultivated *and* trained, who are awake to every refinement of thought, and yet ready for action. But the press and hurry of our times and the clamour for *useful* knowledge are driving classical culture out of the field; and parents will have to make up their minds, not only that they must supplement the moral training of

"They must be educated up to it. Some children, by right of descent, take to books as ducks to the water; but delight in a fine thought, well set, does not come by nature."

the school, but must supply the intellectual culture, without which knowledge may be power, but is not pleasure, nor the means of pleasure" (Vol. 5, pp. 213, 214).

### 7. Select your child's lesson books carefully; they should convey that knowledge is attractive and reading is delightful.

"A child has not begun his education until he has acquired the habit of reading to himself, with interest and pleasure, books fully on a level with his intelligence. I am speaking now of his lesson-books, which are all too apt to be written in a style of insufferable twaddle, probably because they are written by persons who have never chanced to meet a child. All who know children know that they do not talk twaddle and do not like it, and prefer that which appeals to their understanding. Their lesson-books should offer matter for their reading, whether aloud or to themselves; therefore they should be written with literary power. As for the matter of these books, let us remember that children can take in ideas and principles, whether the latter be moral or mechanical, as quickly and clearly as we do ourselves (perhaps more so); but detailed processes, lists and summaries, blunt the edge of a child's delicate mind. Therefore, the selection of their first lesson-books is a matter of grave importance, because it rests with these to give children the idea that knowledge is supremely attractive and that reading is delightful. Once the habit of reading his lesson-books with delight is set up in a child, his education is—not completed, but—ensured" (Vol. 1, p. 229).

### 8. Introduce the author to your child and get out of the way.

"From their earliest days they should get the habit of reading literature which they should take hold of for themselves, much or little, in their own way. As the object of every writer is to explain himself in his own book, the child and the author must be trusted together, without the intervention of the middle-man. What his author does not tell him he must go without knowing for the present. No explanation will really help him, and explanations of words and phrases spoil the text and should not be attempted unless children ask" (Vol. 6, pp. 191, 192).

"Children should read books, not about books and about authors" (Vol. 6, p. 341).

"The direct and immediate impact of great minds upon his own mind is necessary to the education of a child. Most of us can get into touch with original minds chiefly through books" (Vol. 6, p. 303).

### 9. Encourage your child to read the Bible itself for instruction.

"How, then, shall we study our Bible, bearing in mind that our aim is not textual criticism, or even textual knowledge, but the knowledge of God?

"The interpreter is too much with us. We lean on him—whether in commentary, essay, sermon, poem, critique—and are content that he should think for us. It is better that we should, in the first place, try our own efforts at interpretation; when we fail or are puzzled is the time to compare our thought with that of others, choosing as interpreters men of devout mind and scholarly accomplishment. Orderly study, with the occasional help of a sound commentary, is to be recommended. To use 'good books,' by way of a spiritual stimulus, deadens in the end the healthy appetite

---

**Notes**

"Once the habit of reading his lesson-books with delight is set up in a child, his education is—not completed, but—ensured."

for truth. The same remark applies to little text-books, with remarks meant to stimulate certain virtues or states of mind. The error that underlies these aids to private devotion (public worship is another matter) is, that their tendency is to magnify ourselves and our occasions, while they create in us little or no desire for the best knowledge. It is probable that even our lame efforts at reading with understanding are more profitable than the best instruction. The preparedness we need is of the mind and heart; we must pray to be delivered from prejudices and prepossessions, and wait upon God as the thirsty earth waits for rain" (Vol. 4, Book 2, pp. 83, 84).

### 10. Expecting a narration after a single attentive reading will encourage your child to read slowly and carefully.

"He should be trained from the first to think that one reading of any lesson is enough to enable him to narrate what he has read, and will thus get the habit of slow, careful reading, intelligent even when it is silent, because he reads with an eye to the full meaning of every clause" (Vol. 1, p. 227).

"I have already spoken of the importance of a single reading. If a child is not able to narrate what he has read once, let him not get the notion that he may, or that he must, read it again. A look of slight regret because there is a gap in his knowledge will convict him. The power of reading with perfect attention will not be gained by the child who is allowed to moon over his lessons. For this reason, reading lessons must be short; ten minutes or a quarter of an hour of fixed attention is enough for children of the ages we have in view, and a lesson of this length will enable a child to cover two or three pages of his book. The same rule as to the length of a lesson applies to children whose lessons are read to them because they are not yet able to read for themselves" (Vol. 1, pp. 229, 230).

### 11. Do not ask direct questions on the subject in order to test reading comprehension.

"When a child is reading, he should not be teased with questions as to the meaning of what he has read, the signification of this word or that; what is annoying to older people is equally annoying to children" (Vol. 1, p. 228).

"Direct questions on the subject-matter of what a child has read are always a mistake" (Vol. 1, p. 228).

"To read a passage with full attention and to tell it afterwards has a curiously different effect. M. Bergson makes the happy distinction between *word* memory and *mind* memory, which, once the force of it is realised, should bring about sweeping changes in our methods of education.

"Trusting to mind memory we visualise the scene, are convinced by the arguments, take pleasure in the turn of the sentences and frame our own upon them; in fact that particular passage or chapter has been received into us and become a part of us just as literally as was yesterday's dinner; nay, more so, for yesterday's dinner is of little account to-morrow; but several months, perhaps years hence, we shall be able to narrate the passage we had, so to say, consumed and grown upon with all the vividness, detail and accuracy of the first telling. All

---

*Charlotte was discussing children under the age of nine in this section.*

*See page 43 for the Charlotte Mason way of assessing reading comprehension: narration.*

"The power of reading with perfect attention will not be gained by the child who is allowed to moon over his lessons."

powers of the mind which we call faculties have been brought into play in dealing with the intellectual matter thus afforded; so we may not ask questions to help the child to reason, paint fancy pictures to help him to imagine, draw out moral lessons to quicken his conscience. These things take place as involuntarily as processes of digestion" (Vol. 6, pp. 173, 174).

"Give children the sort of knowledge that they are fitted to assimilate, served in a literary medium, and they will pay great attention. What next? A clever *questionnaire?* Questions, as Dr. Johnson told us, are an intrusion and a bore; but here we have a word of ancient wisdom for our guidance; "The mind can know nothing except what it can express in the form of an answer to a question put by the mind to itself." Observe, not a question put by an outsider, but, put by the mind to itself. We all know the trick of it. If we want to tell the substance of a conversation, a sermon, a lecture, we 'go over it in our minds' first and the mind puts its question to itself, the same question over and over again, no more than,—What next?—and lo, we have it, the whole thing complete!" (Vol. 6, pp. 257, 258).

### 12. Too many oral lessons robs a child of developing the habit of reading for instruction.

"The most common and the monstrous defect in the education of the day is that children fail to acquire the habit of reading. Knowledge is conveyed to them by lessons and talk, but the studious habit of using books as a means of interest and delight is not acquired" (Vol. 1, p. 227).

"No education seems to be worth the name which has not made children at home in the world of books, and so related them, mind to mind, with thinkers who have dealt with knowledge. We reject epitomes, compilations, and their like, and put into children's hands books which, long or short, are *living*. Thus it becomes a large part of the teacher's work to help children to deal with their books; so that the oral lesson and lecture are but small matters in education, and are used chiefly to summarise or to expand or illustrate.

"Too much faith is commonly placed in oral lessons and lectures; 'to be poured into like a bucket,' as says Carlyle, 'is not exhilarating to any soul'; neither is it exhilarating to have every difficulty explained to weariness, or to have the explanation teased out of one by questions. 'I will not be put to the *question*. Don't you consider, sir, that these are not the manners of a gentleman? I will not be baited with *what* and *why*; what is this? what is that? why is a cow's tail long? why is a fox's tail bushy?' said Dr Johnson. This is what children think, though they say nothing. Oral lessons have their occasional use, and when they are fitly given it is the children who ask the questions. Perhaps it is not wholesome or quite honest for a teacher to pose as a source of all knowledge and to give 'lovely' lessons. Such lessons are titillating for the moment, but they give children the minimum of mental labour, and the result is much the same as that left on older persons by the reading of a magazine. We find, on the other hand, that in working through a considerable book, which may take two or three years to master, the interest of boys and girls is well sustained to the end; they develop an intelligent curiosity as to causes and consequences, and are in fact educating themselves" (Vol. 3, pp. 226, 227).

"The much-diluted, or over-condensed, teaching of the oral lesson, or the

*Reading for Instruction*

## Notes

lecture, gives place to the well thought out, consecutive treatment of the right book, a *living* book in which facts are presented as the outcome of ideas.

"Children taught in this way are remarkable for their keenness after knowledge, and do well afterwards in any examination for which they may have to prepare; and, what is of much more consequence, are prepared to take their full share of all that life offers of intellectual and practical interests" (Vol. 3, Preface).

### 13. Reading good books for instruction encourages just and carefully formed opinions.

"We must read our newspaper, of course—newspapers on both sides; but he who founds upon his newspaper is an ignorant patriot and an illiberal citizen. His opinions are no more than parrot-like repetitions of other men's sayings; whereas he who dwells with dutiful interest upon the history of his own country, distressed over her ignominies, proud when she has shown herself great; who has pondered the history of another great empire—admiring the temperate justice with which its distant colonies were administered, and scrutinising the causes of its fall—he gradually acquires some insight as to the meaning of national life. He is able to express an opinion which is not a mere echo, and gains convictions which will certainly be of use to his country, even if they are known only to the people about his own fireside.

"He learns to esteem Xerxes as a great gardener, a planter, whose aim it was that every man should have his little 'paradise.' Lycurgus is to him more than a lawgiver, he is a hero able to keep the laws he made. Such a person regards, with half-envious interest, the records of those small yet great republics, distinguished in the arts of peace and of war, in whose open schools every man picked up philosophy, and the best men made it the study of a lifetime.

"He who reads history in this way, not to pass examinations, nor to obtain culture, nor even for his own pleasure (delightful as such reading is), but because he knows it to be his duty to his country to have some intelligent knowledge of the past, of other lands as well as of his own, must add solid worth to the nation that owns him. It is something to prepare for the uses of the State a just, liberal, and enlightened patriotism in the breast of a single citizen" (Vol. 4, Book 2, pp. 74, 75).

"Your opinions about books and other things will very likely be wrong, and you will yourself correct them by and by when you have read more, thought more, know more. Indeed, no wise person, however old, is sure of his opinions. He holds them fast, but he holds them modestly; and, should he be like Numa, convinced that the opinion of others is more sound than his own, why, he has no shame in what we call 'changing his mind.' 'We are none of us infallible, not even the youngest!' was said by a wise and witty man, who knew that young people are apt to be cocksure—that is, to take up opinions at second hand and stick to them obstinately. The word opinion literally means 'a thinking'; what I think, with modesty and hesitation, and not what I am certain-sure about" (Vol. 4, Book 1, pp. 184, 185).

### 14. Casual reading of twaddle can undermine the habit of reading good literature for instruction.

"The habit of casual reading, about which Sir John Lubbock says such wise and

> "Many who would not read even a brilliant novel of a certain type, sit down to read twaddle without scruple."

pleasant words, is a form of mild intellectual dissipation which does more harm than we realise. Many who would not read even a brilliant novel of a certain type, sit down to read twaddle without scruple. Nothing is too scrappy, nothing is too weak to 'pass the time!' The 'Scraps' literature of railway bookstalls is symptomatic. We do not all read scraps, under whatever piquant title, but the locust-swarm of this class of literature points to the small reading power amongst us. The mischief begins in the nursery. No sooner can a child read at all than hosts of friendly people show their interest in him by a present of a 'pretty book.' A 'pretty book' is not necessarily a picture-book, but one in which the page is nicely broken up in talk or short paragraphs. Pretty books for the schoolroom age follow those for the nursery, and, nursery and schoolroom outgrown, we are ready for 'Mudie's' lightest novels; the succession of 'pretty books' never fails us; we have no time for works of any intellectual fibre, and we have no more assimilating power than has the schoolgirl who feeds upon cheese-cakes. Scott is dry as dust, even Kingsley is 'stiff.' We remain, though in another sense than that of the cottage dame, 'poor readers' all our days. Very likely these strictures do not touch a single reader of this page, and I am like a parson of the three-decker age inveighing against the ways of the thieves and drunkards who were *not* in the pews. But the mischief is catching, and the children of even reading parents are not safe" (Vol. 5, pp. 214, 215).

**15. Most adults read and forget because they do not read with attention for instruction.**

"As for the amount covered in each Form, it is probably about the amount most of us cover in the period of time included in a school term, but while we grown-up persons read and forget because we do not take the pains to *know* as we read, these young students have the powers of perfect recollection and just application because they have read with attention and concentration and have in every case reproduced what they have read in narration, or, the gist of some portion of it, in writing" (Vol. 6, p. 185).

**16. Reading for instruction helps your child learn how to self-educate.**

"The children, not the teachers, are the responsible persons; they do the work by self-effort.

"The teachers give sympathy and occasionally elucidate, sum up or enlarge, but the actual work is done by the scholars" (Vol. 6, p. 6).

"As we have already urged, there is but one right way, that is, children must do the work for themselves. They must read the given pages and tell what they have read, they must perform, that is, what we may call the *act of knowing*. We are all aware, alas, what a monstrous quantity of printed matter has gone into the dustbin of our memories, because we have failed to perform that quite natural and spontaneous 'act of knowing,' as easy to a child as breathing and, if we would believe it, comparatively easy to ourselves" (Vol. 6, p. 99).

"The teachers give the uplift of their sympathy in the work and where necessary elucidate, sum up or enlarge, but the actual work is done by the scholars" (Vol. 6, p. 241).

---

## Notes

*Charles Mudie founded a lending library in England in the 1800s and stocked it with novels. His selections became, in a sense, the best-seller list for that era.*

*A Form is somewhat similar to a Grade.*

"The teachers give the uplift of their sympathy in the work and where necessary elucidate, sum up or enlarge, but the actual work is done by the scholars."

*17. Once your child has the habit of reading for instruction, his education is ensured for life.*

"Once the habit of reading his lesson-books with delight is set up in a child, his education is—not completed, but—ensured; he will go on for himself in spite of the obstructions which school too commonly throws in his way" (Vol. 1, p. 229).

## Grades 1–3

*18. From the beginning, teach your child to read with care and deliberation.*

"In teaching to read, as in other matters, *c'est le premier pas qui coute*. The child who has been taught to read with care and deliberation until he has mastered the words of a limited vocabulary, usually does the rest for himself" (Vol. 1, p. 226).

> **C'est le premier pas qui coute** means *"It is the first step that counts."*

*19. As the teacher, focus on two points: encouraging the habit of reading and not allowing slipshod habits in reading.*

"The attention of his teachers should be fixed on two points—that he acquires the *habit* of reading, and that he does not fall into *slipshod habits* of reading" (Vol. 1, p. 226).

*20. During your child's sixth through ninth years, concentrate on cultivating the habit of reading for instruction.*

"The period of a child's life between his sixth and his ninth year should be used to lay the basis of a liberal education, and of the *habit* of reading for instruction" (Vol. 1, Preface).

"Supposing that between the child's sixth and his ninth year half a dozen well-chosen standard books of travel have been read with him in this way, he has gained distinct ideas of the contours, the productions, and the manners of the people, of every great region of the world; has laid up a store of reliable, valuable knowledge, that will last his lifetime; and besides, has done something to acquire a taste for books and the habit of reading" (Vol. 1, p. 276).

"Our great failure seems to me to be caused by the fact that we do not form the *habit of reading books that are worth while* in children while they are at school and are under twelve years of age" (Vol. 3, Preface).

## Grades 4–12

*21. As soon as your child can read, encourage him to read good books for himself.*

"This habit should be begun early; so soon as the child can read at all, he should read for himself, and to himself, history, legends, fairy tales, and other suitable matter" (Vol. 1, p. 227).

*22. Be careful not to read too much to a child who can read for himself; it may become a crutch.*

> "The attention of his teachers should be fixed on two points—that he acquires the *habit* of reading, and that he does not fall into *slipshod habits* of reading."

"It is a delight to older people to read aloud to children, but this should be only an occasional treat and indulgence, allowed before bedtime, for example. We must remember the natural inertness of a child's mind; give him the habit of being read to, and he will steadily shirk the labour of reading for himself; indeed, we all like to be spoon-fed with our intellectual meat, or we should read and think more for ourselves and be less eager to run after lectures" (Vol. 1, p. 228).

**23. Compiling a Book of Mottoes or reading diary can help a person read for instruction.**

"It is very helpful to read with a commonplace book or reading-diary, in which to put down any striking thought in your author, or your own impression of the work, or of any part of it; but *not* summaries of facts. Such a diary, carefully kept through life, should be exceedingly interesting as containing the intellectual history of the writer; besides, we never forget the book that we have made extracts from, and of which we have taken the trouble to write a short review" (Vol. 5, p. 260).

## Questions to Ask about Reading for Instruction

### General Guidelines for All Grades

- Am I mistakenly assuming that my child's love for reading is the same as a habit of reading for instruction?
- Do I understand how reading for instruction is foundational to learning?
- Am I integrating the habit of reading for instruction in all subjects?
- Are my child's lesson books interesting, on his level, and written with literary power?
- Am I finding that my child can cover more ground in fewer hours because he is reading for instruction?
- Do I understand how reading for instruction from good literature can take more effort than is commonly required in a traditional school?
- Do I try to select my child's lesson books carefully, making sure they present that knowledge is attractive and reading is delightful?
- Am I introducing the author to my child and getting out of the way?
- Do I encourage my child to read the Bible itself, not just devotional books, for instruction?
- Am I expecting my child to narrate after a single attentive reading?
- Am I careful not to ask questions on the reading to try to assess comprehension?
- Do I understand how too many oral lessons from the teacher can sabotage the habit of reading for instruction?
- Am I encouraging my child to form just and careful opinions based on reading for instruction?
- Do I understand how twaddle and casual reading can undermine my child's ability to read good literature for instruction?
- Am I trying to demonstrate a good example of reading for instruction myself, as an adult?

"Give him the habit of being read to, and he will steadily shirk the labour of reading for himself."

- Is my child learning how to self-educate by developing the habit of reading for instruction?
- Do I understand how the habit of reading for instruction can ensure my child's learning for life?

### Grades 1–3

- Am I trying to teach my child to read with care and deliberation?
- Am I focusing on the two points of encouraging the habit of reading and not allowing slipshod habits in reading?
- Am I concentrating on cultivating this habit in my six- to nine-year-old child?

### Grades 4–12

- Am I encouraging my child to read good books for himself as soon as he is ready?
- Am I inadvertently providing a crutch to my fluent reader by reading too much to him?
- Might my child enjoy compiling a Book of Mottoes or entries in a reading diary to help him read for instruction?

## More Quotes on Reading for Instruction

"All men who have turned out worth anything have had the chief hand in their own education."—Sir Walter Scott

"Man's mind, once stretched by a new idea, never regains its original dimensions."—Oliver Wendell Holmes

"Read not to contradict and confute, nor to believe and take for granted, nor to find talk and discourse; but to weigh and consider."— Francis Bacon

"A book is a garden, an orchard, a storehouse, a party, a company by the way, a counselor, a multitude of counselors."— Henry Ward Beecher

Force yourself to reflect on what you read, paragraph by paragraph.—Samuel Taylor Coleridge

Tis the good reader that makes the good book; a good head cannot read amiss: in every book he finds passages which seem confidences or asides hidden from all else and unmistakably meant for his ear.—Ralph Waldo Emerson

Readers may be divided into four classes:
1.) Sponges, who absorb all that they read and return it in nearly the same state, only a little dirtied.
2.) Sand-glasses, who retain nothing and are content to get through a book for the sake of getting through the time.

> "It is very helpful to read with a commonplace book or reading-diary, in which to put down any striking thought in your author, or your own impression of the work, or of any part of it; but *not* summaries of facts."

3.) Strain-bags, who retain merely the dregs of what they read.

4.) Mogul diamonds, equally rare and valuable, who profit by what they read, and enable others to profit by it also.—Samuel Taylor Coleridge

## Notes

"We should read and think more for ourselves."

# Chapter 6
# *Narration*

"All right, Dee," said Mom. "I'm going to read this only once, and I want you to pay close attention. When I'm done reading, I'm going to ask you to tell me all about what I read. Ready?"

Dee nodded and Mom started reading, not too fast but not too slow. As she read, she could see Dee concentrating on what was being said. It wasn't difficult, since the story was captivating, and she was careful to stop before Dee lost her focus.

"Now tell me what you remember," Mom instructed.

Dee took a moment to collect her thoughts and determine how to begin, then she recounted the reading in good detail and in her own words.

Mom listened with satisfaction, knowing that Dee was learning an important skill that would serve her well into adulthood.

## Charlotte's Thoughts on Narration

### *General Guidelines for All Grades*

**1. Your child should show what he knows by narrating—either orally or in written form—what he has read or heard.**

"As knowledge is not assimilated until it is reproduced, children should 'tell back' after a single reading or hearing: or should write on some part of what they have read" (Vol. 6, Preface and p. 155).

"Oral teaching was to a great extent ruled out; a large number of books on many subjects were set for reading in morning school-hours; so much work was set that there was only time for a single reading; all reading was tested by a narration of the whole or a given passage, whether orally or in writing. Children working on these lines know months after that which they have read and are remarkable for their power of concentration (attention); they have little trouble with spelling or composition and become well-informed, intelligent persons" (Vol. 6, p. 15).

"What they receive under this condition they absorb immediately and show that they *know* by that test of knowledge which applies to us all, that is, they can tell it with power, clearness, vivacity and charm" (Vol. 6, p. 63).

"It is our part to see that every child *knows* and *can tell*, whether by way of oral narrative or written essay" (Vol. 6, p. 171).

"Whatever a child or grown-up person can tell, that we may be sure he knows, and what he cannot tell, he does not know" (Vol. 6, pp. 172, 173).

---

**Notes**

*Narration is a method that should be integrated into regular subjects.*

"As knowledge is not assimilated until it is reproduced, children should 'tell back' after a single reading or hearing: or should write on some part of what they have read."

## Notes

"Children shew the same surprising power of knowing, evinced by the one sure test,—they are able to 'tell' each work they have read not only with accuracy but with spirit and originality" (Vol. 6, p. 182).

"The reading is tested by narration, or by writing on a test passage" (Vol. 6, p. 241).

"What the children have read they know, and write on any part of it with ease and fluency, in vigorous English" (Vol. 6, p. 241).

"Let the child . . . tell what he has read in whole or in part on the instant, and again, in an examination paper months later" (Vol. 6, p. 258).

"Let the boy read and he knows, that is, if he must tell again what he has read.
"This, of telling again, sounds very simple but it is really a magical creative process by means of which the narrator sees what he has conceived, so definite and so impressive is the act of narrating that which has been read only once" (Vol. 6, p. 261).

"It is true that we all read and that narration is as natural as breathing, its value depending solely upon what is narrated. What we have perhaps failed to discover hitherto is the immense hunger for knowledge (curiosity) existing in everyone and the immeasurable power of attention with which everyone is endowed; that everyone likes knowledge best in a literary form; that the knowledge should be exceedingly various concerning many things on which the mind of man reflects; but that knowledge is acquired only by what we may call "the *act of knowing*," which is both encouraged and tested by narration, and which further requires the later test and record afforded by examinations" (Vol. 6, pp. 290, 291).

"They master a few pages at a single reading so thoroughly that they can 'tell it back' at the time or months later" (Vol. 6, p. 291).

### 2. Require a narration after only one reading.

"He should be trained from the first to think that one reading of any lesson is enough to enable him to narrate what he has read, and will thus get the habit of slow, careful reading, intelligent even when it is silent, because he reads with an eye to the full meaning of every clause" (Vol. 1, p. 227).

"I have already spoken of the importance of a single reading. If a child is not able to narrate what he has read once, let him not get the notion that he may, or that he must, read it again. A look of slight regret because there is a gap in his knowledge will convict him. The power of reading with perfect attention will not be gained by the child who is allowed to moon over his lessons" (Vol. 1, pp. 229, 230).

"The simplest way of dealing with a paragraph or a chapter is to require the child to narrate its contents after a single attentive reading,—*one* reading, however slow, should be made a condition; for we are all too apt to make sure we shall have another opportunity of finding out 'what 'tis all about' There is the weekly review if

"Whatever a child or grown-up person can tell, that we may be sure he knows, and what he cannot tell, he does not know."

we fail to get a clear grasp of the news of the day; and, if we fail a second time, there is a monthly or a quarterly review or an annual summing up: in fact, many of us let present-day history pass by us with easy minds, feeling sure that, in the end, we shall be *compelled* to see the bearings of events. This is a bad habit to get into; and we should do well to save our children by not giving them the vague expectation of second and third and tenth opportunities to do that which should have been done at first" (Vol. 3, pp. 179, 180).

"A *single reading* is insisted on, because children have naturally great power of attention; but this force is dissipated by the re-reading of passages, and also, by questioning, summarising, and the like" (Vol. 6, Preface).

"This is what happens in the narrating of a passage read: each new consecutive incident or statement arrives because the mind asks itself,—"What next?" For this reason it is important that only one reading should be allowed; efforts to memorise weaken the power of attention, the proper activity of the mind" (Vol. 6, p. 17).

"From twenty to sixteen consecutive readings a week might be afforded in a wide selection of books,—literature, history, economics, etc.,—books read with the concentrated attention which makes a single reading suffice" (Vol. 6, p. 86).

"A *single reading* is a condition insisted upon because a naturally desultory habit of mind leads us all to put off the effort of attention as long as a second or third chance of coping with our subject is to be hoped for" (Vol. 6, p. 171).

"I dwell on the single reading because, let me repeat, it is impossible to fix attention on that which we have heard before and know we shall hear again" (Vol. 6, p. 261).

"Their knowledge should be tested, not by questions, but by the oral (and occasionally the written) reproduction of a passage after one reading" (Vol. 6, pp. 341, 342).

*3. Before reading the portion for today, help your child talk a little about what happened last time in order to anticipate what might happen in today's reading.*

"Before the reading for the day begins, the teacher should talk a little (and get the children to talk) about the last lesson, with a few words about what is to be read, in order that the children may be animated by expectation; but she should beware of explanation, and, especially, of forestalling the narrative" (Vol. 1, pp. 232, 233).

*4. Write any key names or words from the reading on a small whiteboard or sheet of paper for your child to see as he listens and narrates.*

"Proper names are written on the blackboard; and, at the end, children narrate the substance of the lesson" (Vol. 3, p. 280).

*5. Read enough to include a full episode, then ask your child to narrate.*

"Then, she may read two or three pages, enough to include an episode; after

### Notes

"He should be trained from the first to think that one reading of any lesson is enough to enable him to narrate what he has read."

*Narration*

## Notes

that, let her call upon the children to narrate,—in turns, if there be several of them. They not only narrate with spirit and accuracy, but succeed in catching the style of their author" (Vol. 1, p. 233).

"Literature at its best is always direct and simple and a normal child of six listens with delight to the tales both of Old and New Testament read to him passage by passage, and by him narrated in turn, with delightful touches of native eloquence" (Vol. 6, p. 160).

### *6. Make sure the book is interesting and enjoyable to your child.*

"The book should always be deeply interesting" (Vol. 1, p. 233).

"The children must enjoy the book. The ideas it holds must each make that sudden, delightful impact upon their minds, must cause that intellectual stir, which mark the inception of an idea" (Vol. 3, p. 178).

### *7. Read through the book consecutively, not just excerpts here and there.*

"In every case the reading should be consecutive from a well-chosen book" (Vol. 1, p. 232).

### *8. Avoid asking direct questions on the subject-matter of the reading; have your child narrate instead.*

"Direct questions on the subject-matter of what a child has read are always a mistake. Let him *narrate* what he has read, or some part of it. He enjoys this sort of consecutive reproduction, but abominates every question in the nature of a riddle. If there must be riddles, let it be his to ask and the teacher's to direct him the answer" (Vol. 1, p. 228).

"The points to be borne in mind are, that he should have no book which is not a child's classic; and that, given the right book, it must not be diluted with talk or broken up with questions, but given to the boy in fit proportions as wholesome meat for his mind, in the full trust that a child's mind is able to deal with its proper food" (Vol. 1, p. 232).

"A *single reading* is insisted on, because children have naturally great power of attention; but this force is dissipated by the re-reading of passages, and also, by questioning, summarising, and the like" (Vol. 6, Preface).

"Long ago, I was in the habit of hearing this axiom quoted by a philosophical old friend:—"The mind can know nothing save what it can produce in the form of an answer to a question put to the mind by itself." I have failed to trace the saying to its source, but a conviction of its importance has been growing upon me during the last forty years. It tacitly prohibits questioning from without; (this does not, of course, affect the Socratic use of questioning for purposes of *moral* conviction); and it is necessary to intellectual certainty, to the act of knowing. For example, to secure a conversation or an incident, we 'go over it in our minds'; that is, the mind puts itself through the process of self-questioning which I have indicated" (Vol. 6, pp. 16, 17).

"The children must enjoy the book."

"Given a book of literary quality suitable to their age and children will know how to deal with it without elucidation. Of course they will not be able to answer questions because questions are an impertinence which we all resent, but they will tell you the whole thing with little touches of individual personality in the narrative" (Vol. 6, p. 260).

"Their knowledge should be tested, not by questions, but by the oral (and occasionally the written) reproduction of a passage after one reading" (Vol. 6, pp. 341, 342).

### 9. Encourage your child to narrate by a genuinely-interested look or word, but be careful not to deluge him with a flood of talk.

"The points to be borne in mind are, that he should have no book which is not a child's classic; and that, given the right book, it must not be diluted with talk or broken up with questions, but given to the boy in fit portions as wholesome meat for his mind, in the full trust that a child's mind is able to deal with its proper food" (Vol. 1, p. 232).

"The teacher's part in this regard is to see and feel for himself, and then to rouse his pupils by an appreciative look or word; but to beware how he deadens the impression by a flood of talk. Intellectual sympathy is very stimulating; but we have all been in the case of the little girl who said, 'Mother, I think I could understand if you did not explain *quite* so much.' A teacher said of her pupil, 'I find it so hard to tell whether she has really grasped a thing or whether she has only got the mechanical hang of it.' Children are imitative monkeys, and it is the 'mechanical hang' that is apt to arrive after a douche of explanation" (Vol. 3, pp. 178, 179).

"The teacher's own really difficult part is to keep up sympathetic interest by look and occasional word, by remarks upon a passage that has been narrated, by occasionally shewing pictures, and so on" (Vol. 6, p. 172).

"The teachers give the uplift of their sympathy in the work and where necessary elucidate, sum up or enlarge, but the actual work is done by the scholars" (Vol. 6, p. 241).

### 10. Do not interrupt your child while he is narrating.

"The teacher does not talk much and is careful never to interrupt a child who is called upon to 'tell' " (Vol. 6, p. 172).

"Corrections must not be made during the act of narration, nor must any interruption be allowed" (Vol. 6, p. 191).

### 11. Do not correct your child's sentence structure or grammar during his narration.

"It is not wise to tease them with corrections; they may begin with an endless chain of 'ands,' but they soon leave this off, and their narrations become good enough in style and composition to be put in a 'print book'!" (Vol. 1, p. 233).

> "Questions are an impertinence which we all resent."

## Narration

### Notes

**12. Correct any mistakes on content when the narration is over, not during the telling.**

"The teacher probably allows other children to correct any faults in the telling when it is over" (Vol. 6, p. 172).

"Corrections must not be made during the act of narration, nor must any interruption be allowed" (Vol. 6, p. 191).

**13. In a group, you may call on children to take turns narrating.**

"Then, she may read two or three pages, enough to include an episode; after that, let her call upon the children to narrate,—in turns, if there be several of them" (Vol. 1, p. 233).

"Ask the children in turn to narrate, each narrating a part of what was read" (Vol. 3, p. 334).

"The time appropriated in the time-table at this stage to the teaching of some half-dozen more or less literary subjects such as Scripture, and the subjects I have indicated, is largely spent by the teachers in reading, say, two or three paragraphs at a time from some one of the set books, which children, here and there in the class, narrate" (Vol. 6, p. 244).

*In Charlotte's foreign language classes, the children would narrate in the language they were learning.*

"As soon as the reading ended, on the instant, without hesitation of any kind, narration began in French, different members of the class taking up the story in turn till it was finished" (Vol. 6, p. 212).

**14. After your child narrates, you may illustrate or elaborate on any lessons drawn from the reading.**

"When the narration is over, there should be a little talk in which moral points are brought out, pictures shown to illustrate the lesson, or diagrams drawn on the blackboard" (Vol. 1, p. 233).

"Then the teacher will read the Bible passage in question which the children will narrate, the commentary serving merely as a background for their thoughts. The narration is usually exceedingly interesting; the children do not miss a point and often add picturesque touches of their own. Before the close of the lesson, the teacher brings out such new thoughts of God or new points of behaviour as the reading has afforded, emphasising the moral or religious lesson to be learnt rather by a reverent and sympathetic manner than by any attempt at personal application" (Vol. 6, p. 163).

"The teachers give the uplift of their sympathy in the work and where necessary elucidate, sum up or enlarge, but the actual work is done by the scholars" (Vol. 6, p. 241).

*"The teacher does not talk much and is careful never to interrupt a child who is called upon to 'tell.'"*

**15. Asking questions on a side issue or about personal opinion are fine.**

"Questions that lead to a side issue or to a personal view are allowable because these interest children—'What would you have done in his place?' " (Vol. 1, pp. 228, 229).

**16. Use other discussion points after the narration to make sure your child is reading intelligently, not just cramming the contents.**

"There is much difference between intelligent reading, which the pupil should do in silence, and a mere parrot-like cramming up of contents; and it is not a bad test of education to be able to give the points of a description, the sequence of a series of incidents, the links in a chain of argument, correctly, after a single careful reading. This is a power which a barrister, a publisher, a scholar, labours to acquire; and it is a power which children can acquire with great ease, and once acquired, the gulf is bridged which divides the reading from the non-reading community.

"But this is only *one* way to use books: others are to enumerate the statements in a given paragraph or chapter; to analyse a chapter, to divide it into paragraphs under proper headings, to tabulate and classify series; to trace cause to consequence and consequence to cause; to discern character and perceive how character and circumstance interact; to get lessons of life and conduct, or the living knowledge which makes for science, out of books; all this is possible for school boys and girls, and *until* they have begun to use books for themselves in such ways, they can hardly be said to have begun their education" (Vol. 3, p. 180).

"If it is desirable to ask questions in order to emphasize certain points, these should be asked after and not before, or during, the act of narration" (Vol. 6, p. 17).

**17. Look over the portion to be read ahead of time and note any discussion points that would be good to use to encourage mental discipline.**

"The teacher's part is, in the first place, to see what is to be done, to look over the work of the day in advance and see what mental discipline, as well as what vital knowledge, this and that lesson afford; and then to set such questions and such tasks as shall give full scope to his pupils' mental activity" (Vol. 3, pp. 180, 181).

**18. Teach your child to make neat marginal notes or underlines in his books.**

"Let marginal notes be freely made, as neatly and beautifully as may be, for books should be handled with reverence. Let numbers, letters, underlining be used to help the eye and to save the needless fag of writing abstracts" (Vol. 3, p. 181).

**19. Sometimes ask your child to write a few questions that cover the passage he read.**

"Let the pupil write for himself half a dozen questions which cover the passage studied; he need not write the answers if he be taught that the mind can know nothing but what it can produce in the form of an answer to a question put by the mind to itself" (Vol. 3, p. 181).

**20. Be careful that discussion points and mental disciplines like those mentioned above do not dampen your child's relation with the living book itself.**

"These few hints by no means cover the disciplinary uses of a good school-book; but let us be careful that our disciplinary devices, and our mechanical devices to

*Notes*

"There is much difference between intelligent reading, which the pupil should do in silence, and a mere parrot-like cramming up of contents."

secure and tabulate the substance of knowledge, do not come between the children and that which is the *soul* of the book, the living thought it contains. Science is doing so much for us in these days, nature is drawing so close to us, art is unfolding so much meaning to us, the world is becoming so rich for us, that we are a little in danger of neglecting the art of deriving sustenance from books. Let us not in such wise impoverish our lives and the lives of our children" (Vol. 3, p. 181).

### 21. The Bible should also be read and narrated, then discussed briefly.

"Method of Bible Lessons.—The method of such lessons is very simple. Read aloud to the children a few verses covering, if possible, an episode. Read reverently, carefully, and with just expression. Then require the children to narrate what they have listened to as nearly as possible in the words of the Bible. It is curious how readily they catch the rhythm of the majestic and simple Bible English. Then, talk the narrative over with them in the light of research and criticism. Let the teaching, moral and spiritual, reach them without much personal application" (Vol. 1, p. 251).

"Read your Bible story to the child, bit by bit; get him to tell you in his own words (keeping as close as he can to the Bible words) what you have read, and then, if you like, talk about it; but not much. Above all, do not let us attempt a 'practical commentary on every verse in Genesis' to quote the title of a work lately published" (Vol. 2, p. 110).

"Read bit by bit (of the Old Testament anyway) to the children, as beautifully as may be, requiring them to tell the story, after listening, as nearly in the Bible words as they can" (Vol. 2, p. 112).

"Literature at its best is always direct and simple and a normal child of six listens with delight to the tales both of Old and New Testament read to him passage by passage, and by him narrated in turn, with delightful touches of native eloquence" (Vol. 6, p. 160).

"The knowledge of God is the principal knowledge, and no teaching of the Bible which does not further that knowledge is of religious value. Therefore the children read, or if they are too young to read for themselves the teacher reads to them, a passage of varying length covering an incident or some definite teaching. If there are remarks to be made about local geography or local custom, the teacher makes them before the passage has been read, emphasizing briefly but reverently any spiritual or moral truth; the children narrate what has been read after the reading; they do this with curious accuracy and yet with some originality, conveying the spiritual teaching which the teacher has indicated" (Vol. 6, p. 272).

### 22. Short lesson times should include the narration.

"For this reason, reading lessons must be short; ten minutes or a quarter of an hour of fixed attention is enough for children of the ages we have in view, and a lesson of this length will enable a child to cover two or three pages of his book. The same rule as to the length of a lesson applies to children whose lessons are read to them because they are not yet able to read for themselves" (Vol. 1, p. 230).

---

*Short lessons in Charlotte's schools meant*
*Grades 1–3: 15–20 minutes*
*Grades 4–6: 20–30 minutes*
*Grades 7–9: 30–45 minutes*

"The mind can know nothing but what it can produce in the form of an answer to a question put by the mind to itself."

"This sort of narration lesson should not occupy more than a quarter of an hour" (Vol. 1, p. 233).

**23. Use narration questions for end-of-term examinations—one or two on each book read during the term.**

"At the end of the term an examination paper is sent out containing one or two questions on each book. Here are a few of the answers. The children in the first two classes narrate their answers, which someone writes from their dictation" (Vol. 3, p. 272).

"These read in a term one, or two, or three thousand pages, according to their age, school and Form, in a large number of set books. The quantity set for each lesson allows of only a single reading; but the reading is tested by narration, or by writing on a test passage. When the terminal examination is at hand so much ground has been covered that revision is out of the question; what the children have read they know, and write on any part of it with ease and fluency, in vigorous English; they usually spell well" (Vol. 6, p. 6)

"Scholars should know their books, many pages in many books, at a single reading, in such a way that months later they can write freely and accurately on any part of the term's reading" (Vol. 6, p. 7)

"Examination papers representing tens of thousands of children working in Elementary Schools, Secondary Schools and home schoolrooms have just passed under my eye. How the children have revelled in knowledge! and how good and interesting all their answers are! How well they spell on the whole and how well they write! We do not need the testimony of their teachers that the work of the term has been joyous; the verve with which the children tell what they know proves the fact. Every one of these children knows that there are hundreds of pleasant places for the mind to roam in" (Vol. 6, p. 45).

"Much use is made according to this method of the years from 6 to 8, during which children must learn to read and write; they get at the same time, however, a good deal of consecutive knowledge of history and geography, tale and fable, some of which at the end of the term they dictate in answer to questions and their answers form well-expressed little essays on the subjects they deal with" (Vol. 6, p. 244).

"Let the child . . . tell what he has read in whole or in part on the instant, and again, in an examination paper months later" (Vol. 6, p. 258).

**24. Knowing that he will have to narrate after a single reading helps your child put forth the effort to pay full attention.**

"We all stir our minds into action the better if there is an implied 'must' in the background; for children in class the 'must' acts through the *certainty* that they will be required to narrate or write from what they have read with no opportunity of 'looking 'up,' or other devices of the idle. Children find the act of narrating so pleasurable in itself that urgency on the part of the teacher is seldom necessary" (Vol. 6, p. 17).

---

## Notes

*See pages 139–158 for these examples of end-of-term questions and narrations.*

*A Form is somewhat similar to a Grade.*

*Terms usually lasted about twelve weeks, so end-of-term exams occurred about three times per school year.*

"What the children have read they know."

## Notes

**25. Seeing the story in his mind's eye will help your child assimilate and remember the events of the reading.**

"Trusting to mind memory we visualise the scene, are convinced by the arguments, take pleasure in the turn the sentences and frame our own upon them; in fact that particular passage or chapter has been received into us and become a part of us just as literally as was yesterday's dinner; nay, more so, for yesterday's dinner is of little account tomorrow; but several months, perhaps years hence, we shall be able to narrate the passage we had, so to say, consumed and grown upon with all the vividness, detail and accuracy of the first telling" (Vol. 6, p. 173).

"Just so in their small degree do the children narrate; they see it all so vividly that when you read or hear their versions the theme is illuminated for you too" (Vol. 6, p. 182).

"Children cannot tell what they have not seen with the mind's eye, which we know as imagination, and they cannot see what is not told in their books with some vividness and some grasp of the subject" (Vol. 6, p. 227).

**26. Children narrate naturally if something interests them, and we can use this natural tendency as an educational tool.**

"Narrating is an *art*, like poetry-making or painting, because it is *there*, in every child's mind, waiting to be discovered, and is not the result of any process of disciplinary education. A creative fiat calls it forth. 'Let him narrate'; and the child narrates, fluently, copiously, in ordered sequence, with fit and graphic details, with a just choice of words, without verbosity or tautology, so soon as he can speak with ease. This amazing gift with which normal children are born is allowed to lie fallow in their education. Bobbie will come home with a heroic narrative of a fight he has seen between 'Duke' and a dog in the street. It is wonderful! He has seen everything, and he tells everything with splendid vigour in the true epic vein; but so ingrained is our contempt for children that we see nothing in this but Bobbie's foolish childish way! Whereas here, if we have eyes to see and grace to build, is the ground-plan of his education" (Vol. 1, p. 231).

"That is how we all learn, we tell again, to ourselves if need be, the matter we wish to retain, the sermon, the lecture, the conversation. The method is as old as the mind of man, the distressful fact is that it has been made so little use of in general education" (Vol. 6, pp. 159, 160).

**27. If you are reading from a book that contains parts that may need to be edited, read it aloud; do not give it to your child to read himself.**

"Where it is necessary to make omissions, as in the Old Testament narratives and Plutarch's *Lives*, for example, it is better that the teacher should always read the lesson which is to be narrated" (Vol. 1, p. 233).

"We find Plutarch's *Lives* exceedingly inspiring. These are read aloud by the teacher (with suitable omissions) and narrated with great spirit by the children" (Vol. 6, p. 185).

> "Children cannot tell what they have not seen with the mind's eye."

*28. Oral narration is good practice for public speaking.*

"Organising capacity, business habits, and some power of public speaking, should be a part of our fitness as citizens. To secure the power of speaking, I think it would be well if the habit of narration were more encouraged, in place of written composition. On the whole, it is more useful to be able to speak than to write, and the man or woman who is able to do the former can generally do the latter" (Vol. 3, p. 88).

"They will welcome the preparation for public speaking, an effort for which everyone must qualify in these days, which the act of narration offers" (Vol. 6, p. 124).

"The act of narrating what has been read might well be useful to boys who should be prepared for public speaking" (Vol. 6, p. 86).

*29. Narration is not parroting back or reciting from rote memory.*

"Narrations which are mere feats of memory are quite valueless" (Vol. 1, p. 289).

"But, it will be said, reading or hearing various books read, chapter by chapter, and then narrating or writing what has been read or some part of it,—all this is mere memory work. The value of this criticism may be readily tested; will the critic read before turning off his light a leading article from a newspaper, say, or a chapter from Boswell or Jane Austen, or one of Lamb's Essays; then, will he put himself to sleep by narrating silently what he has read. He will not be satisfied with the result but he will find that in the act of narrating every power of his mind comes into play, that points and bearings which he had not observed are brought out; that the whole is visualized and brought into relief in an extraordinary way; in fact, that scene or argument has become a part of his personal experience; he *knows*, he has assimilated what he has read. *This is not memory work.* In order to memorise, we repeat over and over a passage or a series of points or names with the aid of such clues as we can invent; we do memorise a string of facts or words, and the new possession serves its purpose for a time, but it is not assimilated; its purpose being served, we know it no more. This is memory work by means of which examinations are passed with credit. I will not try to explain (or understand!) this power to memorise;—it has its subsidiary use in education, no doubt, but it must not be put in the place of the prime agent which is *attention*" (Vol. 6, p. 16).

*30. You'll be able to tell whether your child has gained real knowledge or just information from his book by noting if his narrations demonstrate an ability to condense, illustrate, and narrate with freedom or if he simply parrots phrases from the passage.*

"Perhaps the chief function of a teacher is to distinguish information from knowledge in the acquisitions of his pupils. Because knowledge is power, the child who has got knowledge will certainly show power in dealing with it. He will recast, condense, illustrate, or narrate with vividness and with freedom in the arrangement of his words. The child who has got only information will write and speak in the

---

*Notes*

"That is how we all learn, we tell again, to ourselves if need be, the matter we wish to retain, the sermon, the lecture, the conversation."

stereotyped phrases of his text-book, or will mangle in his notes the words of his teacher" (Vol. 3, p. 225).

"Children shew the same surprising power of knowing, evinced by the one sure test,—they are able to 'tell' each work they have read not only with accuracy but with spirit and originality" (Vol. 6, p. 182).

### 31. Children's personalities will show in their narrations; allow them to narrate in their own ways.

"Indeed, it is most interesting to hear children of seven or eight go through a long story without missing a detail, putting every event in its right order. These narrations are never a slavish reproduction of the original. A child's individuality plays about what he enjoys, and the story comes from his lips, not precisely as the author tells it, but with a certain spirit and colouring which express the narrator. By the way, it is very important that children should be allowed to narrate in their own way, and should not be pulled up or helped with words and expressions from the text" (Vol. 1, p. 289).

"Literature at its best is always direct and simple and a normal child of six listens with delight to the tales both of Old and New Testament read to him passage by passage, and by him narrated in turn, with delightful touches of native eloquence" (Vol. 6, p. 160).

"The narration is usually exceedingly interesting; the children do not miss a point and often add picturesque touches of their own" (Vol. 6, p. 163).

"Given a book of literary quality suitable to their age and children will know how to deal with it without elucidation. Of course they will not be able to answer questions because questions are an impertinence which we all resent, but they will tell you the whole thing with little touches of individual personality in the narrative" (Vol. 6, p. 260).

"They throw individuality into this telling back so that no two tell quite the same tale" (Vol. 6, p. 292).

### 32. Drawing a favorite scene is a form of narration.

"History readings afford admirable material for narration, and children enjoy narrating what they have read or heard. They love, too, to make illustrations. Children who had been reading *Julius Caesar* (and also, Plutarch's *Life*), were asked to make a picture of their favourite scene, and the results showed the extraordinary power of visualising which the little people possess. Of course that which they visualise, or imagine clearly, they know; it is a life possession" (Vol. 1, p. 292).

### 33. Acting out a favorite scene is a form of narration.

"Children have other ways of expressing the conceptions that fill them when they are duly fed. They play at their history lessons, dress up, make tableaux, act scenes; or they have a stage, and their dolls act, while they paint the scenery and

> "Narrations which are mere feats of memory are quite valueless."

speak the speeches. There is no end to the modes of expression children find when there is anything in them to express" (Vol. 1, p. 294).

"Children are born poets, and they dramatise all the life they see about them, after their own hearts, into an endless play. There is no reason why this natural gift should not be pressed into the service of education. Indeed, it might be safe to go further: the child who does not dramatise his lessons, who does not play at Richard and Saladin, who does not voyage with Captain Cook and excavate with Mr Flinders Petrie, is not learning. The knowledge he gets by heart is not assimilated and does not become part of himself.

"Therefore it is well that children should, at any rate, have the outlet of *narration*, that they should tell the things they know in full detail; and, when the humour takes them, 'play' the persons, act the scenes that interest them in their reading" (Vol. 5, pp. 305, 306).

*34. When your child is acting out a narration, be careful not to make the trappings of the presentation more important than the content.*

"On the other hand, there is the danger that their representation of facts may become more to them than the facts themselves, that the show of things may occupy their whole minds. For this reason it may be well not to indulge children with anything in the form of a stage or stage properties, not with so much as a puppet-show. They will find all they want in the chair which serves as a throne, the sofa which behaves as a ship, the ruler which plays the part of rapier, gun, or sceptre, as occasion demands. In fact, preoccupation with tawdry and trivial things will be avoided if children are let alone: imagination will furnish them with ample properties, delightful scenes, upon the merest suggestion of reality" (Vol. 5, p. 306).

*35. One criteria for selecting a book is whether your child can narrate it.*

"I have already spoken of the sorts of old chronicles upon which children should be nourished; but these are often too diffuse to offer good matter for narration, and it is well to have quite fitting short tales for this purpose" (Vol. 1, p. 289).

"The completeness with which hundreds of children reject the wrong book is a curious and instructive experience, not less so than the avidity and joy with which they drain the right book to the dregs; children's requirements in the matter seem to be quantity, quality and variety: but the question of books is one of much delicacy and difficulty. After the experience of over a quarter of a century in selecting the lesson books proper to children of all ages, we still make mistakes, and the next examination paper discovers the error! Children cannot answer questions set on the wrong book; and the difficulty of selection is increased by the fact that what they like in books is no more a guide than what they like in food" (Vol. 6, p. 248).

*36. Narration requires your child to do the mental work and form his own relation with the book.*

"As we have already urged, there is but one right way, that is, children must do the work for themselves. They must read the given pages and tell what they have read, they must perform, that is, what we may call the *act of knowing*" (Vol. 6, p. 99).

# Notes

*For more forms of narration, read the Narration Ideas on page 175.*

"A narration should be original as it comes from the child—that is, his own mind should have acted upon the matter it has received."

> Notes

*Yes, narration is a natural skill that most children use, but it may take time to transition from using that skill whenever desired to employing it purposefully for education.*

"That which they visualise, or imagine clearly, they know; it is a life possession."

"This, of getting ideas out of them, is by no means all we must do with books. 'In all labour there is profit,' at any rate in some labour; and the labour of thought is what his book must induce in the child. He must generalise, classify, infer, judge, visualise, discriminate, labour in one way or another, with that capable mind of his, until the substance of his book is assimilated or rejected, according as he shall determine; for the determination rests with him and not with his teacher" (Vol. 3, p. 179).

"As for all the teaching in the nature of 'told to the children,' most children get their share of that whether in the infant school or at home, but this is practically outside the sphere of that part of education which demands a *conscious mental effort*, from the scholar, the mental effort of telling again that which has been read or heard" (Vol. 6, p. 159).

"While we grown-up persons read and forget because we do not take the pains to *know* as we read, these young students have the powers of perfect recollection and just application because they have read with attention and concentration and have in every case reproduced what they have read in narration, or, the gist of some portion of it, in writing" (Vol. 6, p. 185).

"The children, not the teachers, are the responsible persons; they do the work by self-effort.
"The teachers give the uplift of their sympathy in the work and where necessary elucidate, sum up or enlarge, but the actual work is done by the scholars" (Vol. 6, pp. 6, 241).

"They should read to know" (Vol. 6, p. 341).

### 37. Give your child time to "hit his stride" in narrating.

"It is not wise to tease them with corrections; they may begin with an endless chain of 'ands,' but they soon leave this off, and their narrations become good enough in style and composition to be put in a 'print book'!" (Vol. 1, p. 233).

"The first efforts may be stumbling but presently the children get into their 'stride' and 'tell' a passage at length with surprising fluency" (Vol. 6, p. 172).

### 38. Various students may narrate better in different subjects.

"It rarely happens that all the children in a class are not able to answer all the questions set in such subjects as history, literature, citizenship, geography, science. But here differences manifest themselves; some children do better in history, some in science, some in arithmetic, others in literature; some, again, write copious answers and a few write sparsely; but practically all know the answers to the set questions" (Vol. 6, p. 241).

### 39. Narration helps knowledge grow in your child, and therefore, is the chief part of education.

"Here is an example of how such knowledge grows. I heard a class of girls aged about thirteen read an essay on George Herbert. Three or four of his poems were included, and none of the girls had read either essay or poems before. They 'narrated' what they had read and in the course of their narration gave a full paraphrase of *The Elixir, The Pulley,* and one or two other poems. No point made by the poet was omitted and his exact words were used pretty freely. The teacher made comments upon one or two unusual words and that was all; to explain or enforce (otherwise than by a reverently sympathetic manner, the glance and words that showed that she too, cared), would have been impertinent. It is an interesting thing that hundreds of children of this age in Secondary and Elementary Schools and in families scattered over the world read and narrated the same essay and no doubt paraphrased the verses with equal ease. I felt humbled before the children knowing myself incapable of such immediate and rapid apprehension of several pages of new matter including poems whose intention is by no means obvious. In such ways the great thoughts of great thinkers illuminate children and they grow in knowledge, chiefly the knowledge of God.

"And yet this, the chief part of education, is drowned in torrents of talk, in tedious repetition, in objurgation and recrimination, in every sort of way in which the mind may be bored and the affections deadened" (Vol. 6, pp. 64, 65).

"Now this art of telling back is *Education* and is very enriching. We all practise it, we go over in our minds the points of a conversation, a lecture, a sermon, an article, and we are so made that only those ideas and arguments which we go over are we able to retain. Desultory reading or hearing is entertaining and refreshing, but is only educative here and there as our attention is strongly arrested. Further, we not only retain but realise, understand, what we thus go over. Each incident stands out, every phrase acquires new force, each link in the argument is riveted, in fact we have performed THE ACT OF KNOWING, and that which we have read, or heard, becomes a part of ourselves, it is assimilated after the due rejection of waste matter" (Vol. 6, p. 292).

"The child must read to know; his teacher's business is to see that he knows. All the acts of generalization, analysis, comparison, judgment, and so on, the mind performs for itself in the act of knowing. If we doubt this, we have only to try the effect of putting ourselves to sleep by relating silently and carefully, say, a chapter of Jane Austen or a chapter of the Bible, read once before going to bed. The degree of insight, the visualization, that comes with this sort of mental exercise is surprising" (Vol. 6, p. 304).

**40. You may want to memorize these summary mottos.**

"A few pedagogic maxims should help us, such as, 'Do not explain,' 'Do not question,' 'Let one reading of a passage suffice,' 'Require the pupil to relate the passage he has read' " (Vol. 6, p. 304).

## Grades 1–3

**41. Do not require narrations from children younger than six years old.**

"Until he is six, let Bobbie narrate only when and what he has a mind to. He must not be called upon to *tell* anything. Is this the secret of the strange long talks we watch with amusement between creatures of two, and four, and five? Is it possible

"The labour of thought is what his book must induce in the child."

# Narration

## Notes

that they narrate while they are still inarticulate, and that the other inarticulate person takes it all in? They try us, poor dear elders, and we reply 'Yes,' 'Really!' 'Do you think so?' to the babble of whose meaning we have no comprehension. Be this as it may; of what goes on in the dim region of 'under two' we have no assurance. But wait till the little fellow has words and he will 'tell' without end to whomsoever will listen to the tale, but, for choice, to his own compeers" (Vol. 1, pp. 231, 232).

### 42. Until your child can read fluently for himself, read aloud his books to him and have him narrate.

"When the child is six, not earlier, let him narrate the fairy-tale which has been read to him, episode by episode, upon one hearing of each; the Bible tale read to him in the words of the Bible; the well-written animal story; or all about other lands from some such volume as *The World at Home*. The seven-years-old boy will have begun to read for himself, but must get most of his intellectual nutriment, by ear, certainly, but read to him out of books" (Vol. 1, p. 232).

"Literature at its best is always direct and simple and a normal child of six listens with delight to the tales both of Old and New Testament read to him passage by passage, and by him narrated in turn, with delightful touches of native eloquence" (Vol. 6, p. 160).

"Our plan in each of these subjects is to read him the passage for the lesson (a good long passage), talk about it a little, avoiding much explanation, and then let him narrate what has been read. This he does very well and with pleasure, and is often happy in catching the style as well as the words of the author" (Vol. 3, p. 272).

"Children cannot of course themselves read a book which is by no means written down to the 'child's level' so the teacher reads and the children 'tell' paragraph by paragraph, passage by passage" (Vol. 6, p. 172).

### 43. Start by having your child narrate paragraphs, then gradually move to whole chapters.

"For this reason, reading lessons must be short; ten minutes or a quarter of an hour of fixed attention is enough for children of the ages we have in view, and a lesson of this length will enable a child to cover two or three pages of his book" (Vol. 1, p. 230).

"The simplest way of dealing with a paragraph or a chapter is to require the child to narrate its contents after a single attentive reading" (Vol. 3, p. 179).

"Children cannot of course themselves read a book which is by no means written down to the 'child's level' so the teacher reads and the children 'tell' paragraph by paragraph, passage by passage" (Vol. 6, p. 172).

"Form IA (7 to 9) hears and tells chapter by chapter" (Vol. 6, p. 180).

> "The child must read to know; his teacher's business is to see that he knows."

"Probably young children should be allowed to narrate paragraph by paragraph, while children of seven or eight will 'tell' chapter by chapter" (Vol. 6, p. 191).

"The time appropriated in the time-table at this stage to the teaching of some half-dozen more or less literary subjects such as Scripture, and the subjects I have indicated, is largely spent by the teachers in reading, say, two or three paragraphs at a time from some one of the set books, which children, here and there in the class, narrate" (Vol. 6, p. 244).

*44. Children under nine may occasionally be asked to write part of their narration or to write a short account of something familiar to them.*

"For children under nine, the question of composition resolves itself into that of narration, varied by some such simple exercise as to write a part and narrate a part, or write the whole account of a walk they have taken, a lesson they have studied, or of some simple matter that they know" (Vol. 1, p. 247).

*45. Record your child's narration in writing as he tells, if desired.*

"Children of six can tell to amazing purpose. The grown-up who writes the tale to their 'telling' will cover many pages before getting to the end of 'Hans and Gretel' or 'The Little Match Girl' or a Bible story. The facts are sure to be accurate and the expression surprisingly vigorous, striking and unhesitating" (Vol. 6, p. 190).

"The children in the first two classes narrate their answers, which someone writes from their dictation" (Vol. 3, p. 272).

## *Grades 4–12*

*46. As soon as your child can read fluently, transition to having him read the books himself and narrate them.*

"As soon as children are able to read with ease and fluency, they read their own lesson, either aloud or silently, with a view to narration" (Vol. 1, p. 233).

## Questions to Ask about Narration

### *General Guidelines for All Grades*
- Am I having my child show what he knows by narrating what he has read or heard?
- Do I require him to narrate after only one reading?
- Am I using pre-reading review narrations?
- Do I write key names or words from the reading on a small whiteboard or sheet of paper for my child to look at during the reading and narration?
- Am I trying to read a full episode?

---

*Older children do more written narrations. See page 70 for details.*

" 'Do not explain,' 'Do not question,' 'Let one reading of a passage suffice,' 'Require the pupil to relate the passage he has read.' "

# Notes

- Am I making sure the books are interesting and enjoyable to my child?
- Am I being careful to read through books consecutively, rather than random excerpts?
- Am I not asking direct questions on the content of the reading?
- Am I trying to encourage my child who is narrating by giving a genuinely-interested look or word?
- Am I being careful not to flood my child with my own thoughts and talk on the passage?
- Am I remembering not to interrupt my child when he is narrating?
- Am I trying not to correct my child's sentence structure or grammar during his narration?
- Do I wait until after my child is done narrating before I correct any mistakes on the passage's content?
- Am I allowing the children to take turns narrating in a group?
- Do I illustrate or elaborate on any lessons drawn from the reading after my child has finished narrating?
- Do I sometimes ask questions on a side issue or to gather my child's opinion?
- Am I occasionally using discussion points after the narration to make sure my child is reading intelligently?
- Am I looking over the passage ahead of time to find any discussion points that would be good to use?
- Am I teaching my child to make neat marginal notes or underlines in his books as appropriate?
- Do I sometimes ask my child to write a few questions that cover the passage he read?
- Am I being careful that any discussion points do not dampen my child's relation with the living book itself?
- Am I including the Bible as a book to be read, narrated, and discussed?
- Am I allowing time for narrations within the short lesson time period?
- Am I using one or two narration questions per book for end-of-term examinations?
- Am I consistently asking for narration in order to help my child pay full attention to a single reading?
- Do I encourage my child to see the story in his mind's eye as it is read?
- Do I understand how narration is a natural skill for most children?
- Am I reading aloud, editing, and keeping in my possession any books that may have inappropriate parts for my child?
- Do I understand how oral narration is good practice for public speaking?
- Am I satisfied that narration lays the groundwork for and provides practice in composition?
- Am I encouraging my child to occasionally write his narration as poetry?
- Do I understand that narrating is not the same as reciting from rote memory?
- Am I able to tell how well my child has assimilated the passage by the freedom he shows in narrating it?
- Am I encouraging my child to express his personality in his narrations?

"The simplest way of dealing with a paragraph or a chapter is to require the child to narrate its contents after a single attentive reading."

- Do I sometimes have my child draw or act a favorite scene from the reading as narration?
- Am I being careful to make the content of the acted narration more important than the set, costumes, or other trappings?
- Am I willing to replace a book that my child cannot narrate?
- Am I requiring my child to do the work himself and form his own relation with the book?
- Am I trying to be patient, calm, and encouraging until my child "hits his stride" in narrating?
- Do I understand that some students may narrate better in some subjects?
- Am I making narration a chief part of my child's education?
- Can I narrate or recite the four mottoes for a lesson with narration?

### Grades 1–3

- Am I careful not to require a narration from any child younger than six years old?
- Am I reading aloud the lesson books for my less-than-fluent reader?
- Am I allowing my child to start with narrating paragraphs until he is ready to move to longer passages?
- Do I occasionally ask a child younger than nine years old to write a part of his narration or a short account of something that is familiar to him?
- Do I occasionally write or type my child's narration as he tells it?

### Grades 4–12

- Do I have my fluent reader read his lesson books for himself?

## More Quotes on Narration

Let us tenderly and kindly cherish, therefore, the means of knowledge. Let us dare to read, think, speak, and write.—John Adams

Knowledge which is acquired under compulsion obtains no hold on the mind.—Plato

We ought to be ten times as hungry for knowledge as for food for the body.—Henry Ward Beecher

"Information is not knowledge."—Albert Einstein

"Children of six can tell to amazing purpose."

# Chapter 7
# *Composition*

"I still remember the composition class I took in high school," Carlie said. "We had to write about all sorts of strange things."

"Like what?" asked Simone.

"Topics we didn't care about and didn't really know anything about," explained Carlie. "For example, we had to write an essay on What Is Happiness? and a three-page paper on Life Inside a Ping-Pong Ball. Who comes up with those assignments?"

Simone laughed. "I know what you mean. So how do you do composition with your children?"

"We do mostly oral composition during the first three grades."

"Oral composition? What's that?" asked Simone.

Carlie smiled. "Do you remember the hardest part about writing those composition assignments? It was coming up with what you were going to say, right? Well, we practice just the thought process for a while in the early grades, and they tell their compositions instead of writing them. Later we add the element of the hand trying to keep up with the thoughts."

Simone nodded. "Makes sense. And how do you pick your topics?"

"We stick to talking and writing about people and events that the children know about and care about," replied Carlie. "For example, they tell me about a character in one of their books or about something that happened that day."

"So they never have an actual composition lesson?"

"When they get older, we will fine-tune their writing with some specific instruction," Carlie said. "But I am *not* going to make them write three pages about Life inside a Ping-Pong Ball!"

## Charlotte's Thoughts on Composition

### *General Guidelines for All Grades*

*1. Oral composition should be used habitually throughout all grades.*

"Oral composition is the habit of the school from the age of six to eighteen" (Vol. 6, pp. 269, 270).

*2. Oral narration lays the foundation for composition, and written narration provides practice in composition.*

"For children under nine, the question of composition resolves itself into that of narration, varied by some such simple exercise as to write a part and narrate a part, or write the whole account of a walk they have taken, a lesson they have studied, or of some simple matter that they know. . . . They should narrate in the first place, and they will compose, later, readily enough" (Vol. 1, p. 247).

---

**Notes**

*Composition is a natural outflowing of narration, a method that should be integrated into regular subjects.*

*For more on oral and written "telling back," narration, see page 43.*

"Oral composition is the habit of the school from the age of six to eighteen."

## Notes

*The P.U.S. was the Parents' Union School founded on Charlotte Mason's philosophy and methods.*

"If we would believe it, composition is as natural as jumping and running to children who have been allowed due use of books."

*3. Oral narration is more important than written, and those who can orally narrate can usually write their thoughts, as well.*

"To secure the power of speaking, I think it would be well if the habit of narration were more encouraged, in place of written composition. On the whole, it is more useful to be able to speak than to write, and the man or woman who is able to do the former can generally do the latter" (Vol. 3, p. 88).

*4. Narration/composition—whether written or oral—is natural to most children and does not need to be taught.*

"If we would believe it, composition is as natural as jumping and running to children who have been allowed due use of books. They should narrate in the first place, and they will compose, later, readily enough; but they [children under ten] should not be taught 'composition' " (Vol. 1, p. 247).

"All their work lends itself to oral composition and the power of such composition is innate in children and is not the result of instruction" (Vol. 6, p. 191).

"In few things do certain teachers labour in vain more than in the careful and methodical way in which they teach composition to young children. The drill that these undergo in forming sentences is unnecessary and stultifying, as much so perhaps as such drill would be in the acts of mastication and deglutination. Teachers err out of their exceeding goodwill and generous zeal. They feel that they cannot do too much for children and attempt to do for them those things which they are richly endowed to do for themselves. Among these is the art of composition" (Vol. 6, p. 190).

"But let me again say there must be no attempt to teach composition. Our failure as teachers is that we place too little dependence on the intellectual power of our scholars, and as they are modest little souls what the teacher kindly volunteers to do for them, they feel that they cannot do for themselves. But give them a fair field and no favour and they will describe their favourite scene from the play they have read, and much besides" (Vol. 6, p. 192).

*5. Directed composition lessons usually result in inferior work than that of students who have read good books and been given practice in oral narration.*

"Then follows a series of writing lessons, 'simple compositions on the subject of the lessons. . . . the children framed the sentences which the teacher wrote on the blackboard and the class copied afterwards.' Here is one composition,—'Robinson spent his first night in a tree. In the morning he was hungry but he saw nothing round him but grass and trees without fruit. On the sea-shore he found some shell-fish which he ate.' Compare this with the voluminous output of children of six or seven working on the P.U.S. scheme upon any subject that they know; with, indeed, the pages they will dictate after a single reading of a chapter of *Robinson Crusoe, not* a 'child's edition' " (Vol. 6, p. 115).

*6. Many traditional composition courses and classes violate a child's conscience and encourage plagiarism.*

" 'What a prodigiously well-read and delightful person the Reverend Lawrence

Veal was, George's master! He knows *everything*,' Amelia said. 'He says there is no place in the bar or the senate that Georgy may not aspire to. Look here,' and she went to the piano-drawer and drew out a theme of George's composition. This great effort of genius, which is still in the possession of Georgy's mother, is as follows:—

" '*On Selfishness.*—Of all the vices which degrade the human character, Selfishness is the most odious and contemptible. An undue love of Self leads to the most monstrous crimes and occasions of the greatest misfortunes both in *States and Families*. As a selfish man will impoverish his family and often bring them to ruin; so a selfish king brings ruin on his people and often plunges them into war. Example: The selfishness of Achilles, as remarked by the poet Homer, occasioned a thousand woes to the Greeks—μυρί᾽ Ἀχαιοῖς ἄλγε᾽ ἔθηκέ—(Hom., *Il.* A. 2). The selfishness of the late Napoleon Bonaparte occasioned innumerable wars in Europe, and caused him to perish, himself, in a miserable island—that of St. Helena in the Atlantic Ocean.

" 'We see by these examples that we are not to consult our own interest and ambition, but that we are to consider the interests of others as well as our own.

George S. Osborne.

" 'Athene House, 24 *April* 1827.'

" ' Think of him' (George was 10) 'writing such a hand, and quoting Greek too, at his age,' the delighted mother said.

"And well might Mrs George Sedley be delighted. Would not many a mother to-day triumph in such a literary effort? What can Thackeray be laughing at? Or does he, in truth, give us this little 'theme' as a *tour de force*?

"I think this great moral teacher here throws down the gauntlet in challenge of an educational futility which is practised, and an educational fallacy which is accepted, even in the twentieth century. That futility is the extraction of original composition from schoolboys and schoolgirls. The proper function of the mind of the young scholar is to collect material for the generalisations of after-life. If a child is asked to generalise, that is, to write an essay upon some abstract theme, a double wrong is done him. He is brought up before a stone wall by being asked to do what is impossible to him, and that is discouraging. But a worse moral injury happens to him in that, having no thought of his own to offer on the subject, he puts together such tags of commonplace thought as have come in his way and offers the whole as his 'composition,' an effort which puts a strain upon his conscience while it piques his vanity. In these days masters do not consciously put their hand to the work of their pupils as did that 'prodigiously well-read and delightful' master who had the educating of George Osborne. But, perhaps without knowing it, they give the ideas which the cunning schoolboy seizes to 'stick' into the 'essay' he hates" (Vol. 1, pp. 243–245).

"We must disabuse our minds of the theory that the functions of education are in the main gymnastic, a continual drawing out without a corresponding act of putting in. The modern emphasis upon 'self-expression' has given new currency to this idea; we who know how little there is in us that we have not received, that the most we can do is to give an original twist, a new application, to an idea that has been passed on to us; who recognise, humbly enough, that we are but torch-bearers, passing on our light to the next as we have received it from the last, even we invite children to 'express themselves' about a tank, a Norman castle, the Man

## Notes

**Tour de force** *means an exceptionally creative achievement.*

"They should narrate in the first place, and they will compose, later, readily enough."

## Notes

in the Moon, not recognising that the quaint things children say on unfamiliar subjects are no more than a patchwork of notions picked up here and there. One is not sure that so-called original composition is wholesome for children, because their consciences are alert and they are quite aware of their borrowings; it may be better that they should read on a theme before they write upon it, using then as much latitude as they like" (Vol. 6, p. 108).

**7. Traditional composition courses can be an insult to a child's intelligence.**

"Sometimes they do more. They deliberately teach children how to 'build a sentence' and how to 'bind sentences' together.

"Lessons in Composition.—Here is a series of preliminary exercises (or rather a part of a series, which numbers 40) intended to help a child to write an essay on 'An Umbrella,' from a book of the hour proceeding from one of our best publishing houses:—

*"Step I.*

"1. What are you?
"2. How did you get your name?
"3. Who uses you?
"4. What were you once?
"5. What were you like then?
"6. Where were you obtained or found?
"7. Of what stuff or materials are you made?
"8. From what sources do you come?
"9. What are your parts?
"10. Are you made, grown, or fitted together?

• • • • • •

*"Step II.*

"I am an umbrella, and am used by many people, young and old.

"I get my name from a word which means a shade.

"The stick came perhaps from America, and is quite smooth, even, and polished, so that the metal ring may slide easily up and down the stick.

"My parts are a frame and a cover. My frame consists of a stick about a yard long, wires, and a sliding metal band. At the lower end of the stick is a steel ferrule or ring. This keeps the end from wearing away when I am used in walking.

*"Step III.*

"Now use *it, is,* and *was,* instead of *I, have, my,* and *am.*

• • • • • •

*"Exercise.*

"Now write out your own description of it."

"And this is work intended for Standards VI. And VII.! That is to say, this kind of thing is the final literary effort to be exacted from children in our elementary schools!

"The two volumes (I quote from near the end of the second and more advanced

> "One is not sure that so-called original composition is wholesome for children, because their consciences are alert and they are quite aware of their borrowings."

volume) are not to be gibbeted as exceptionally bad. A few years ago the appalling discovery was made that, both in secondary and elementary schools, 'composition' was dreadfully defective, and, therefore, badly taught. Since then many volumes have been produced, more or less on the lines indicated in the above citation, and distinguished publishers have not perceived that to offer to the public, with the sanction of their name, works of this sterilising and injurious character, is an offence against society. The body of a child is sacred in the eye of the law, but his intellectual powers may be annihilated on such starvation diet as this, and nothing said! The worst of it is, both authors and publishers in every case act upon the fallacy that well-intentioned effort is always excusable, if not praiseworthy. They do not perceive that no effort is permissible towards the education of children without an intelligent conception, both of children, and of what is meant by education" (Vol. 1, pp. 245–247).

*8. Children should write of what they know and care about through their readings or experiences.*

"Children reject the notion of writing an 'Essay on Happiness' " (Vol. 6, p. 10).

"The point to be considered is that the subject be one on which, to quote again Jane Austen's expression, the imagination of the children has been 'warmed.' They should be asked to write upon subjects which have interested them keenly" (Vol. 6, p. 193).

"They will describe their favourite scene from The Tempest or Woodstock. They write or 'tell' stories from work set in Plutarch or Shakespeare or tell of the events of the day. They narrate from English, French and General History, from the Old and the New Testament, from *Stories from the History of Rome*, from Bulfinch's *Age of Fable*, from, for example, Goldsmith's or Wordsworth's poems, from *The Heroes of Asgard*: in fact, Composition is not an adjunct but an integral part of their education in every subject. The exercise affords very great pleasure to children, perhaps we all like to tell what we know, and in proportion as their composition is entirely artless, it is in the same degree artistic and any child is apt to produce a style to be envied for its vigour and grace" (Vol. 6, p. 192).

*9. Reading worthwhile books as a habit usually results in easy and vigorous composition.*

"Our great failure seems to me to be caused by the fact that we do not form *the habit of reading books that are worth while* in children while they are at school and are under twelve years of age. The free use of books implies correct spelling and easy and vigorous composition without direct teaching of these subjects" (Vol. 3, Preface).

"By means of the free use of books the mechanical difficulties of education—reading, spelling, composition, etc.—disappear, and studies prove themselves to be 'for delight, for ornament, and for ability' " (Vol. 3, p. 214).

"Examination papers representing tens of thousands of children working in Elementary Schools, Secondary Schools and home schoolrooms have just passed

*Notes*

"How the children have revelled in knowledge!"

under my eye. How the children have revelled in knowledge! and how good and interesting all their answers are! How well they spell on the whole and how well they write!" (Vol. 6, p. 45).

**10. *Knowing something of history and literature is foundational to writing.***

"The educational outlook is rather misty and depressing both at home and abroad. That science should be a staple of education, that the teaching of Latin, of modern languages, of mathematics, must be reformed, that nature and handicrafts should be pressed into service for the training of the eye and hand, that boys and girls must learn to write English and therefore must know something of history and literature; and, on the other hand, that education must be made more technical and utilitarian—these, and such as these, are the cries of expedience with which we take the field" (Vol. 1, Preface).

**11. *Composition/written narrations should include letter writing.***

"Have we not all correspondents whose epistles are delightful in their rippling, sparkling flow of talk, with just the little touches of tenderness and confidence which make a letter a personal thing? Do we not know what it is to open an envelope with the certainty that we shall take pure delight in every line of its enclosure? Because we love the writer? Not necessarily. The morning's post may bring you an epistle from an unknown correspondent which shall captivate you, fill you with a sense of well-being for a whole day; and this, not because of the contents, but simply because the gracious courtesy of it puts you on good terms with yourself and the world. One man may refuse a favour and another grant it; and the way in which the refusal is couched may give you more pleasure than the concession.

"Possibly, sincere deference is the ingredient which gives flavour to a gracious letter; and if we do not write epistles as charming as those of our grandfathers and grandmothers, is it because we do not think enough of one another to make a spontaneous outpouring worth while? The children of parents living in India usually write and receive interesting letters, and this, because children and parents are glad to make the most of the only means of knowing each other. Perhaps no opportunity of writing detailed, animated letters to children should be omitted. Let them grow up with the idea that it is worth while to write good letters. That schoolboy whose correspondence for a term was comprised in two post-cards, 'All right:' 'Which train?' is not a good model, except as brevity is the soul of wit!" (Vol. 5, pp. 218, 219).

**12. *Occasionally ask your older child to write his narration as poetry.***

"Sometimes they are asked to write verses about a personage or an event; the result is not remarkable by way of poetry, but sums up a good deal of thoughtful reading in a delightful way" (Vol. 6, p. 242).

## Grades 1–3
**13. *For children six to nine years old, composition is accomplished by oral narration and occasional written narration.***

" 'Composition' comes by Nature.—In fact, lessons on '*composition*' should follow the model of that famous essay on 'Snakes in Ireland'—'There are none.'

---

*Notes*

*See pages 139–171 for examples of written narrations/compositions by students in Charlotte's schools. Notice the various kinds of composition styles used: poetry, letter, play, narrative, etc.*

"Before they are ten, children who have been in the habit of using books will write good, vigorous English with ease and freedom; that is, if they have not been hampered by instructions."

For children under nine, the question of composition resolves itself into that of narration, varied by some such simple exercise as to write a part and narrate a part, or write the whole account of a walk they have taken, a lesson they have studied, or of some simple matter that they know" (Vol. 1, p. 247).

"Children are in Form IA from 7 to 9 and their reading is wider and their composition more copious. They will 'tell' in their examinations about the Feeding of the Four Thousand, about the Building of the Tabernacle, How Doubting Castle was demolished, about the burning of Old St. Paul's, How we know that the world is round and a great deal besides; for all their work lends itself to oral composition and the power of such composition is innate in children and is not the result of instruction" (Vol. 6, p. 191).

**14. *There need not be any direct teaching of composition, written or oral, in the early grades.***

"Composition in Form I (A and B) is almost entirely oral and is so much associated with Bible history, English history, geography, natural history, that it hardly calls for a special place on the programme, where however it does appear as 'Tales' " (Vol. 6, p. 190).

"Before they are ten, children who have been in the habit of using books will write good, vigorous English with ease and freedom; that is, if they have not been hampered by instructions. It is well for them not even to learn rules for the placing of full stops and capitals until they notice how these things occur in their books. Our business is to provide children with material in their lessons, and, *leave the handling of such material to themselves.* If we would believe it, composition is as natural as jumping and running to children who have been allowed due use of books. They should narrate in the first place, and they will compose, later, readily enough; but they should not be taught 'composition' " (Vol. 1, p. 247).

"Some Syntax is necessary and a good deal of what may be called historical Grammar, but, *not* in order to teach the art of correct writing and speaking; this is a native art, and the beautiful consecutive and eloquent speech of young scholars in narrating what they have read is a thing to be listened to not without envy" (Vol. 6, p. 269).

**15. *Do not worry too much about punctuation or capitalization in beginning written narrations.***

"Children must not be teased or instructed about the use of stops or capital letters. These things too come by nature to the child who reads, and the teacher's instructions are apt to issue in the use of a pepper box for commas" (Vol. 6, p. 191).

"It is well for them not even to learn rules for the placing of full stops and capitals until they notice how these things occur in their books" (Vol. 1, p 247).

## Grades 4–6

**16. *Beginning around ages 9–12, your child should write his own narrations.***

"Form II (A and B), (ages 9 to 12). Children in this Form have a wider range

## Notes

*Children ages 6 to 8 may dictate their narrations to you as you record them in writing.*

*A Form is somewhat similar to a Grade.*

"All their work lends itself to oral composition and the power of such composition is innate in children."

of reading, a more fertile field of thought, and more delightful subjects for composition. They write their little essays themselves, and as for the accuracy of their knowledge and justice of their expression, why, 'still the wonder grows' " (Vol. 6, p. 192).

***17. Begin helping your child improve his writing skills when he is old enough to take a critical interest in the use of words of his own accord.***

"Let me repeat that what is called 'composition' is an inevitable consequence of this free yet exact use of books and requires no special attention until the pupil is old enough to take naturally a critical interest in the use of words" (Vol. 6, p. 274).

***18. Composition improvement should be addressed one or two points at a time.***

"Perhaps the method of a University tutor is the best that can be adopted; that is, a point or two might be taken up in a given composition and suggestions or corrections made with little talk" (Vol. 6, pp. 193, 194).

## Grades 7–9

***19. Children eleven to fifteen years old should write more narrations than younger students, but there is still no teaching of composition as a separate subject.***

"In Class III. the range of age is from eleven or twelve to fifteen. . . .The reader will notice from the subjoined specimens that the papers are still written *con amore,* and show an intelligent grasp of the several subjects. Though there are errors in many of the papers, they are not often the mistakes of ignorance or stupidity, nor are they those of a person who has never understood what he is writing about. 'Composition' is never taught as a subject; well-taught children compose as well-bred children behave—by the light of nature. It is probable that no considerable writer was ever taught the art of 'composition' " (Vol. 3, p. 286).

***20. Start asking for poetry compositions/narrations around ages eleven to fifteen.***

"The measured cadences of verse are as pleasing to children as to their elders. Many children write verse as readily as prose, and the conciseness and power of bringing their subject matter to a point which this form of composition requires affords valuable mental training. One thing must be borne in mind. Exercises in scansion are as necessary in English as in Latin verse. Rhythm and accent on the other hand take care of themselves in proportion as a child is accustomed to read poetry" (Vol. 6, p. 193).

"Sometimes they are asked to write verses about a personage or an event; the result is not remarkable by way of poetry, but sums up a good deal of thoughtful reading in a delightful way" (Vol. 6, p. 242).

## Grades 10–12

***21. Children sixteen to eighteen years old need some definite teaching in the art of composition, but not too much.***

---

### Notes

**Con amore** *means "with love."*

*See examples of students' poetry writing on pages 159–171.*

"If we would believe it, composition is as natural as jumping and running to children who have been allowed due use of books."

"Forms V and VI. In these Forms some definite teaching in the art of composition is advisable, but not too much, lest the young scholars be saddled with a stilted style which may encumber them for life. Perhaps the method of a University tutor is the best that can be adopted; that is, a point or two might be taken up in a given composition and suggestions or corrections made with little talk. Having been brought up so far upon stylists the pupils are almost certain to have formed a good style; because they have been thrown into the society of *many* great minds, they will not make a servile copy of any one but will shape an individual style out of the wealth of material they possess; and because they have matter in abundance and of the best they will not write mere verbiage" (Vol. 6, pp. 193, 194).

## Questions to Ask about Composition

### General Guidelines for All Grades

- Am I using oral composition (narration) throughout all the grades?
- Am I laying a good foundation with oral narration, since oral narration is more important than written?
- Do I understand that oral narration/composition is natural to most children and does not need to be taught?
- Am I getting inferior results from my child's compositions because I'm giving formulaic, teacher-directed lessons?
- If I am using a composition course, does it violate my child's conscience and encourage plagiarism?
- If I am using a composition course, am I insulting my child's intelligence with its approach?
- Am I careful to have my child write about things he knows and cares about, rather than random topics?
- Am I supporting good composition skills by having my child read worthwhile books?
- Am I laying a good foundation in composition by giving my child good history and literature books?
- Am I trying to include letter-writing as part of my child's written narrations/compositions?

### Grades 1–3

- Am I satisfied that the only composition my six- to nine-year-old needs is oral narration and occasional written narration?
- Do I avoid direct teaching of composition as a separate subject for my child through fifteen years old?
- Am I trying not to worry about punctuation or capitalization in beginning written narrations?

### Grades 4–6

- Am I asking my nine- to twelve-year-old child to write his own narrations?
- Is my child taking an interest in the use of words of his own accord and is, therefore, ready for me to help him improve his writing skill?

---

## Notes

*Most language arts composition courses include these four types of writing:*
- *Narrative—Telling a story, either fact or fiction.*
- *Expository—Informing or explaining a subject.*
- *Descriptive – A type of expository writing. Painting a picture by incorporating imagery and specific details.*
- *Persuasive—Stating an opinion and attempting to influence the reader.*

*Charlotte included all four types in her narration questions, as well as asking for various styles of writing:*
- *Story*
- *Poetry*
- *Letter*
- *Script*
- *Essay*
- *Dialogue*
- *Diary*
- *Exposition*
- *Diagram drawing*

*See page 173 for examples of the narration questions Charlotte used.*

"It is probable that no considerable writer was ever taught the art of 'composition.'"

- Am I addressing those composition improvements only one or two points at a time?

### Grades 7–9
- Am I requiring my older child to write more narrations?
- Am I occasionally asking for narrations in poetry form beginning with ages 11 to 15?

### Grades 10–12
- Am I giving my child, ages 16 to 18, some definite teaching in the art of composition?

## More Quotes on Composition

Fill your paper with the breathings of your heart.—William Wordsworth

The difference between the right word and the almost right word is the difference between lightning and a lightning bug.—Mark Twain

Proofread carefully to see if you any words out.—Author Unknown

Words—so innocent and powerless as they are, as standing in a dictionary, how potent for good and evil they become in the hands of one who knows how to combine them.—Nathaniel Hawthorne

You could compile the worst book in the world entirely out of selected passages from the best writers in the world.—G.K. Chesterton

The two most engaging powers of an author are to make new things familiar and familiar things new.—Samuel Johnson

"Having been brought up so far upon stylists the pupils are almost certain to have formed a good style."

# Chapter 8
# *Reading Aloud*

> Reading aloud is a method that should be integrated into regular subjects.

"I love listening to your children read to my little ones," said Paula. "How did you teach them to read so well?"

"I guess I just try to set a good example and give them plenty of practice," Mikel replied.

"Did you have them practice imitating you?" Paula was curious.

"Not at all," said Mikel. "I read aloud every day after lunch, and I consciously try to slow down my speaking so my eyes can run ahead and see what's coming up. I look for clues about who is speaking and how they're feeling, and try to reflect that in my voice. Oh, and punctuation. The punctuation can give you lots of clues about when to pause. It takes some effort, but it gets easier with practice."

"Well, your children have certainly picked up the knack of it," Paula replied. "It's so pleasant to listen to them read. I'll have to start working on slowing down my mouth and letting my eyes run ahead."

"And you're welcome to come listen to our lunchtime read-aloud any time you want to," added Mikel with a twinkle in her eye.

## Charlotte's Thoughts on Reading Aloud

### *General Guidelines for All Grades*

*1. Give your child plenty of practice reading aloud from his school books and a good deal of poetry.*

"He should have practice, too, in reading aloud, for the most part, in the books he is using for his term's work. These should include a good deal of poetry" (Vol. 1, p. 227).

*2. Good reading aloud is distinct, easy, and sympathetic.*

"If reading is to be pleasant to the listeners, the reading itself must be distinct, easy, and sympathetic" (Vol. 5, p. 220).

*3. Teach your child to speak beautiful words in a beautiful way.*

"He should have practice, too, in reading aloud, for the most part, in the books he is using for his term's work. These should include a good deal of poetry, to accustom him to the delicate rendering of shades of meaning, and especially to make him aware that words are beautiful in themselves, that they are a source of pleasure, and are worthy of our honour; and that a beautiful word deserves to be beautifully said, with a certain roundness of tone and precision of utterance" (Vol. 1, p. 227).

*4. Parents are best equipped to help their children learn how to read aloud for the listeners' pleasure.*

> Beginning readers, ages 6–8, should have practice in reading aloud as they learn to decode the words. However, their school books should be read aloud to them at that age.

> "Sympathetic" means sharing in another's feelings. So sympathetic reading would understand and convey the emotions of the characters or the author.

> "A beautiful word deserves to be beautifully said, with a certain roundness of tone and precision of utterance."

## Notes

*Charlotte advocated a family read-aloud time, which is a great opportunity for children to practice and perfect their reading aloud skills.*

*Remember that much of a child's enunciation and inflection will be influenced by listening to the parent or teacher read aloud.*

*Your eyes can take in words faster than your mouth can say them. So let your mouth take its time while your eyes run ahead and reconnoiter.*

**"Intelligent reading comes only of the habit of reading with understanding."**

"And here is something more which parents must do for their children themselves, for nobody else will get them into the habit of reading for the pleasure of other people from the moment when they can read fluently at all" (Vol. 5, p. 220).

### 5. Encourage your child to read with expression, but don't teach him simply to imitate you.

"Quite young children are open to this sort of teaching, conveyed, not in a lesson, but by a word now and then" (Vol. 1, p. 227).

"In this connection the teacher should not trust to setting, as it were, a copy in reading for the children's imitation. They do imitate readily enough, catching tricks of emphasis and action in an amusing way; but these are mere tricks, an aping of intelligence. The child must express what *he* feels to be the author's meaning; and this sort of intelligent reading comes only of the habit of reading with understanding" (Vol. 1, pp. 227, 228).

### 6. Three common mistakes when reading aloud are (1) poor enunciation, (2) not looking ahead, and (3) yawning while reading.

"After indistinct and careless enunciation, perhaps the two most trying faults in a reader are, the slowness which does not see what is coming next, and stumbles over the new clause, and the habit of gasping, like a fish out of water, several times in the course of a sentence" (Vol. 5, pp. 220, 221).

### 7. An easy way to stop yawning while reading is to breathe through the nose, not through the mouth.

"The last fault is easy of cure: 'Never breathe through the lips, but always through the nostrils, in reading,' is a safe rule: if the lips be closed in the act of taking breath, enough air is inhaled to inflate the lungs, and supply 'breath' to the reader: if an undue supply is taken in by mouth and nostrils both, the inconvenience is caused which relieves itself in gasps" (Vol. 5, p. 221).

### 8. You can use simple breathing exercises to remind your child of the proper way to breathe when reading aloud.

"It is important that, when reading aloud, children should make due use of the vocal organs, and, for this reason, a reading lesson should be introduced by two or three simple breathing exercises, as, for example, a long inspiration with closed lips and a slow expiration with open mouth" (Vol. 1, p. 230).

### 9. Try to look a line ahead when reading aloud.

"The stumbling reader spoils his book from sheer want of attention. He should train himself to look on, to be always a line in advance; so that he may be ready for what is coming" (Vol. 5, p. 221).

### 10. Reading aloud with pauses in the correct places, reflecting the punctuation, comes from understanding the passage.

"The habit of 'minding your stops' comes of intelligent reading. A child's understanding of the passage will lead him to correct pointing" (Vol. 1, p. 230).

*11. Correct poor enunciation one point at a time.*

"Faults in enunciation should be dealt with one by one. For instance, one week the reader takes pains to secure the 'd' in 'and'; the other letters will take care of themselves, and the less they are heard the better. Indeed, if the final consonants are secured, *d, t,* and *ng* especially, the reading will be distinct and finished" (Vol. 5, p. 221).

*12. Teach your child that careful and proper enunciation reflects the respect due to well-written words.*

"Provincial pronunciation and slipshod enunciation must be guarded against. Practice in pure vowel sounds, and the respect for words which will not allow of their being hastily slurred over, should cure these defects. By the way, quite little children commonly enunciate beautifully, because a big word is a new acquirement which they delight in and make the most of; our efforts should be directed to make older children hold words in like esteem" (Vol. 1, p. 230).

*13. Help your child realize that his listeners' pleasure in the book depends on his reading well.*

"Let everybody take his night or his week for reading, with the certainty that the pleasure of the whole family depends on his reading well" (Vol. 5, p. 221).

## Questions to Ask on Reading Aloud

### General Guidelines for All Grades
- Am I seeking to give my child plenty of practice reading aloud from his school books, including a good deal of poetry?
- Am I encouraging my child to read aloud distinctly, easily, and with sympathy?
- Am I teaching my child to speak beautiful words in a beautiful way?
- Do I accept the fact that parents are best equipped to help children learn how to read aloud pleasantly?
- Am I encouraging my child to read with good expression, not just imitating someone else's reading?
- Do I or my child struggle with poor enunciation, not looking ahead, or yawning while reading aloud?
- Am I trying to breathe through my nose, so as not to yawn while reading aloud?
- Am I using simple breathing exercises to remind my child to breathe through his nose when reading aloud?
- Am I trying to look a line ahead when reading aloud, and encouraging my child to do the same when he is reading aloud?
- Am I trying to read with understanding and pause in the correct places while reading aloud?
- Am I being careful to correct any poor enunciation one point at a time?

> "Quite little children commonly enunciate beautifully, because a big word is a new acquirement which they delight in and make the most of; our efforts should be directed to make older children hold words in like esteem."

- Am I communicating to my child how careful and proper enunciation shows respect due to well-written words?
- Am I communicating how others' pleasure in a book can depend on the reader's skill?

## Other Quotes on Reading

"A book reads the better which is our own, and has been so long known to us, that we know the topography of its blots, and dog's ears, and can trace the dirt in it to having read it at tea with buttered muffins."—Charles Lamb

"How many a man has dated a new era in his life from the reading of a book."—Henry David Thoreau

"The love of learning, the sequestered nooks,
And all the sweet serenity of books."—Henry Wadsworth Longfellow

"That is a good book which is opened with expectation and closed with profit."—Amos Bronson Alcott

"Some books are to be tasted, others to be swallowed, and some few to be chewed and digested."—Francis Bacon

---

"The pleasure of the whole family depends on his reading well."

# Part 3

# Language Arts Lessons

# Chapter 9
# *Beginning Reading*

*Beginning reading is taught as specific language arts lessons.*

"I'm stuck," Pam greeted her sister as she came through the door.

"Hello to you too," joked Bethany. "What's up?"

"You know that Ben knows all his letters and the sounds they make. Well, now he's starting to put together three-letter words with short vowels, and I don't have a clue what to do next," Pam sighed as she flopped into a chair.

"Sounds like he's making good progress," remarked Bethany. "You're not pushing him, right?"

"No, of course not," replied Pam. "He's the one pushing. He *so* wants to read!"

Bethany smiled. "Sounds like Ben. Okay, here's what you do next."

Pam rummaged in her bag for a spiral notebook and clicked her pen. "Ready."

"Keep going with the three-letter short-vowel words. When he's ready for something a little different, show him how you can add a silent-e to the end of many of those words to make the vowel long."

"Got it." Pam kept her eyes on the notebook and wrote furiously.

"After that, mix in some blends like *ng* and *th* to keep it interesting. When he has mastered all that, you're ready for actual reading lessons."

Pam stopped writing and looked up at Bethany. "Isn't that what we've been doing?"

"Not really. You've been laying the foundation, but this is where Ben will discover the delight in reading for himself," explained Bethany. "Take a poem that he's heard and type it up on your computer. Print one copy as is. Enlarge the font and print a second copy to cut apart into individual words. Then mix up the word order and print a third copy."

"Hang on," interrupted Pam. " . . . mix up word order and print. Okay, go."

"No, wait. Stop writing for a minute and listen to the big idea," Bethany instructed. "We'll go over the details after tea."

Pam set down her pen.

"You're going to use the words of the poem for your lessons. You'll be teaching Ben to recognize those words like he recognizes his friends' faces, no matter where he sees them. And you will alternate teaching sight words and teaching word families. Ben will learn hundreds and thousands of words; you will be his hero; and he will love reading for the rest of his life," Bethany finished with a flourish.

Laughing, Pam laid her notebook on the table. "Perfect. Now where's that tea?"

## Charlotte's Thoughts on Beginning Reading

*Stage One: The Alphabet Letters and Their Sounds*

*1. Give your child letters that he can touch and handle—whether lettered wooden blocks, magnetic letters, or whatever—both upper case and lower case.*

*The ideas given in Stage One on playing with letters can be used during the early years and set the foundation for beginning reading lessons.*

"The learning of the alphabet should be made a means of cultivating the child's observation."

## Beginning Reading

### Notes

*Let your child progress at his own pace in learning the alphabet. Please don't feel like these activities are requirements for your toddlers!*

"As for his letters, the child usually teaches himself. He has his box of ivory letters and picks out *p* for pudding, *b* for blackbird, *h* for horse, big and little, and knows them both" (Vol. 1, p. 201).

*2. Draw letters in the air and see if your child can name them, thus encouraging the habit of careful observation.*

"But the learning of the alphabet should be made a means of cultivating the child's observation: he should be made to *see* what he looks at. Make big *B* in the air, and let him name it" (Vol. 1, p. 201).

*3. Let your child draw letters in the air or in a tray of sand and you name them.*

"Then let him make round *O*, and crooked *S*, and *T* for Tommy, and you name the letters as the little finger forms them with unsteady strokes in the air. To make the small letters thus from memory is a work of more art, and requires more careful observation on the child's part. A tray of sand is useful at this stage. The child draws his finger boldly through the sand, and then puts a back to his *D*; and behold, his first essay in making a straight line and a curve" (Vol. 1, p. 201).

*4. Be creative and use whatever you have to teach the alphabet.*

"But the devices for making the learning of the '*A B C*' interesting are endless" (Vol. 1, p. 201).

*5. Do not hurry your child to learn all the A B C's.*

"There is no occasion to hurry the child" (Vol. 1, p. 201).

*6. Let your child find all the uppercase d's and lowercase d's (or another letter he has learned) on a page of large print.*

"Let him learn one form at a time, and know it so well that he can pick out the *d*'s, say, big and little, in a page of large print" (Vol. 1, p. 201).

*7. Teach your child the sounds that the letters make.*

"Let him say *d* for duck, dog, doll, thus: *d*-uck, *d*-og, prolonging the sound of the initial consonant, and at last sounding *d* alone, not *dee*, but *d'*, the mere sound of the consonant separated as far as possible from the following vowel" (Vol. 1, p. 201).

*8. Many children will learn the alphabet on their own, but there is no harm in teaching it when approached as play.*

"Let the child alone, and he will learn the alphabet for himself: but few mothers can resist the pleasure of teaching it; and there is no reason why they should, for this kind of learning is no more than play to the child, and if the alphabet be *taught* to the little student, his appreciation of both form and sound will be cultivated" (Vol. 1, pp. 201, 202).

*9. You can begin teaching the alphabet whenever the child shows an interest in his box of letters, as long as you keep it a game.*

"There is no occasion to hurry the child."

"When should he begin? Whenever his box of letters begins to interest him. The baby of two will often be able to name half a dozen letters; and there is nothing against it so long as the finding and naming of letters is a game to him" (Vol. 1, p. 202).

### 10. Be careful not to push, tease, or show off your child's progress in learning the alphabet.

"But he must not be urged, required to show off, teased to find letters when his heart is set on other play" (Vol. 1, p. 202).

### 11. Recognize that different children are ready to read at different ages.

"It is open to discussion whether the child should acquire the art unconsciously, from his infancy upwards, or whether the effort should be deferred until he is, say, six or seven, and then made with vigour" (Vol. 1, p. 199).

"I would have children taught *to read* before they learn the mechanical arts of reading and writing; and they learn delightfully; they give perfect attention to paragraph or page read to them and are able to relate the matter point by point, *in their own words*; but they demand classical English and cannot learn to read in this sense upon anything less. They begin their 'schooling' in 'letters' at six, and begin at the same time to learn mechanical reading and writing. A child does not lose by spending a couple of years in acquiring these because he is meanwhile 'reading' the Bible, history, geography, tales, with close attention and a remarkable power of reproduction, or rather, of translation into his own language; he is acquiring a copious vocabulary and the habit of consecutive speech. In a word, he is an educated child from the first, and his power of dealing with books, with several books in the course of a morning's 'school,' increases with his age.

"But children are not all alike; there is as much difference between them as between men or women; two or three months ago, a small boy, not quite six, came to school (by post); and his record was that he could read anything in five languages, and was now teaching himself the Greek characters" (Vol. 6, pp. 30, 31).

### 12. Many children teach themselves to read, so don't let the idea of teaching reading intimidate you.

"Many persons consider that to learn to read a language so full of anomalies and difficulties as our own is a task which should not be imposed too soon on the childish mind. But, as a matter of fact, few of us can recollect how or when we learned to read: for all we know, it came by nature, like the art of running; and not only so, but often mothers of the educated classes do not know how their children learned to read. 'Oh, he taught himself,' is all the account his mother can give of little Dick's proficiency. Whereby it is plain, that this notion of the extreme difficulty of learning to read is begotten by the elders rather than by the children" (Vol. 1, p. 200).

### 13. At the same time, recognize that learning to read does require effort, so do all you can to make the task easy and inviting.

"Probably that vague whole which we call 'Education' offers no more difficult and repellent task than that to which every little child is (or ought to be) set down—

*Notes*

*While children are still learning to read fluently, you can read their other lesson books to them. See page 43 for more on reading and narrating lesson books.*

"Children are not all alike."

the task of learning to read. We realise the labour of it when some grown man makes a heroic effort to remedy shameful ignorance, but we forget how contrary to Nature it is for a little child to occupy himself with dreary hieroglyphics—all so dreadfully alike!—when the world is teeming with interesting objects which he is agog to know. But we cannot excuse our volatile Tommy, nor is it good for him that we should. It is quite necessary he should know how to read; and not only so—the discipline of the task is altogether wholesome for the little man. At the same time, let us recognise that learning to read is to many children hard work, and let us do what we can to make the task easy and inviting" (Vol. 1, p. 214).

### 14. Be prepared to use a combination of sight words and phonics to teach reading.

"Definitely, what is it we propose in teaching a child to read? *(a)* that he shall know at sight, say, some thousand words; *(b)* That he shall be able to build up new words with the elements of these. Let him learn ten new words a day, and in twenty weeks he will be to some extent able to read, without any question as to the number of letters in a word. For the second, and less important, part of our task, the child must know the sounds of the letters, and acquire power to throw given sounds into new combinations" (Vol. 1, pp. 215, 216).

## Stage Two: Preparation for Reading
### 15. Make a game of putting together the words in word families.

"Exercises treated as a game, which yet teach the powers of the letters, will be better to begin with than actual sentences. Take up two of his letters and make the syllable 'at': tell him it is the word we use when we say 'at home,' 'at school.' Then put *b* to 'at'—*bat; c* to 'at'—*cat; fat, hat, mat, sat, rat,* and so on" (Vol. 1, p. 202).

### 16. Use actual words and let the child say each one with its initial consonant added.

"First, let the child say what the word becomes with each initial consonant; then let him add the right consonant to 'at,' in order to make *hat, pat, cat.* Let the syllables all be actual words which he knows. Set the words in a row, and let him read them off" (Vol. 1, p. 202).

### 17. Continue the process with other short-vowel three-letter words.

"Do this with the short vowel sounds in combination with each of the consonants, and the child will learn to read off dozens of words of three letters, and will master the short-vowel sounds with initial and final consonants without effort. Before long he will do the lesson for himself. 'How many words can you make with "en" and another letter, with "od" and another letter?' etc." (Vol. 1, p. 202).

### 18. Do not hurry your child.

"Do not hurry him" (Vol. 1, p. 202).

### 19. After he has mastered short-vowel three-letter words, teach the silent-e that makes a long vowel in the word in the same way.

"When this sort of exercise becomes so easy that it is no longer interesting, let

> "Let us do what we can to make the task easy and inviting."

the long sounds of the vowels be learnt in the same way: use the same syllables as before with a final *e*; thus 'at' becomes 'ate,' and we get *late, pate, rate,* etc. The child may be told that *a* in 'rate' is *long a; a* in 'rat' is *short a*. He will make the new sets of words with much facility, helped by the experience he gained in the former lessons" (Vol. 1, pp. 202, 203).

*20. Continue the process with consonant combinations, like "ng" and "th."*

"Then the same sort of thing with final 'ng'—'ing,' 'ang,' 'ong,' 'ung'; as in *ring, fang, long, sung*: initial 'th,' as *then, that*: final 'th,' as *with, pith, hath, lath*, and so on, through endless combinations which will suggest themselves" (Vol. 1, p. 203).

*21. These word games are not reading, but they lay the foundation for future reading lessons.*

"This is not reading, but it is preparing the ground for reading; words will be no longer unfamiliar, perplexing objects, when the child meets with them in a line of print" (Vol. 1, p. 203).

*22. Encourage your child to pronounce correctly any word that he learns.*

"Require him to pronounce the words he makes with such finish and distinctness that he can himself hear and count the sounds in a given word" (Vol. 1, p. 203).

*23. Encourage him to shut his eyes and spell the word he has made, thus preparing him for future spelling lessons.*

"Accustom him from the first to shut his eyes and spell the word he has made. This is important. Reading is not spelling, nor is it necessary to spell in order to read well; but the good speller is the child whose eye is quick enough to take in the letters which compose it, in the act of reading off a word; and this is a habit to be acquired from the first: *accustom* him to *see* the letters in the word, and he will do so without effort.

"If words were always made on a given pattern in English, if the same letters always represented the same sounds, learning to read would be an easy matter; for the child would soon acquire the few elements of which all words would, in that case, be composed. But many of our English words are, each, a law unto itself: there is nothing for it, but the child must learn to know them at sight; he must recognise 'which,' precisely as he recognises '*B*,' because he has seen it before, been made to look at it with interest, so that the pattern of the word is stamped on his retentive brain. This process should go on side by side with the other—the learning of the powers of the letters; for the more variety you can throw into his reading lessons, the more will the child enjoy them. Lessons in word-making help him to take intelligent interest in *words*; but his progress in the art of reading depends chiefly on the 'reading at sight' lessons" (Vol. 1, pp. 203, 204).

### Stage Three: Reading Lessons Guidelines
*24. Proceed slowly, making sure your child has mastered a concept before moving on to the next.*

"The teacher must be content to proceed very slowly, securing the ground under her feet as she goes" (Vol. 1, p. 204).

> "The teacher must be content to proceed very slowly, securing the ground under her feet as she goes."

## Notes

*See pages 179–185 for more on this style of reading lessons.*

**25. Use real words that represent real things to teach reading, not meaningless combinations of letters.**

"The child cares for things, not words; his analytic power is very small, his observing faculty is exceedingly quick and keen; nothing is too small for him; he will spy out the eye of a fly; nothing is too intricate, he delights in puzzles. But the thing he learns to know by looking at it, is a thing which interests him. Here we have the key to reading. No meaningless combinations of letters, no *cla, cle, cli, clo, clu*, no *ath, eth, ith, oth, uth*, should be presented to him. The child should be taught from the first to regard the printed word as he already regards the spoken word, as the symbol of fact or idea full of interest. How easy to read 'robin redbreast,' 'buttercups and daisies'; the number of letters in the words is no matter; the words themselves convey such interesting ideas that the general form and look of them fixes itself on the child's brain by the same law of association of ideas which makes it easy to couple the objects with their spoken names. Having got a word fixed on the sure peg of the idea it conveys, the child will use his knowledge of the sounds of the letters to make up other words containing the same elements with great interest. When he knows 'butter' he is quite ready to make 'mutter' by changing the *b* for an *m*" (Vol. 1, p. 216).

**26. Read aloud a short portion of a children's poem or prose, pointing to each word as you say it.**

"Say—
  'Twinkle, twinkle, little star,
  How I wonder what you are,'
is the first lesson; just those two lines. Read the passage for the child, very slowly, sweetly, with just expression, so that it is pleasant to him to listen. Point to each word as you read" (Vol. 1, p. 204).

**27. Point to the words out of order and have your child say each with careful enunciation.**

"Then point to 'twinkle,' 'wonder,' 'star,' 'what,'—and expect the child to pronounce each word in the verse taken promiscuously" (Vol. 1, p. 204).

"The little people will probably have to be pulled up on the score of pronunciation. They must render 'high,' 'sky,' 'like,' 'world,' with delicate precision; 'diamond,' they will no doubt wish to hurry over, and say as 'di'mond,' just as they will reduce 'history' to 'hist'ry.' But here is another advantage of slow and steady progress—the *saying* of each word receives due attention, and the child is trained in the habit of careful enunciation" (Vol. 1, p. 206).

**28. When he shows that he knows each word by itself, let him read the two lines with good enunciation and expression.**

"Then, when he shows that he knows each word by itself, and not before, let him *read* the two lines with clear enunciation and expression: insist from the first on clear, beautiful reading, and do not let the child fall into a dreary monotone, no more pleasant to himself than to his listener. Of course, by this time he is able to say the two lines; and let him say them clearly and beautifully. In his after lessons he will learn the rest of the little poem" (Vol. 1, p. 204).

> "Having got a word fixed on the sure peg of the idea it conveys, the child will use his knowledge of the sounds of the letters to make up other words containing the same elements with great interest."

"A beautiful word deserves to be beautifully said, with a certain roundness of tone and precision of utterance. Quite young children are open to this sort of teaching, conveyed, not in a lesson, but by a word now and then" (Vol. 1, p. 227).

### 29. Have your child identify on a few pages of printed type the words he has learned.

"The child should hunt through two or three pages of good clear type for 'little,' 'star,' 'you,' 'are,' each of the words he has learned, until the word he knows looks out upon him like the face of a friend in a crowd of strangers, and he is able to pounce upon it anywhere. Lest he grow weary of the search, the teacher should guide him, unawares, to the line or paragraph where the word he wants occurs. Already the child has accumulated a little capital; he knows eight or ten words so well that he will recognise them anywhere, and the lesson has occupied probably ten minutes" (Vol. 1, p. 205).

### 30. Children can recognize words as they recognize the faces of friends. Don't feel like you must have a rule for every sound every letter can make in every word.

"In the first place, let us bear in mind that reading is not a science nor an art. Even if it were, the children must still be the first consideration with the educator; but it is not. Learning to read is no more than picking up, how we can, a knowledge of certain arbitrary symbols for objects and ideas. There are absolutely no right and necessary 'steps' to reading, each of which leads to the next; there is no true beginning, middle, or end. For the arbitrary symbols we must know in order to read are not *letters*, but *words*. By way of illustration, consider the delicate differences of sound represented by the letter 'o' in the last sentence; to analyse and classify the sounds of 'o' in 'for,' 'symbols,' 'know,' 'order,' 'to,' 'not,' and 'words,' is a curious, not especially useful, study for a philologist, but a laborious and inappropriate one for a child. It is time we faced the fact that the letters which compose an English word are full of philological interest, and that their study will be a valuable part of education by-and-by; but meantime, sound and letter-sign are so loosely wedded in English, that to base the teaching of reading on the sounds of the letters only, is to lay up for the child much analytic labour, much mental confusion, due to the irregularities of the language; and some little moral strain in making the sound of a letter in a given word fall under any of the 'sounds' he has been taught" (Vol. 1, p. 215).

### 31. Begin the next lesson by reviewing familiar words in printed type first, then repeat the process described above with the next lines of the poem or passage.

"The next 'reading at sight' lesson will begin with a hunt for the familiar words, and then—
 'Up above the world so high,
 Like a diamond in the sky,'
should be gone through in the same way" (Vol. 1, p. 205).

### 32. Keep reading lessons interesting.

"In the first place, her lessons must be made *interesting*. Do not let her scramble through a page of 'reading,' for instance, spelling every third word and then waiting to be told what it spells, but let every day bring the complete mastery of a few new words, as well as the keeping up of the old ones" (Vol. 5, p. 30).

### 33. Encourage him to recite the poems and passages that he has learned as he masters each.

"At this stage, his reading lessons must advance so slowly that he may just as well learn his reading exercises, both prose and poetry, as recitation lessons. Little poems suitable to be learned in this way will suggest themselves at once; but perhaps prose is better, on the whole, as offering more of the words in everyday use, of Saxon origin, and of anomalous spelling" (Vol. 1, pp. 204, 205).

### 34. Use good poetry and prose even at this stage, not twaddle.

"Even for their earliest reading lessons, it is unnecessary to put twaddle into the hands of children" (Vol. 1, p. 205).

"When there is so much noble poetry within a child's compass, the pity of it, that he should be allowed to learn twaddle!" (Vol. 1, p. 226).

### 35. Randomly ask your child to spell one of the shorter words he has learned. Do not make him study it, but ask periodically to encourage him to cultivate the habit of looking at how words are spelled.

"As spelling is simply the art of *seeing*, seeing the letters in a word as we see the features of a face—say to the child, 'Can you spell sky?'—or any of the shorter words. He is put on his mettle, and if he fail this time, be sure he will be able to spell the word when you ask him next; but do not let him *learn* to spell or even say the letters aloud with the word before him" (Vol. 1, pp. 205, 206).

### 36. Don't worry about reading comprehension; your child will understand what he reads in his lesson if you use this method.

"As for understanding what they read, the children will be full of bright, intelligent remarks and questions, and will take this part of the lesson into their own hands; indeed, the teacher will have to be on her guard not to let them carry her away from the subject" (Vol. 1, p. 206).

### 37. Keep the reading lesson short and gradually lengthen it as your child knows more words.

"Every day increases the number of words he is able to read at sight, and the more words he knows already, the longer his reading lesson becomes in order to afford the ten or dozen new words which he should master every day" (Vol. 1, p. 206).

"But do not let the lesson last more than ten minutes, and insist, with brisk, bright determination, on the child's full concentrated attention of eye and mind for the whole ten minutes. Do not allow a moment's dawdling at lessons" (Vol. 5, p. 30).

*38. Using this method, your child will learn 2,000–3,000 words in a year.*

" 'But what a snail's progress!' you are inclined to say. Not so slow, after all: a child will thus learn, without appreciable labour, from two to three thousand words in the course of a year; in other words, he will learn *to read*, for the mastery of this number of words will carry him with comfort through most of the books that fall in his way" (Vol. 1, p. 206).

*39. Focus on setting up good habits of reading and reading with care.*

"The child who has been taught to read with care and deliberation until he has mastered the words of a limited vocabulary, usually does the rest for himself. The attention of his teachers should be fixed on two points—that he acquires the *habit* of reading, and that he does not fall into *slipshod habits* of reading" (Vol. 1, p. 226).

## Questions to Ask about Beginning Reading

### Stage One: The Alphabet

- Does my child have letters that he can touch and handle, both upper case and lower case?
- Do I draw letters in the air and see if my child can name them?
- Do I encourage my child to draw letters in the air or in a tray of sand for me to name?
- Am I using whatever I have handy to teach the alphabet?
- Am I being careful not to hurry my child to learn all the A B C's?
- Do I give my child opportunities to find the letters he knows on a page of printed words in large type?
- Am I teaching my child the sounds that the letters make?
- Am I approaching these lessons as play for my child?
- Has my child shown an interest in his box of letters? If not, am I being careful not to push him into learning the alphabet?
- Am I trying not to push, tease, or show off my child's progress?
- Do I recognize that different children are ready to read at different ages?
- Am I trying not to let the idea of teaching reading intimidate me?
- Am I doing all I can to make the task of learning to read easy and inviting?
- Am I prepared to use both sight words and phonics to teach reading?

### Stage Two: Preparation for Reading

- Do I make a game of putting together words in word families?
- Am I being careful to use actual words?
- Am I encouraging my child to say each new word we make in a word family?
- Have we covered short-vowel three-letter words in this way?
- Am I being careful not to hurry my child?
- Have we covered how silent-e makes long-vowel words?

"The child who has been taught to read with care and deliberation until he has mastered the words of a limited vocabulary, usually does the rest for himself."

- Have we covered combinations in words like "ng" and "th"?
- Am I trying to lay a good foundation for real reading lessons?
- Am I encouraging my child to pronounce words correctly as he learns them?
- Am I encouraging my child occasionally to shut his eyes and spell a word he has made?

### Stage Three: Reading Lessons

- Am I making sure my child has mastered a concept before moving on to the next?
- Am I using real words that represent real things?
- Do I read aloud a short portion of a poem or prose, pointing to each word as I say it?
- Am I asking my child to say each word as I point to it out of order?
- Am I encouraging my child to read with good enunciation and expression?
- Am I asking my child to identify on a page of printed type the words he has learned?
- Am I comfortable that I don't have to give a rule for every sound every letter can make in every word?
- Am I beginning each lesson with review of the words already learned?
- Am I trying to keep reading lessons interesting?
- Do I encourage my child to recite the poem or passage he learned?
- Am I trying to use good poetry and prose, not twaddle?
- Do I occasionally ask my child to spell one of the shorter words he has learned?
- Am I comfortable that my child will understand what he is reading?
- Do I keep reading lessons short?
- Am I focusing on setting up the good habits of reading and reading with care?

## More Quotes about Beginning Reading

"What we want is to see the child in pursuit of knowledge, and not knowledge in pursuit of the child."—George Bernard Shaw

"The man who can make hard things easy is the educator."—Ralph Waldo Emerson

"Teachers open the door, but you must enter by yourself."—Chinese Proverb

"The stories of childhood leave an indelible impression, and their author always has a niche in the temple of memory from which the image is never cast out to be thrown on the rubbish heap of things that are outgrown and outlived."—Howard Pyle

"It is a great thing to start life with a small number of really good books which are your very own."— Arthur Conan Doyle

---

*Notes*

*See a sample of beginning reading lessons of this style on page 183.*

"Do not allow a moment's dawdling at lessons."

"Once you learn to read, you will be forever free."— Frederick Douglass

"To learn to read is to light a fire; every syllable that is spelled out is a spark."— Victor Hugo

> "The more variety you can throw into his reading lessons, the more will the child enjoy them."

# Chapter 10
# Copywork and Transcription

*Notes*

*Copywork and transcription are taught as specific language arts lessons.*

"Quality, not quantity," remarked Katherine.

"Maybe that's where I'm off target," Maggie said. "Tommy's handwriting lessons are taking a good thirty minutes, and we're both frustrated. He gets so tired of drawing lines and lines of letters, he quits trying. I get upset because it's sloppy, so we do the same page over again the next day. And we're getting nowhere."

"Exactly," Katherine replied. "And you're inadvertently setting up a habit of sloppy work. Back off how much you require, but require that it be his best effort."

"So how much do you think I should require?" asked Maggie

"Set a small goal that emphasizes doing his best. If he already knows how to form each letter, start with a word or two and gradually work your way up to a line," explained Katherine. "And use meaningful words that give him something to think about."

Maggie nodded. "That makes sense. We could write his memory verse a little at a time."

"Yes, or a Thank You note, or a short poem, or a letter to a friend," said Katherine. "Set the goal so he knows how much he needs to do, and once he has accomplished that goal the lesson is done."

"Even if it takes only five minutes?" Maggie was surprised.

"Even if it takes only five minutes." Katherine smiled. "You'll be surprised how much his handwriting will improve with five minutes of best effort instead of thirty minutes of sloppiness."

*Vulgar means "lacking refinement, culture, or taste."*

*A sample of Mrs. Bridges' new handwriting.*

## Charlotte's Thoughts on Copywork and Transcription

*General Guidelines for All Grades*

**1. A beautiful style of handwriting helps cultivate your child's taste for beauty. Do not allow vulgar handwriting.**

"Some years ago I heard of a lady who was elaborating, by means of the study of old Italian and other manuscripts, a 'system of beautiful handwriting' which could be taught to children. I waited patiently, though not without some urgency, for the production of this new kind of 'copy-book.' The need for such an effort was very great, for the distinctly commonplace writing taught from existing copy-books, however painstaking and legible, cannot but have a rather vulgarising effect both on the writer and the reader of such manuscript. At last the lady, Mrs Robert Bridges, has succeeded in her tedious and difficult undertaking, and this book for teachers will enable them to teach their pupils a style of writing which is pleasant to acquire because it is beautiful to behold. It is surprising how quickly young children, even

*"Variety and beauty of form are attractive, even to little children."*

## Notes

*An example of an elaborate heading and copperplate handwriting.*

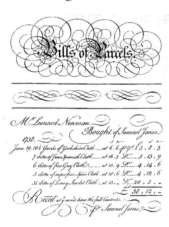

"In this, as in everything else, the care of the educator must be given, not only to the formation of good, but to the prevention of bad habits."

those already confirmed in 'ugly' writing, take to this 'new handwriting' " (Vol. 1, pp. 235, 236).

*2. A beautiful model of the letters or words and interesting content should keep copywork lessons interesting and pleasant.*

"I should say that variety and beauty of form are attractive, even to little children, and that the attempt to create something which interests them, cheers and crowns their stupendous efforts with a pleasure that cannot be looked for in the task of copying monotonous shapes" (Vol. 1, p. 237).

"A sense of beauty in their writing and in the lines they copy should carry them over this stage of their work with pleasure" (Vol. 1, p. 239).

*3. Your child should continue writing a medium size until he can make his letters with ease.*

" 'Text-hand,' the medium size, should be continued until he makes the letters with ease" (Vol. 1, p. 235).

*4. Do not hurry your child into writing small; it can instigate bad habits.*

"One word more; do not hurry the child into 'small hand'; . . . . It is much easier for the child to get into an irregular scribble by way of 'small-hand,' than to get out of it again. In this, as in everything else, the care of the educator must be given, not only to the formation of good, but to the prevention of bad habits" (Vol. 1, p. 235).

*5. Do not require your child to copy elaborate or ornamental writing.*

"If he write in books with copperplate headlines (which are, on the whole, to be eschewed), discrimination should be exercised in the choice of these; in many of them the writing is atrocious, and the letters are adorned with flourishes which increase the pupil's labour but by no means improve his style" (Vol. 1, p. 235).

*6. Make sure your child's work surface is well lit and that his body is not casting a shadow across his work.*

"For the writing position children should sit so that light reaches them from the left" (Vol. 1, p. 239).

*7. The desk or table should be at a comfortable height for your child.*

"Desk or table should be at a comfortable height" (Vol. 1, p. 239).

*8. Teach your child to hold a pencil or pen correctly.*

"It would be a great gain if children were taught from the first to hold the pen between the first and second fingers, steadying it with the thumb. This position avoids the uncomfortable strain on the muscles produced by the usual way of holding a pen—a strain which causes writer's cramp in later days when there is much writing to be done. The pen should be held in a comfortable position, rather near the point, fingers and thumb somewhat bent, and the hand resting on the paper. The writer should also be allowed to support himself with the left hand on the paper, and should write in an easy position, with bent head but not with stooping figure" (Vol. 1, p. 239).

## Grade 1

**9. Teach a young child to write only if he is interested in it.**

"A child will have taught himself to paint, paste, cut paper, knit, weave, hammer and saw, make lovely things in clay and sand, build castles with his bricks; possibly, too, will have taught himself to read, write, and do sums, besides acquiring no end of knowledge and notions about the world he lives in, by the time he is six or seven. What I contend for is that he shall do these things because he chooses (provided that the standard of perfection in his small works be kept before him)" (Vol. 1, pp. 193, 194).

**10. Beginning writing lessons require your child to learn how to control his hand and make it draw what he sees in his mind's eye.**

"A child must first learn to control his hand and constrain it to obey his eye" (Vol. 1, p. 236).

**11. Practice letters first on the chalkboard or whiteboard, later with pencil on paper, then with pen and ink.**

"In all writing lessons, free use should be made of the blackboard by both teacher and children by way of model and practice" (Vol. 1, p. 239).

"At this stage the chalk and blackboard are better than pen and paper, as it is well that the child should rub out and rub out until his own eye is satisfied with the word or letter he has written" (Vol. 1, p. 234).

"The method of using Mrs Bridges' *Handwriting*, which we find most effectual, is to practise each form on the blackboard from the plate, and later to use pencil, and still later pen and ink" (Vol. 1, p. 237).

**12. Beginning writing lessons should be short, not more than five or ten minutes.**

"Let the writing lesson be short; it should not last more than five or ten minutes" (Vol. 1, p. 233).

**13. Encourage your child to accomplish something perfectly in every writing lesson, whether a stroke or a letter. Avoid forming the habit of careless work.**

"I can only offer a few hints on the teaching of *writing*, though much might be said. First, let the child accomplish something perfectly in every lesson—a stroke, a pothook, a letter. . . . Ease in writing comes by practice; but that must be secured later. In the meantime, the thing to be avoided is the habit of careless work— humpy *m*'s, angular *o*'s" (Vol. 1, pp. 233, 234).

" 'Throw perfection into all you do' is a counsel upon which a family may be brought up with great advantage. We English, as a nation, think too much of persons, and too little of *things, work, execution*. Our children are allowed to make

> "Let the child accomplish something perfectly in every lesson—a stroke, a pothook, a letter."

their figures or their letters, their stitches, their dolls' clothes, their small carpentry, anyhow, with the notion that they will do better by-and-by. Other nations—the Germans and the French, for instance—look at the question philosophically, and know that if children get the *habit* of turning out imperfect work, the men and women will undoubtedly keep that habit up. I remember being delighted with the work of a class of about forty children, of six and seven, in an elementary school at Heidelberg. They were doing a writing lesson, accompanied by a good deal of oral teaching from a master, who wrote each word on the blackboard. By-and-by the slates were shown, and I did not observe *one faulty or irregular letter* on the whole forty slates. The same principle of 'perfection' was to be discerned in a recent exhibition of schoolwork held throughout France. No faulty work was shown, to be excused on the plea that it was the work of children" (Vol. 1, pp. 159, 160).

*14. Give your child good copies to imitate.*

"Set good copies before him, and see that he imitates his model dutifully" (Vol. 1, p. 234).

*15. Have your child evaluate his writing compared to the model and have him point out what is wrong.*

"Set him six strokes to copy; let him, not bring a slateful, but six perfect strokes, at regular distances and at regular slopes. If he produces a faulty pair, get *him* to point out the fault, and persevere until he has produced his task" (Vol. 1, p. 160).

*16. Set a goal for your child of producing a few perfect letters or a single line copied exactly. When he reaches the goal, the lesson is done.*

"His writing task is to produce six perfect *m*'s: he writes six lines with only one good *m* in each line; the time for the writing lesson is over and he has none for himself; or, he is able to point out six good *m*'s in his first line, and he has the rest of the time to draw steamboats and railway trains" (Vol. 1, p. 143).

"The writing lesson being, not so many lines, or 'a copy'—that is, a page of writing—but a single line which is as exactly as possible a copy of the characters set. The child may have to write several lines before he succeeds in producing this" (Vol. 1, p. 235).

"If he does not do it to-day, let him go on to-morrow and the next day, and when the six perfect strokes appear, let it be an occasion of triumph" (Vol. 1, p. 160).

*17. Teach printing before cursive, possibly italics style.*

"But the child should have practice in printing before he begins to write" (Vol. 1, p. 234).

*18. Teach capital letters before lowercase letters.*

"First, let him print the simplest of the capital letters with single curves and straight lines. When he can make the capitals and large letters, with some firmness and decision, he might go on to the smaller letters" (Vol. 1, p. 234).

*19. Your child should write simple, large letters for beginning writing lessons.*

"When he can make the capitals and large letters, with some firmness and decision, he might go on to the smaller letters—'printed' as in the type we call 'italics,' only upright,—as simple as possible, and large" (Vol. 1, p. 234).

*20. Writing lessons should group letters with similar strokes. Charlotte's students followed this sequence.*

1. Learn to draw a straight line.
2. Learn to draw a hooked line.
3. Learn to draw letters that are made up of a straight line and a hooked line: *n, m, v, w, r, h, p, y.*
4. Learn to draw a circle.
5. Learn to draw letters with a curve in them: *a, c, g, e, x, s, q.*
6. Learn looped and irregular letters: *b, l, f, t,* etc.

"Let the stroke be learned first; then the pothook; then the letters of which the pothook is an element—*n, m, v, w, r, h, p, y*; then *o,* and letters of which the curve is an element—*a, c, g, e, x, s, q*; then looped and irregular letters—*b, l, f, t,* etc." (Vol. 1, p. 234).

*21. Writing lessons should follow this technique.*

1. Day One: Form one letter perfectly.
2. Day Two: Form another letter that uses the same element.
3. Repeat until that element and its letters are familiar.
4. Form letters into words as soon as possible for the student to copy. The goal is to write the word once without a mistake.
5. Continue in this fashion with an emphasis on making perfect letters.

"One letter should be perfectly formed in a day, and the next day the same elemental forms repeated in another letter, until they become familiar. By-and-by copies, three or four of the letters they have learned grouped into a word—'man,' 'aunt'; the lesson to be the production of the written word *once* without a single fault in any letter" (Vol. 1, p. 234).

*22. Do not hurry or pressure a child to have beautiful handwriting; that will come by and by.*

"Of the further stages, little need be said. Secure that the child *begins* by making perfect letters and is never allowed to make faulty ones, and the rest he will do for himself; as for 'a good hand,' do not hurry him; his 'handwriting' will come by-and-by out of the character that is in him; but, as a child, he cannot be said, strictly speaking, to have character" (Vol. 1, p. 234).

*23. Once your child has mastered the mechanics of writing, move on to transcription.*

"By-and-by the children will be promoted to transcribe little poems, and so on,

## Notes

*These letter groupings are based on the style of handwriting that Charlotte used for her students. You may need to reorganize which letters should be grouped together if you are using a different style.*

"Secure that the child begins by making perfect letters and is never allowed to make faulty ones, and the rest he will do for himself."

in this very pleasing script" (Vol. 1, p. 237).

## Grades 2, 3

*24. Children of seven or eight can begin transcription in their copywork lessons.*

"The earliest practice in writing proper for children of seven or eight should be, not letter-writing or dictation, but transcription, slow and beautiful work" (Vol. 1, p. 238).

*25. In transcription, your child looks at the word until he can see it in his mind's eye, then writes it from memory.*

"Transcription should be an introduction to spelling. Children should be encouraged to look at the word, see a picture of it with their eyes shut, and then write from memory" (Vol. 1, p. 238).

*26. Allow your child to select a favorite verse of a poem, rather than an entire poem, for his transcription.*

"A certain sense of possession and delight may be added to this exercise if children are allowed to choose for transcription their favourite verse in one poem and another. This is better than to write a favourite poem, an exercise which stales on the little people before it is finished" (Vol. 1, p. 238).

*27. A handwritten journal of your child's chosen verses will give him pleasure.*

"A book of their own, made up of their own chosen verses, should give them pleasure" (Vol. 1, p. 238).

*28. Use lined paper with lines wide enough to encourage neat writing; too narrow of lines can result in sloppy writing.*

"Double-ruled lines, small text-hand, should be used at first, as children are eager to write very minute 'small hand,' and once they have fallen into this habit it is not easy to get good writing" (Vol. 1, pp. 238, 239).

*29. Transcription lessons should last no longer than ten or fifteen minutes.*

"Not more than ten minutes or a quarter of an hour should be given to the early writing-lessons. If they are longer the children get tired and slovenly" (Vol. 1, p. 239).

## Questions to Ask on Copywork and Transcription

### General Guidelines for All Grades

- Am I teaching my child a beautiful style of handwriting, rather than a vulgar style?
- Am I trying to supply my child with a beautiful model to copy, as well as interesting content?
- Am I encouraging my child to write in a medium size until he can make his letters with ease?

*Transcription is the precursor to dictation. See page 99 for more on dictation.*

"Transcription should be an introduction to spelling."

- Am I being careful not to hurry my child into writing small, and thus, instigating bad habits?
- Do I not require my child to copy elaborate or ornamental writing?
- Is my child's work surface well lit and his body not casting a shadow across his work?
- Is my child's desk or table at a comfortable height for him?
- If my child is using a pencil or pen, is he holding it correctly?

## Grade 1

- Is my child interested in learning to write?
- Is my child physically able to control his hand and make it draw what he sees in his mind's eye?
- Am I using a chalkboard or whiteboard for beginning writing lessons?
- Am I limiting beginning writing lessons to five or ten minutes?
- Am I encouraging my child to do his best work?
- Am I giving my child good copies to imitate?
- Am I having my child compare his writing to the model?
- Am I setting a goal in each lesson that encourages best effort, and stopping the lesson when that goal is reached?
- Am I teaching printing before cursive, possibly in italics style?
- Am I teaching capital letters before lowercase letters?
- Am I encouraging my child to write simple, large letters for beginning writing lessons?
- Am I teaching letters grouped by similar strokes?
- Am I following this technique?
  1. Day One: Form one letter perfectly.
  2. Day Two: Form another letter that uses the same element.
  3. Repeat until that element and its letters are familiar.
  4. Form letters into words as soon as possible for the student to copy. The goal is to write the word once without a mistake.
  5. Continue in this fashion with an emphasis on making perfect letters.
- Am I being careful not to hurry or pressure my child to have beautiful handwriting right away?

## Grades 2, 3

- Has my seven- or eight-year-old child started transcription work?
- Am I encouraging my child to look at a word until he can see it in his mind's eye, then write it from memory?
- Am I allowing my child to select a favorite verse from a poem to transcribe?
- Have I provided a nice journal for my child's chosen verses?
- Does the journal have lined paper with lines that are wide enough to encourage neat writing?
- Am I limiting transcription lessons to ten or fifteen minutes?

---

**Notes**

*You can download free manuscript copywork at SimplyCharlotteMason.com.*

"A certain sense of possession and delight may be added to this exercise if children are allowed to choose for transcription their favourite verse in one poem and another."

## More Quotes on Copywork and Transcription

"A man's penmanship is an unfailing index of his character, moral and mental, and a criterion by which to judge his peculiarities of taste and sentiments."—Philip Dormer Stanhope, 4th Earl of Chesterfield

"Thou shalt in any wise set him king over thee, whom the Lord thy God shall choose: . . . And it shall be, when he sitteth upon the throne of his kingdom, that he shall write him a copy of this law in a book out of that which is before the priests the Levites: And it shall be with him, and he shall read therein all the days of his life: that he may learn to fear the Lord his God, to keep all the words of this law and these statutes, to do them" (Deuteronomy 17:15, 18, 19).

---

"A book of their own, made up of their own chosen verses, should give them pleasure."

# Chapter 11
# *Dictation*

*Notes*

*Dictation is taught as specific language arts lessons.*

"No lists?" asked Peter.

"No lists," Shantay replied.

"Then how do you teach it?" Peter was curious.

"I teach spelling with interesting quotes and passages from good books," answered Shantay.

"Really? Tell me how it works," said Peter.

Shantay grabbed *Robinson Crusoe* off the shelf and opened it to the chapter she had just finished reading. "Let's take this paragraph as an example," she said, pointing to a paragraph on the page. "Joey and I read through this paragraph together and identify the words that he needs to study—any word that he isn't sure he knows how to spell."

"I'm with you so far," Peter said.

"Joey studies those words, and I check to make sure he knows how to spell them. Then he looks over the passage again, getting familiar with the capitalization and punctuation. Once he's ready, I dictate the passage to him, phrase by phrase, and he writes it down. I watch while he writes to make sure he is spelling everything correctly," Shantay explained.

Peter was deep in thought. "So he is constantly seeing the words in context."

"Right. It's also reinforcing capitalization and punctuation and good writing style. Plus, he's learning to look at how words are spelled as he reads, which is a skill that will carry him into his adult life."

"Interesting."

Shantay smiled. "Yes, it is much more interesting than using lists. The passages give Joey an idea to think about, as well as a spelling lesson. He really enjoys this method."

## Charlotte's Thoughts on Dictation

### *General Guidelines for All Grades*
**1. Spelling and reading are two different things.**

"But spelling and reading are *two* things. You must learn to spell in order to *write* words, not to *read* them. A child is droning over a reading-lesson, spells c o u g h; you say 'cough,' and she repeats. By dint of repetition, she learns at last to associate the look of the word with the sound, and says 'cough' without spelling it; and you think she has arrived at 'cough' through c o u g h. Not a bit of it; c o f spells cough!" (Vol. 1, p. 210).

**2. Cold turkey dictation (in which the child does not study the passage ahead of time) is mischievous and counteractive to Charlotte Mason's philosophy.**

"Of all the mischievous exercises in which children spend their school hours,

*Phonics rules work well for teaching your child how to read; however, spelling phonetically does not work well.*

"Spelling and reading are two things."

dictation, as commonly practised, is perhaps the most mischievous; and this, because people are slow to understand that there is no part of a child's work at school which some philosophic principle does not underlie" (Vol. 1, p. 240).

*3. Your child should never be encouraged to look carefully at or copy a misspelled word.*

"The common [incorrect] practise is for the teacher to dictate a passage, clause by clause, repeating each clause, perhaps, three or four times under a fire of questions from the writers. Every line has errors in spelling, one, two, three, perhaps. The conscientious teacher draws her pencil under these errors, or solemnly underlines them with red ink. The children correct in various fashions; sometimes they change books, and each corrects the errors of another, copying the word from the book or from the blackboard. A few benighted teachers still cause children to copy their own error along with the correction, which last is written three or four times, learned, and spelt to the teacher. The latter is astonished at the pure perversity which causes the same errors to be repeated again and again, notwithstanding all these painstaking efforts" (Vol. 1, pp. 240, 241).

*4. Help your child cultivate the habit of being able to see the word in his mind's eye.*

"But the fact is, the gift of spelling depends upon the power the eye possesses to 'take' (in a photographic sense) a detailed picture of a word; and this is a power and habit which must be cultivated in children from the first. When they have read 'cat,' they must be encouraged to see the word with their eyes shut, and the same habit will enable them to image 'Thermopylae' " (Vol. 1, p. 241).

*5. Studying a misspelled word, even along with its correct spelling, sets up a mental debate as to which spelling is correct.*

"This picturing of words upon the retina appears to me to be the only royal road to spelling; an error once made and corrected leads to fearful doubt for the rest of one's life, as to which was the wrong way and which the right. Most of us are haunted by some such doubt as to whether 'balance,' for instance, should have one 'l' or two; and *the doubt is born of a correction.* Once the eye sees a misspelt word, that image remains; and if there is also the image of the word rightly spelt, we are perplexed as to which is which" (Vol. 1, p. 241).

*6. Cold turkey dictation reinforces spelling errors.*

"Now we see why there could not be a more ingenious way of making bad spellers than 'dictation' as it is commonly taught. Every misspelt word is an image in the child's brain not to be obliterated by the right spelling" (Vol. 1, p. 241).

*7. The teacher's business is to prevent or hide away any false spelling.*

"It becomes, therefore, the teacher's business to prevent false spelling, and, if an error has been made, to hide it away, as it were, so that the impression may not become fixed" (Vol. 1, p. 241).

*8. The habit of reading worthwhile books for instruction encourages correct spelling.*

"Our great failure seems to me to be caused by the fact that we do not form the *habit of reading books that are worth while* in children while they are at school and are under twelve years of age. The free use of books implies correct spelling and easy and vigorous composition without direct teaching of these subjects" (Vol. 3, Preface).

" 'Composition' is never taught as a subject; well-taught children compose as well-bred children behave—by the light of nature. It is probable that no considerable writer was ever taught the art of 'composition.' The same remark may be made about spelling: excepting for an occasional 'inveterate' case, the habit of reading teaches spelling" (Vol. 3, p. 286).

"Oral teaching was to a great extent ruled out; a large number of books on many subjects were set for reading in morning school-hours; so much work was set that there was only time for a single reading; all reading was tested by a narration of the whole or a given passage, whether orally or in writing. Children working on these lines know months after that which they have read and are remarkable for their power of concentration (attention); they have little trouble with spelling or composition and become well-informed, intelligent persons" (Vol. 6, p. 15).

"This is what we have established in many thousands of cases, even in those of dull and backward children, that any person can understand any book of the right calibre (a question to be determined mainly by the age of the young reader); that the book must be in literary form; that children and young persons require no elucidation of what they read; that their attention does not flag while so engaged; that they master a few pages at a single reading so thoroughly that they can 'tell it back' at the time or months later whether it be the *Pilgrim's Progress* or one of Bacon's Essays or Shakespeare's plays; that they throw individuality into this telling back so that no two tell quite the same tale; that they learn incidentally to write and speak with vigour and style and usually to spell well" (Vol. 6, pp. 291, 292).

"What the children have read they know, and write on any part of it with ease and fluency, in vigorous English; they usually spell well" (Vol. 6, pp. 6, 241).

**9. Children who are constantly read to do not gain the advantage of seeing the correct spelling of words. When they are ready, they need to transition to reading their books for themselves.**

"It is impossible to teach children to spell when they do not read for themselves; we hear complaints of the difficulties of spelling, of the necessity to do violence to the language which is dear to us all in order to make 'spelling made easy'; but in thousands of cases that come before us we find that children who use their books for themselves spell well because they visualise the words they read. Those who merely listen to their teacher have no guide (in English at any rate) to the spelling of the words they hear. We are, perhaps, opposed to oral lessons or lectures except by way of occasional review or introduction. For actual education children must do their own work out of their own books under the sympathetic guidance of an intelligent teacher" (Vol. 6, p. 271).

## Notes

*See page 29 for more on reading for instruction.*

"The free use of books implies correct spelling and easy and vigorous composition without direct teaching of these subjects."

## Notes

**10. Poor spelling may be caused by reading too little or reading too quickly.**

"Illiterate spelling is usually a sign of sparse reading; but, sometimes, of hasty reading without the habit of *seeing* the words that are skimmed over" (Vol. 1, pp. 242, 243).

**11. You can incorporate spelling into other subjects' lessons by writing any difficult word from the reading and encouraging your child to look at it until he can see it in his mind's eye.**

"Spelling must not be lost sight of in the children's other studies, though they should not be teased to spell. It is well to write a difficult proper name, for example, on the blackboard in the course of history or geography readings, rubbing the word out when the children say they can see it. The whole secret of spelling lies in the habit of visualising words from memory, and children must be trained to visualise in the course of their reading. They enjoy this way of learning to spell" (Vol. 1, p. 243).

### Grades 1–3

**12. Dictation is not for younger children (ages 7 or 8).**

"The earliest practice in writing proper for children of seven or eight should be, not letter-writing or dictation, but transcription, slow and beautiful work" (Vol. 1, p. 238).

*See page 91 for more on copywork and transcription.*

**13. Copywork and transcription can be an introduction to this type of spelling lessons.**

"Transcription should be an introduction to spelling. Children should be encouraged to look at the word, see a picture of it with their eyes shut, and then write from memory" (Vol. 1, p. 238).

*Charlotte started prepared dictation lessons when the child was 9 or 10 years old.*

### Grades 3–12

**14. A prepared dictation lesson would follow these steps.**

1. The student and teacher read the passage and identify any words that the student doesn't know how to spell.

2. The student prepares the passage by studying the word(s) he is not sure of and lets the teacher know when he is ready.

3. The teacher double-checks the student's readiness, using the chalkboard or whiteboard.

4. The teacher dictates the passage, clause by clause, stating each clause one time only.

*Dictation was usually scheduled once or twice a week in Charlotte's schools.*

5. If the student misspells a word, the teacher covers it with a small slip of paper.

6. The student studies any misspelled word and writes it correctly on the slip of paper. (See details below for each step.)

**15. A child eight or nine years old can prepare a paragraph; an older child, one to three pages.**

*"It is impossible to teach children to spell when they do not read for themselves."*

"A child of eight or nine prepares a paragraph, older children a page, or two or three pages" (Vol. 1, pp. 241, 242).

*16. Your child generally knows which words he needs to study, but you may point out some that might cause stumbling.*

"Before he begins, the teacher asks what words he thinks will need his attention. He generally knows, but the teacher may point out any word likely to be a cause of stumbling" (Vol. 1, p. 242).

*17. When studying a word, your child should look at it until he can see it in detail with his eyes shut.*

"The child prepares by himself, by looking at the word he is not sure of, and then seeing it with his eyes shut" (Vol. 1, p. 242).

*18. When your child says he is ready, ask if there are any words he is not certain of the spelling. Write those words, one at a time, on a chalkboard or whiteboard and have him look at it again. Then erase the word and ask him to write it on the chalkboard or whiteboard while you stand ready to erase any wrong letter immediately—even before it is complete, if possible.*

"He lets his teacher know when he is ready. The teacher asks if there are any words he is not sure of. These she puts, one by one, on the blackboard, letting the child look till he has a picture, and then rubbing the word out. If anyone is still doubtful he should be called to put the word he is not sure of on the board, the teacher watching to rub out the word when a wrong letter begins to appear, and again helping the child to get a mental picture" (Vol. 1, p. 242).

*19. Dictate the passage clause by clause, stating each clause only once, and using your voice inflection to reinforce the punctuation; but do not state the punctuation marks as part of the clause.*

"Then the teacher gives out the dictation, clause by clause, each clause repeated *once*. She dictates with a view to the pointing, which the children are expected to put in as they write; but they must not be told 'comma,' 'semicolon,' etc." (Vol. 1, p. 242).

*20. After the preparation described, errors should be few and far between.*

"After the sort of preparation I have described, which takes ten minutes or less, there is rarely an error in spelling" (Vol. 1, p. 242).

*21. Cover any misspelled word quickly to try to prevent its image from being imprinted in your child's brain.*

"After the sort of preparation I have described, which takes ten minutes or less, there is rarely an error in spelling. If there be, it is well worth while for the teacher to be on the watch with slips of stamp-paper to put over the wrong word, that its image may be erased as far as possible" (Vol. 1, p. 242).

*22. At the end of the lesson, your child should again study any misspelled word, then write it correctly on the slip of paper that covers the misspelling.*

# Notes

*You could also employ other study methods that suit various learning styles. A kinesthetic learner may want to look at the word and trace the letters on the tabletop or build the word with magnetic letters. A visual learner may want to copy the correct spelling.*

*Feel free to use for copywork a portion or all of the passage being studied. Copywork could be incorporated in the studying phase.*

*Small self-stick notes work well to cover any misspelled words. White-out tape also works well.*

"They enjoy this way of learning to spell."

## Dictation

### Notes

*You can use selections from any of your child's books for dictation. If you would like a collection of dictation exercises already selected from great sources and covering the 6,000 most frequently used words in the English language, take a look at* Spelling Wisdom, *available at SimplyCharlotteMason.com.*

"The teacher gives out the dictation, clause by clause, each clause repeated once."

"At the end of the lesson, the child should again study the wrong word in his book until he says he is sure of it, and should write it correctly on the stamp-paper" (Vol. 1, p. 242).

**23. Children usually enjoy and cooperate with this type of spelling lesson.**

"A lesson of this kind secures the hearty co-operation of children, who feel they take their due part in it" (Vol. 1, p. 242).

**24. Prepared dictation helps your child develop the habit of looking at how words are spelled as he reads.**

"It also prepares them for the second condition of good spelling, which is—much reading combined with the habit of imaging the words as they are read" (Vol. 1, p. 242).

## Questions to Ask about Dictation

### General Guidelines for All Grades

- Do I understand how spelling and reading are two different things?
- Am I avoiding cold-turkey dictation, which is mischievous and counteractive to Charlotte Mason's philosophy?
- Am I mistakenly encouraging my child to look carefully at or copy a misspelled word?
- Am I trying to help my child cultivate the habit of being able to see the word in his mind's eye?
- Do I realize how studying a misspelled word, even along with its correct spelling, sets up a mental debate as to which spelling is correct?
- Am I inadvertently reinforcing spelling errors by using cold-turkey dictation?
- Am I trying to prevent or hide away any false spelling?
- Am I helping my child develop the habit of reading worthwhile books for instruction, which will encourage correct spelling?
- Am I making sure my fluent reader is reading for himself so he can see how the words are spelled?
- Is my child reading too little or too quickly and, thus, not seeing words spelled correctly as he reads?
- Am I incorporating spelling into other subjects' lessons by writing any difficult word from the reading and encouraging my child to look at it until he can see it in his mind's eye?

### Grades 1–3

- Am I encouraging good spelling preparation in my six- to eight-year-old by copywork and transcription, and saving dictation until my child is nine or older?
- Do I understand how copywork and transcription can be an introduction to this type of spelling lessons?

## Grades 3–12

- Am I following these steps for a prepared dictation lesson:
  1. Read the passage and identify words my child doesn't know how to spell.
  2. Have my child prepare the passage by studying those words.
  3. Double-check my child's readiness, using a chalkboard or whiteboard.
  4. Dictate the passage, clause by clause, stating each clause one time only.
  5. Cover any misspelled word with a small slip of paper.
  6. Have my child study any misspelled word and write it correctly on the slip of paper.
- Am I having my eight- or nine-year old study and prepare a paragraph and my older child, one to three pages?
- Am I helping my child identify potential words that need to be studied?
- Am I encouraging my child to look at the word until he can see it in detail with his eyes shut?
- Am I writing on the chalkboard or whiteboard the words he studied to have him look again, and then erasing the words and asking him to write them?
- Am I trying to use my voice inflection to reinforce the punctuation as I dictate, but not stating the punctuation marks?
- Am I careful to state each clause only once during a dictation exercise?
- Am I noticing that errors are few and far between, a result of following all the steps in the lesson?
- Am I trying to cover any misspelled word quickly to prevent its image from being imprinted in my child's brain?
- Am I having my child study any misspelled word at the end of the lesson and write it correctly on the slip of paper or correction tape that covers the misspelling?
- Am I finding that my child enjoys and cooperates with this type of spelling lesson?
- Is my child beginning to form the habit of looking at how words are spelled as he reads?

## More Quotes on Spelling and Dictation

"My spelling is Wobbly. It's good spelling but it Wobbles, and the letters get in the wrong places."—A. A. Milne

"Take care that you never spell a word wrong. Always before you write a word, consider how it is spelled, and, if you do not remember, turn to a dictionary. It produces great praise to a lady to spell well."—Thomas Jefferson to his daughter, Martha

"A lesson of this kind secures the hearty co-operation of children, who feel they take their due part in it."

# Chapter 12
# Poetry and Shakespeare

> *Poetry and Shakespeare are taught as specific language arts lessons.*

Adriana was disappointed as she read the paper hanging on Sue's refrigerator. "Sue, dear, Jimmy is capable of understanding and enjoying much more than

'Apple, apple on the tree,
I know that you are good for me.
You are fun to munch and crunch
For a snack and for my lunch.'

"Really?" Sue seemed doubtful.

"Absolutely," replied Adriana. "The poetry we give our children should convey worthy ideas presented in literary words. It should inspire and educate them while teaching them the beauty of a well-crafted phrase."

"But can my six-year-old understand those kinds of poems?" Sue asked.

"Of course!

'Listen, my children, and you shall hear
Of the midnight ride of Paul Revere.'

"Jimmy could understand that poem. Or

'Under a spreading chestnut-tree
The village smithy stands;
The smith, a mighty man is he,
With large and sinewy hands.'

"Think of the pictures those poems can create in Jimmy's mind, how they will warm his imagination and increase his vocabulary," responded Adriana. "Don't waste your time on twaddle, my dear. Give Jimmy the good stuff."

## Charlotte's Thoughts on Poetry and Shakespeare

### *General Guidelines for All Grades*

**1. Your child's education should include poetry, which is the highest form of literature.**

"The days have gone by when the education befitting either a gentleman or an artisan was our aim. Now we must deal with a child of man, who has a natural desire to know the history of his race and of his nation, what men thought in the past and are thinking now; the best thoughts of the best minds taking form as literature, and at its highest as poetry, or, as poetry rendered in the plastic forms of art: as a child of God, whose supreme desire and glory it is to know about and to know his almighty Father: as a person of many parts and passions who must know how to use, care for, and discipline himself, body, mind and soul: as a person of many relationships,—to family, city, church, state, neighbouring states, the world at large: as the inhabitant of a world full of beauty and interest, the features of which he must recognise and know how to name, and a world too, and a universe, whose every function of every part is ordered by laws which he must begin to know.

> "The best thoughts of the best minds taking form as literature, and at its highest as poetry."

## Notes

"It is a wide programme founded on the educational rights of man; wide, but we may not say it is impossible nor may we pick and choose and educate him in this direction but not in that. We may not even make choice between science and the 'humanities.' Our part it seems to me is to give a child a vital hold upon as many as possible of those wide relationships proper to him. Shelley offers us the key to education when he speaks of 'understanding that grows bright gazing on many truths' " (Vol. 6, p. 157).

### 2. Cultivate your child's taste for the best in literature and poetry.

"Children must be Nurtured on the Best.—For the children? They must grow up upon the best. There must never be a period in their lives when they are allowed to read or listen to twaddle or reading-made-easy. There is never a time when they are unequal to worthy thoughts, well put; inspiring tales, well told. Let Blake's 'Songs of Innocence' represent their standard in poetry; De Foe and Stevenson, in prose; and we shall train a race of readers who will demand *literature*—that is, the fit and beautiful expression of inspiring ideas and pictures of life" (Vol. 2, p. 263).

"I saw it stated the other day that children do not care for poetry, that a stirring narrative in verse is much more to their taste. They do like the tale, no doubt, but poetry appeals to them on other grounds, and Shelley's *Skylark* will hold a child entranced sooner than any moving anecdote" (Vol. 3, p. 121).

### 3. Whether in poetry or prose, good literature can be recognized by the force and beauty of the words.

"The thing is, to keep your eye upon words and wait to feel their force and beauty; and, when words are so fit that no other words can be put in their places, so few that none can be left out without spoiling the sense, and so fresh and musical that they delight you, then you may be sure that you are reading Literature, whether in prose or poetry. A great deal of delightful literature can be recognised only by this test" (Vol. 4, Book 1, p. 41).

"Words, 'a Passion and a Power.'—Later, follows the story of his first enthralment by poetry:—

'Twice five years
Or less I might have seen, when first my mind
With conscious pleasure opened to the charm
Of words in timeful order, found them sweet
For their own *sakes*, a passion and a power;
And phrases pleased me chosen for delight,
For pomp, or love. Oft, in the public roads
Yet unfrequented, while the morning light
Was yellowing the hill tops, I went abroad
With a dear friend, and for the better part
Of two delightful hours we strolled along
By the still borders of the misty lake,
Repeating favourite verses with one voice,
Or conning more, as happy as the birds
That round us chaunted.' " (Vol. 3, p. 199).

---

*This poem is by Ruskin.*

"There is never a time when they are unequal to worthy thoughts, well put; inspiring tales, well told."

### 4. Focus on one poet at a time, rather than a collection of random poetry.

" 'Collections' of poems are to be eschewed; but some one poet should have at least a year to himself, that he may have time to do what is in him towards cultivating the seeing eye, the hearing ear, the generous heart" (Vol. 5, p. 224).

### 5. Read poetry often, daily is best.

"Poetry should be read daily" (Vol. 3, p. 307).

### 6. Introduce the poet to your child and get out of the way.

"The Art of Standing Aside.—I have even known of teachers who have thought well to compose the songs and poems which their children use. Think of it! not even our poets are allowed to interpose between the poor child and the probably mediocre mind of the teacher. The art of standing aside to let a child develop the relations proper to him is the fine art of education" (Vol. 3, p. 67).

"There are still, probably, Kindergartens where a great deal of twaddle is talked in song and story, where the teacher conceives that to make poems for the children herself and to compose tunes for their singing and to draw pictures for their admiration, is to fulfil her function to the uttermost. The children might echo Wordsworth's complaint of 'the world,' and say, the teacher is too much with us, late and soon. Everything is directed, expected, suggested. No other personality out of book, picture, or song, no, not even that of Nature herself, can get at the children without the mediation of the teacher. No room is left for spontaneity or personal initiation on their part" (Vol. 1, p. 188).

### 7. Different poets will appeal to various children.

"There is no space to glance at even the few poets each of whom should have his share in the work of cultivating the mind. After the ploughing and harrowing, the *seed* will be appropriated by a process of natural selection; this poet will draw disciples here, that, elsewhere; but it is the part of parents to bring the minds of their children under the influence of the highest, purest poetic thought we have" (Vol. 5, p. 225).

"It is unnecessary to say a word about the great later poets, Browning, Tennyson, and whoever else stands out from the crowd; each will secure his own following of young disciples from amongst those who have had the poetic taste developed; and to develop this appreciative power, rather than to direct its use, is the business of the parents" (Vol. 5, p. 226).

### 8. Give your child entire poems, not just extracts.

"Selections should be avoided; children should read the whole book or the whole poem to which they are introduced" (Vol. 6, p. 340).

"One other caution; it seems to be necessary to present ideas with a great deal of padding, as they reach us in a novel or poem or history book written with literary power. A child cannot in mind or body live upon tabloids however scientifically prepared; out of a whole big book he may not get more than half a dozen of those

## Notes

*Charlotte specifically mentioned these poets for study (Vol. 5, pp. 211, 224–226):*
*Scott, Cowper, Goldsmith, Milton, Wordsworth, Coleridge, Keats, Shelley, Browning, Tennyson, George Herbert, Vaughan, Keble.*

"It is the part of parents to bring the minds of their children under the influence of the highest, purest poetic thought we have."

## Notes

ideas upon which his spirit thrives; and they come in unexpected places and unrecognised forms, so that no grown person is capable of making such extracts from Scott or Dickens or Milton, as will certainly give him nourishment. It is a case of,—'In the morning sow thy seed and in the evening withhold not thine hand for thou knowest not whether shall prosper, either this or that' " (Vol. 6, pp. 109, 110).

### 9. Children can narrate poetry with little explanation from the teacher.

"They narrate from English, French and General History, from the Old and the New Testament, from *Stories from the History of Rome,* from Bulfinch's *Age of Fable,* from, for example, Goldsmith's or Wordsworth's poems, from *The Heroes of Asgard*" (Vol. 6, p. 192).

"Here is an example of how such knowledge grows. I heard a class of girls aged about thirteen read an essay on George Herbert. Three or four of his poems were included, and none of the girls had read either essay or poems before. They 'narrated' what they had read and in the course of their narration gave a full paraphrase of *The Elixir, The Pulley,* and one or two other poems. No point made by the poet was omitted and his exact words were used pretty freely. The teacher made comments upon one or two unusual words and that was all; to explain or enforce (otherwise than by a reverently sympathetic manner, the glance and words that showed that she too, cared), would have been impertinent" (Vol. 6, pp. 64, 65).

"Their power to understand, visualise, and 'tell' a play of Shakespeare from nine years old and onwards is very surprising. They put in nothing which is not there, but they miss nothing and display a passage or a scene in a sort of curious relief" (Vol. 6, p. 182).

### 10. Poetry can enhance nature study.

"We are doing something; we are trying to open the book of nature to children by the proper key—knowledge, acquaintance by look and name, if not more, with bird and flower and tree; we see, too, that the magic of poetry makes knowledge vital, and children and grown-ups quote a verse which shall add blackness to the ashbud, tender wonder to that 'flower in the crannied wall,' a thrill to the song of the lark" (Vol. 6, pp. 327, 328).

### 11. Your child should memorize poetry.

*See page 119 for more on memorization and recitation.*

"It is well to store a child's memory with a good deal of poetry, learnt without labour" (Vol. 1, p. 224).

### 12. Occasionally ask your older child to write a narration in poetry form.

"They have an enviable power of getting at the gist of a book or subject. Sometimes they are asked to write verses about a personage or an event; the result is not remarkable by way of poetry, but sums up a good deal of thoughtful reading in a delightful way" (Vol. 6, p. 242).

### 13. Though poetry is fiction, it can still contain truth and be valuable for instructing your child's conscience.

"Children should read the whole book or the whole poem to which they are introduced."

"What shall we say of fable, poetry, romance, the whole realm of fiction? There are two sorts of Truth. What we may call *accidental* Truth; that is, that such and such a thing came to pass in a certain place at a certain hour on a certain day; and this is the sort of Truth we have to observe in our general talk. The other, the Truth of Art, is what we may call *essential* Truth; that, for example, given, such and such a character, he must needs have thought and acted in such and such a way, with such and such consequences; given, a certain aspect of nature, and the poet will receive from it such and such ideas; or, certain things of common life, as a dog with a bone, for example, will present themselves to the thinker as fables, illustrating some of the happenings of life. This sort of fiction is of enormous value to us, whether we find it in poetry or romance; it teaches us morals and manners; what to do in given circumstances; what will happen if we behave in a certain way. It shows how, what seems a little venial fault is often followed by dreadful consequences, and our eyes are opened to see that it is not little or venial, but is a deep-seated fault of character; some selfishness, shallowness, or deceitfulness upon which a man or woman makes shipwreck. We cannot learn these things except through what is called fiction, or from the bitter experience of life, from the penalties of which our writers of fiction do their best to spare us" (Vol. 4, Book 1, p. 160).

"The Poet and the Essayist are our Teachers.—A child gets moral notions from the fairy-tales he delights in, as do his elders from tale and verse. So nice a critic as Matthew Arnold tells us that poetry is a criticism of life; so it is, both a criticism and an inspiration; and most of us carry in our minds tags of verse which shape our conduct more than we know;—

'Wisdom is ofttimes nearer when we stoop
Than when we soar.'

'The friends thou hast, and their adoption tried,
Grapple them to thy soul with hooks of steel.'

"A thousand thoughts that burn come to us on the wings of verse" (Vol. 4, Book 2, p. 10).

"Poetry, too, supplies us with tools for the modelling of our lives, and the use of these we must get at for ourselves. The line that strikes us as we read, that recurs, that we murmur over at odd moments—this is the line that influences our living, if it speak only—

'Of old, unhappy, far-off things,
And battles long ago.'

A couplet such as this, though it appear to carry no moral weight, instructs our conscience more effectually than many wise saws. As we 'inwardly digest,' reverence comes to us unawares, gentleness, a wistful tenderness towards the past, a sense of continuance, and of a part to play that shall not be loud and discordant, but of a piece with the whole. This is one of the 'lessons never learned in schools' which comes to each of us only as we discover it for ourselves.

"Many have a favourite poet for a year or two, to be discarded for another and another. Some are happy enough to find the poet of their lifetime in Spenser, Wordsworth, Browning, for example; but, whether it be for a year or a life, let us mark as we read, let us learn and inwardly digest. Note how good this last word is. What we digest we assimilate, take into ourselves, so that it is part and parcel of us,

---

## Notes

*You can see samples of narrations written in poetry form on pages 161–172.*

"The magic of poetry makes knowledge vital."

and no longer separable" (Vol. 4, Book 2, pp. 71, 72).

### 14. Poetry is a wonderful means of cultivating intellectual culture.

"Poetry takes first rank as a means of intellectual culture. Goethe tells us that we ought to see a good picture, hear good music, and read some good poetry every day" (Vol. 5, p. 224).

### 15. Poetry can inspire your child toward good character, noble deeds, and sense of duty.

"Heroic poetry contains such inspiration to noble living as is hardly to be found elsewhere" (Vol. 2, p. 141).

"As a fact, the books which make us think, the poems which we ponder, the lives of men which we consider, are of more use to us than volumes of good counsel" (Vol. 4, Book 1, p. 184).

"Literature is full of teaching, by precept and example, concerning the management of our physical nature. I shall offer a lesson here and there by way of sample, but no doubt the reader will think of many better teachings; and that is as it should be; the way such teaching should come to us is, here a little and there a little, incidentally, from books which we read for the interest of the story, the beauty of the poem, or the grace of the writing" (Vol. 4, Book 2, p. 11).

"The poets give us the best help in this kind of teaching; as, for example, Wordsworth's *Ode to Duty*:—
> 'Stern lawgiver! yet thou dost wear
> The Godhead's most benignant grace;
> Nor know we anything so fair
> As is the smile upon thy face;
> Flowers laugh before thee on their beds;
> And fragrance in thy footing treads;
> Thou dost preserve the stars from wrong;
> And the most ancient heavens, through thee, are
> fresh and strong.'

Or Matthew Arnold's lines on *Rugby Chapel*—
> 'Servants of God!—or sons
> Shall I not call you? because
> Not as servants ye knew
> Your Father's innermost mind,
> His, who unwillingly sees
> One of His little ones lost—
> Yours is the praise, if mankind
> Hath not as yet in its march
> Fainted, and fallen, and died!'

Or this, again, of Tennyson—
> 'Not once or twice in our fair island story

---

"A thousand thoughts that burn come to us on the wings of verse."

> The path of duty was the way to glory:
> He, that ever following her commands,
> On with toil of heart and knees and hands,
> Thro' the long gorge to the far light, has won
> His path upward and prevail'd,—
> Shall find the toppling crags of duty, scaled,
> Are close upon the shining table-lands
> To which our God Himself is moon and sun.'

Or Matthew Arnold's *Morality*—
> How, 'Tasks in hours of insight willed
> Can be through hours of gloom fulfilled.'

"Possibly we could hardly do better than lead children to reflect on some high poetic teaching, adding love to law and devotion to duty, so that children shall know themselves, by duty as by prayer,
> 'Bound by gold chains about the feet of God.'

"In the matter of the ideas that inspire the virtuous life, we miss much by our way of taking things for granted" (Vol. 3, pp. 130, 131).

"This education of the feelings, moral education, is too delicate and personal a matter for a teacher to undertake trusting to his own resources. Children are not to be fed morally like young pigeons with predigested food. They must pick and eat for themselves and they do so from the conduct of others which they hear of or perceive. But they want a great quantity of the sort of food whose issue is conduct, and that is why poetry, history, romance, geography, travel, biography, science and sums must all be pressed into service. No one can tell what particular morsel a child will select for his sustenance. One small boy of eight may come down late because—'I was meditating upon Plato and couldn't fasten my buttons,' and another may find his meat in 'Peter Pan'! But all children must read widely, and know what they have read, for the nourishment of their complex nature" (Vol. 6, p. 59).

### 16. Include the poetry from the Bible.

"The Bible a Classic Literature.—But it is singular that so few educationalists recognise that the Bible is not a single book, but a classic literature of wonderful beauty and interest; that, apart from its Divine sanctions and religious teaching, from all that we understand by 'Revelation,' the Bible, as a mere instrument of education, is, at the very least, as valuable as the classics of Greece or Rome. Here is poetry, the rhythm of which soothes even the jaded brain past taking pleasure in any other" (Vol. 2, p. 104).

### 17. Poems can inspire patriotism, just as good biographies can.

"Of Patriotic Poems.—Next in value to biographies from the point of view of inspiration are the burning words of the poets,—Tennyson's *Ode to the Iron Duke*, for example. Perhaps no poet has done more to stir the fire of patriotism amongst us than Mr Rudyard Kipling: 'We learn from our wistful mothers to call Old England "home," ' opens the door to a flood of patriotic feeling; as indeed do

---

*Notes*

"The line that strikes us as we read, that recurs, that we murmur over at odd moments--this is the line that influences our living."

the whole of the poems, *The Native-born* and *The Flag of England*:—
> 'Never was isle so little,
> Never were seas so lone,
> But over the scud and the palm trees
> The English flag has flown' " (Vol. 3, p. 134).

## Grades 1–3

**18. From the beginning, do not give your child twaddle.**

"Even for their earliest reading lessons, it is unnecessary to put twaddle into the hands of children" (Vol. 1, p. 205).

"When there is so much noble poetry within a child's compass, the pity of it, that he should be allowed to learn twaddle!" (Vol. 1, p. 226).

*Twaddle is talking down to a child, assuming he cannot understand.*

**19. Have your younger child memorize simple poems that he can relate to in his thoughts and imagination.**

"Let the poems the child learns be simple and within the range of his own thought and imagination" (Vol. 1, p. 226).

**20. Use poems for handwriting practice in copywork and transcription.**

"By-and-by the children will be promoted to transcribe little poems, and so on, in this very pleasing script" (Vol. 1, p. 237).

"A certain sense of possession and delight may be added to this exercise if children are allowed to choose for transcription their favourite verse in one poem and another. This is better than to write a favourite poem, an exercise which stales on the little people before it is finished. But a book of their own, made up of their own chosen verses, should give them pleasure" (Vol. 1, p. 238).

*See page 91 for more on copywork and transcription.*

**21. Include poetry in beginning reading lessons.**

"Reading at Sight.—The teacher must be content to proceed very slowly, securing the ground under her feet as she goes. Say—
> 'Twinkle, twinkle, little star,
> How I wonder what you are,'

is the first lesson; just those two lines. Read the passage for the child, very slowly, sweetly, with just expression, so that it is pleasant to him to listen. Point to each word as you read. Then point to 'twinkle,' 'wonder,' 'star,' 'what,'—and expect the child to pronounce each word in the verse taken promiscuously; then, when he shows that he knows each word by itself, and not before, let him *read* the two lines with clear enunciation and expression: insist from the first on clear, beautiful reading, and do not let the child fall into a dreary monotone, no more pleasant to himself than to his listener. Of course, by this time he is able to say the two lines; and let him say them clearly and beautifully. In his after lesson he will learn the rest of the little poem" (Vol. 1, p. 204).

*For more on beginning reading, see pages 79–89.*

"The books which make us think, the poems which we ponder, the lives of men which we consider, are of more use to us than volumes of good counsel."

## Grades 4–12

**22. Let your older child have plenty of practice reading aloud poetry and**

*appreciating its beautiful use of words.*

"He should have practice, too, in reading aloud, for the most part, in the books he is using for his term's work. These should include a good deal of poetry, to accustom him to the delicate rendering of shades of meaning, and especially to make him aware that words are beautiful in themselves, that they are a source of pleasure, and are worthy of our honour; and that a beautiful word deserves to be beautifully said, with a certain roundness of tone and precision of utterance" (Vol. 1, p. 227).

"The transition to Form IIA is marked by more individual reading as well as by a few additional books. The children read their 'Shakespeare play' in character" (Vol. 6, p. 182).

### 23. Older children can create a Book of Mottoes filled with favorite quotes, passages, and poems culled from their readings.

"In the reading of the Bible, of poetry, of the best prose, the culling of mottoes is a delightful and most stimulating occupation, especially if a motto book be kept, perhaps under headings, perhaps not. It would not be a bad idea for children to make their own year-book, with a motto for every day in the year culled from their own reading. What an incentive to a good day it would be to read in the morning as a motto of our very own choice and selection, and not the voice of an outside mentor: 'Keep ye the law; be swift in all obedience'! The theme suggests endless subjects for consideration and direct teaching: for example, lives with a keynote; Bible heroes; Greek heroes; poems of moral inspiration; poems of patriotism, duty, or any single moral quality; moral object-lessons; mottoes and where to find them, etc." (Vol. 3, p. 135).

### 24. Shakespeare should be read by children ages 9 or 10 and older.

"And Shakespeare? He, indeed, is not to be classed, and timed, and treated as one amongst others,—he, who might well be the daily bread of the intellectual life; Shakespeare is not to be studied in a year; he is to be read continuously throughout life, from ten years old and onwards. But a child of ten cannot understand Shakespeare. No; but can a man of fifty? Is not our great poet rather an ample feast of which every one takes according to his needs, and leaves what he has no stomach for? A little girl of nine said to me the other day that she had only read one play of Shakespeare's through, and that was *A Midsummer Night's Dream*. She did not understand the play, of course, but she must have found enough to amuse and interest her. How would it be to have a monthly reading of Shakespeare—a play, to be read in character, and continued for two or three evenings until it is finished? The Shakespeare evening would come to be looked on as a family *festa*; and the plays, read again and again, year after year, would yield more at each reading, and would leave behind in the end rich deposits of wisdom" (Vol. 5, p. 226).

## Grades 10–12
### 25. Poems of a time period can help illustrate a history study.

"But any sketch of the history teaching in Forms V and VI in a given period depends upon a notice of the 'literature' set; for plays, novels, essays, 'lives,' poems,

---

# Notes

*An easy way to study Shakespeare:*
*1. Read a narrative form of the play so your child can get familiar with the plot and characters. Books like* Tales from Shakespeare *by Charles and Mary Lamb and* Beautiful Stories from Shakespeare for Children *by E. Nesbit work well for this step.*
*2. Read lines from the play in Shakespeare's original words.*
*3. Watch a presentation of the play that is true to the original.*

"The way such teaching should come to us is, here a little and there a little, incidentally, from books which we read for the interest of the story, the beauty of the poem, or the grace of the writing."

## Notes

*Forms V and VI included children around ages 17 and 18.*

are all pressed into service and where it is possible, the architecture, painting, etc., which the period produced" (Vol. 6, pp. 177, 178).

"Readings in literature, whether of prose or poetry, should generally illustrate the historical period studied" (Vol. 6, p. 340).

"Literature is hardly a distinct subject, so closely is it associated with history, whether general or English; and whether it be contemporary or merely illustrative; and it is astonishing how much sound learning children acquire when the thought of an age is made to synchronise with its political and social developments. A point which I should like to bring before the reader is the peculiar part which poetry plays in making us aware of this thought of the ages, including our own. Every age, every epoch, has its poetic aspect, its quintessence, as it were, and happy the people who have a Shakespeare, a Dante, a Milton, a Burns, to gather up and preserve its meaning as a world possession" (Vol. 6, p. 274).

## Questions to Ask about Poetry and Shakespeare

### General Guidelines for All Grades

- Am I trying to include poetry in my child's education?
- Am I seeking to use the best in literature and poetry in order to cultivate my child's taste for it?
- Am I learning to recognize good poetry and literature by the force and beauty of the words?
- Am I focusing on one poet at a time?
- Am I trying to read poetry often; daily, if possible?
- Am I introducing the poet to my child and getting out of the way?
- Do I recognize that different poets will appeal to various children?
- Am I giving my child entire poems, not just extracts?
- Am I expecting my child to narrate poetry with little explanation from me?
- Am I using poetry to enhance our nature study?
- Do I occasionally ask my child to write a narration in poetry form?
- Do I realize the value of poetry for instructing my child's conscience?
- Do I realize the value of poetry for cultivating my child's intellectual culture?
- Do I realize the value of poetry for inspiring my child toward good character, noble deeds, and sense of duty?
- Am I including poetry from the Bible?
- Do I realize how poetry can inspire patriotism in my child, just as good biographies can?

### Grades 1–3

- Am I trying not to give my child twaddle, even when he is young?
- Am I starting with simple poems that my child can relate to in his thoughts and imagination?
- Do I use poems as part of my child's handwriting practice in copywork and transcription?

*"When there is so much noble poetry within a child's compass, the pity of it, that he should be allowed to learn twaddle!"*

- Am I including poetry in my young child's beginning reading lessons?

### Grades 4–12
- Am I giving my older child plenty of practice reading aloud poetry and appreciating its beautiful use of words?
- Am I encouraging my older child to create a Book of Mottoes filled with favorite quotes, passages, and poems culled from his readings?
- Am I reading Shakespeare with my children who are ten and older?

### Grades 10–12
- Am I trying to use poetry from certain time periods to illustrate our history studies?

## More Quotes on Poetry and Shakespeare

"Writing a poem is discovering."—Robert Frost

"A man should hear a little music, read a little poetry, and see a fine picture every day of his life, in order that worldly cares may not obliterate the sense of the beauty which God has implanted in the human soul."—Johann Wolfgang von Goethe

"Poetry is when an emotion has found its thought and the thought has found words."—Robert Frost

"Poetry is the art of uniting pleasure with truth."—Samuel Johnson

"A poet dares be just so clear and no clearer. . . . He unzips the veil from beauty, but does not remove it. A poet utterly clear is a trifle glaring."—E. B. White

"Poets have been mysteriously silent on the subject of cheese."—G. K. Chesterton

"When you are describing,
A shape, or sound, or tint;
Don't state the matter plainly,
But put it in a hint;
And learn to look at all things,
With a sort of mental squint."—Lewis Carroll

"Prose, words in their best order.
Poetry, the best words in the best order."—Samuel Taylor Coleridge

"When I read Shakespeare I am struck with wonder
That such trivial people should muse and thunder
In such lovely language."—D. H. Lawrence

"A beautiful word deserves to be beautifully said."

# Chapter 13
# Recitation and Memorization

> Notes
>
> *Recitation and memorization are part of poetry, which is taught as specific language arts lessons.*

"Wow, did you catch that line?" Mom read it again.

'A wretched soul, bruised with adversity
We bid be quiet, when we hear it cry;
But were we burdened with like weight of pain,
As much, or more, we should ourselves complain.'

I think that's one we should memorize."

Kim liked that idea. "Can we recite it for Grandma next time we video chat with her?"

"Yes, absolutely," replied Mom. "I'm sure she would love it."

"So how do we start?" Kim asked.

"We already have," said Mom. "Here, I'll read it one more time for you now. Then I'll read it again while you're brushing your teeth tonight. I'll just read it for you a few times a day for the rest of this week, and I'm sure you'll have it memorized soon."

"That doesn't sound hard," Kim said.

"It's not," Mom agreed. "And I'll help you make sure you can say these beautiful words in a beautiful way."

## Charlotte's Thoughts on Recitation and Memorization

### *General Guidelines for All Grades*

**1. All children can learn to recite beautifully if coached properly.**

"All children have it in them to recite; it is an imprisoned gift waiting to be delivered, like Ariel from the pine" (Vol. 1, p. 223).

**2. Learning to speak beautifully is the first step in good recitation.**

"A child who is not a genius, is not even born of cultivated parents, may be taught the fine art of beautiful and perfect speaking; but that is only the first step in the acquisition of 'The Children's Art' " (Vol. 1, p. 223).

**3. Help your child practice correct enunciation.**

"The training of the ear and voice is an exceedingly important part of physical culture. Drill the children in pure vowel sounds, in the enunciation of final consonants; do not let them speak of 'walkin' ' and 'talkin',' of a 'fi-ine da-ay,' 'ni-ice boy-oys.' Drill them in pronouncing difficult words—'imperturbability,' 'ipecacuanha,' 'Antananarivo,'—with sharp precision after a single hearing; in

> *Ariel is a character from Shakespeare's* The Tempest, *who was imprisoned in a tree and rescued.*

> "All children have it in them to recite; it is an imprisoned gift waiting to be delivered."

## Notes

*Charlotte recommended the carefully graduated steps described in Mr. Arthur Burrell's book,* Recitation: A Handbook for Teachers.

*"My name is Norval" was a satirical poem popular during Charlotte's lifetime.*

"The child should speak beautiful thoughts so beautifully, with such delicate rendering of each *nuance* of meaning, that he becomes to the listener the interpreter of the author's thought."

producing the several sounds of each vowel; and the sounds of the consonants *without* attendant vowels" (Vol. 1, p. 133).

### 4. The longer a bad habit of enunciation is allowed to continue, the harder it will be to correct.

"Here we see how important it is to keep watch over the habits of enunciation, carriage of the head, and so on, which the child is forming hour by hour. The poke, the stoop, the indistinct utterance, is not a mere trick to be left off at pleasure 'when he is older and knows better,' but is all the time growing into him becoming a part of himself, because it is registered in the very substance of his spinal cord. The part of his nervous system where consciousness resides (the brain) has long ago given a standing order, and such are the complications of the administration, that to recall the order would mean the absolute re-making of the parts concerned. And to correct bad habits of speaking, for instance, it will not be enough for the child to intend to speak plainly and to try to speak plainly; he will not be able to do so habitually until some degree of new growth has taken place in the organs of voice whilst he is making efforts to form the new habit" (Vol. 1, pp. 113, 114).

### 5. Good recitation conveys each nuance of meaning and the author's thoughts.

"The child should speak beautiful thoughts so beautifully, with such delicate rendering of each *nuance* of meaning, that he becomes to the listener the interpreter of the author's thought" (Vol. 1, p. 223).

### 6. Interpreting a poem or passage well is a great education in itself.

"Now, consider what appreciation, sympathy, power of expression this implies, and you will grant that 'The Children's Art' is, as Steele said of the society of his wife, 'a liberal education in itself' " (Vol. 1, p. 223).

### 7. Your child should learn to interpret and convey meaning for himself, not just parrot your inflection.

"It is objected—'Children are such parrots! They say a thing as they hear it said; as for troubling themselves to "appreciate" and "interpret," not a bit of it!' Most true of the 'My name is Norval' style of recitation; but throughout this volume the child is led to find the just expression of thought for himself; never is the poor teacher allowed to set a pattern—'say this as I say it.' The ideas are kept well within the child's range, and the expression is his own" (Vol. 1, pp. 223, 224).

### 8. Recitation is great preparation for public speaking.

"I hope that my readers will train their children in the art of recitation; in the coming days, more even than in our own, will it behove every educated man and woman to be able to speak effectively in public; and, in learning to recite you learn to speak" (Vol. 1, p. 224).

### 9. Your child should still memorize poetry, even if he is not preparing those passages for recitation.

"Recitation and committing to memory are not necessarily the same thing, and it is well to store a child's memory with a good deal of poetry, learnt without labour" (Vol. 1, p. 224).

### 10. Your child can memorize a passage simply by hearing it once or twice each day.

"Some years ago I chanced to visit a house, the mistress of which had educational notions of her own, upon which she was bringing up a niece. She presented me with a large foolscap sheet written all over with the titles of poems, some of them long and difficult: *Tintern Abbey*, for example. She told me that her niece could repeat to me any of those poems that I liked to ask for, and that she had never learnt a single verse by heart in her life. The girl did repeat several of the poems on the list, quite beautifully and without hesitation; and then the lady unfolded her secret. She thought she had made a discovery, and I thought so too. She read a poem through to E.; then the next day, while the little girl was making a doll's frock, perhaps, she read it again; once again the next day, while E.'s hair was being brushed. She got in about six or more readings, according to the length of the poem, at odd and unexpected times, and in the end E. could say the poem which she had *not* learned.

"I have tried the plan often since, and found it effectual. The child must not try to recollect or to say the verse over to himself, but, as far as may be, present an open mind to receive an impression of interest. Half a dozen repetitions should give children possession of such poems as—'Dolly and Dick,' 'Do you ask what the birds say?' 'Little lamb, who made thee?' and the like" (Vol. 1, pp. 224, 225).

### 11. This method of memorizing takes the weariness away from the task and helps your child develop the habit of making mental images.

"The gains of such a method of learning are, that the edge of the child's enjoyment is not taken off by wearful verse by verse repetitions, and, also, that the habit of making mental images is unconsciously formed" (Vol. 1, p. 225).

### 12. Scripture stored in your child's heart can bear fruit in the future.

"It is a delightful thing to have the memory stored with beautiful, comforting, and inspiring passages, and we cannot tell when and how this manner of seed may spring up, grow, and bear fruit" (Vol. 1, p. 253).

### 13. Memorizing Scripture should not be done in such a way as to burden your child.

"But the learning of the parable of the Prodigal Son, for example, should not be laid on the children as a burden" (Vol. 1, p. 253).

### 14. A larger passage can be memorized in smaller sections, if desired.

"The whole parable should be read to them in a way to bring out its beauty and tenderness; and then, day by day, the teacher should recite a short passage, perhaps two or three verses, saying it over some three or four times until the children think they know it. Then, but not before, let them recite the passage. Next day the children will recite what they have already learned, and so on, until they are able to say the whole parable" (Vol. 1, p. 253).

---

### Notes

*A foolscap sheet of paper measures about 13 x 16 inches.*

**Tintern Abbey**, *a poem by Wordsworth, is more than 150 lines long.*

*See page 124 for the poems Charlotte recommended young children memorize.*

"It is well to store a child's memory with a good deal of poetry, learnt without labour."

*Recitation and Memorization*

## Notes

*To give you an idea of how much memorization was expected in Charlotte's schools, during one term (12 weeks) a twelve-year-old child was to memorize two Bible passages of 20 verses each and these three poems or selections:* Ode on the Death of the Duke of Wellington, The Charge of the Light Brigade, You Ask Me Why *(Vol. 3, p. 303).*

*See page 124 for some specific poems Charlotte recommended for this age.*

*See page 79 for more details on using poetry for beginning reading lessons.*

**"When there is so much noble poetry within a child's compass, the pity of it, that he should be allowed to learn twaddle!"**

### 15. Read and recite Scripture in a beautiful way.

"The whole parable should be read to them in a way to bring out its beauty and tenderness" (Vol. 1, p. 253).

### 16. Allow ample time to memorize a passage and prepare it for recitation.

"Sometimes events hurry us, and sometimes—is it not true?—we like the little excitement of a rush. The children like it, too, at first. Father's birthday is coming, and Nellie must recite a poem for him; the little *fête* has only been thought of a week in advance, and Nellie is seized at all sorts of odd moments to have some lines of the recitation crammed into her. At first she is pleased and important, and goes joyously to the task; but by-and-by it irks her; she is cross and naughty, is reproached for want of love for father, sheds tears over her verses, and, though finally the little performance may be got through very well, Nellie has suffered physically and morally in doing what, if it had been thought of a month beforehand, would have been altogether wholesome and delightful" (Vol. 3, p. 34).

## Grades 1–3

### 17. Memorizing requires mental effort, so do not require it of your child younger than six.

"Let me again say, every effort of the kind, however unconscious, means wear and tear of brain substance. Let the child lie fallow till he is six" (Vol. 1, p. 226).

### 18. Your younger child should be allowed to memorize shorter and simpler poems, but not twaddle.

"And then, in this matter of memorising, as in others, attempt only a little, and let the poems the child learns be simple and within the range of his own thought and imagination. At the same time, when there is so much noble poetry within a child's compass, the pity of it, that he should be allowed to learn twaddle!" (Vol. 1, p. 226).

### 19. Your young child can learn and recite the graceful passages he is using for reading lessons—both poetry and prose.

"At this stage, his reading lessons must advance so slowly that he may just as well learn his reading exercises, both prose and poetry, as recitation lessons. Little poems suitable to be learned in this way will suggest themselves at once; but perhaps prose is better, on the whole, as offering more of the words in everyday use, of Saxon origin, and of anomalous spelling. Short fables, and such graceful, simple prose as we have in Mrs Gatty's *Parables from Nature*, and, still better, in Mrs Barbauld's prose poems, are very suitable" (Vol. 1, pp. 204, 205).

### 20. Your child should begin memorizing Bible passages when six or seven.

"The learning by heart of Bible passages should begin while the children are quite young, six or seven" (Vol. 1, p. 253).

## Questions to Ask about Recitation and Memorization

### General Guidelines for All Grades

- Do I believe that my child can learn to recite beautifully?
- Am I encouraging my child to speak beautifully, with correct enunciation?
- Am I seeking to correct poor enunciation promptly?
- Do I understand how a good recitation is an expression of every nuance of the author's thoughts?
- Do I consider the thought and effort that goes into interpreting a poem or passage well as a great education in itself?
- Am I encouraging my child to interpret and convey the passage's meaning for himself, not just imitate me?
- Do I understand how recitation is great preparation for public speaking?
- Am I having my child memorize poetry even if he does not prepare it for recitation?
- Am I helping my child memorize a passage by simply saying it once or twice a day in his hearing?
- Do I encourage my child to make mental images as he listens to the passage he is memorizing?
- Do I understand how Scripture stored in my child's heart can bear fruit in the future?
- Am I being careful that Scripture memory is not a burden to my child?
- Am I allowing larger passages to be memorized in smaller sections, if needed?
- Am I trying to read and recite Scripture in a beautiful way for my children to hear?
- Do I allow ample time for my child to memorize a passage and prepare it for recitation?

### Grades 1–3

- Am I not requiring memorization from my child who is younger than six?
- Am I allowing my younger children to memorize shorter and simpler poems, but not twaddle?
- Am I having my beginning reader learn and recite the poems and passages he is using for his reading lessons?
- Am I assigning Bible passages to be memorized by my six- or seven-year-old?

## More Quotes on Recitation and Memorization

"What a poor appearance the tales of poets make when stripped of the colors which music puts upon them, and recited in simple prose."—Plato

"Thy word have I hid in mine heart that I might not sin against Thee" (Psalm 119:11).

"The two offices of memory are collection and distribution."—Samuel Johnson

"To have great poets there must be great audiences too."—Walt Whitman

---

**Notes**

"It is a delightful thing to have the memory stored with beautiful, comforting, and inspiring passages, and we cannot tell when and how this manner of seed may spring up, grow, and bear fruit."

# Beginning Poems for Recitation

Charlotte specifically mentioned these three poems that "would compel any child under the age of nine to recite" (Vol. 1, p. 224).

### Winken, Blinken, and Nod
#### by Eugene Field

Wynken, Blynken, and Nod one night
   Sailed off in a wooden shoe—
Sailed on a river of crystal light,
   Into a sea of dew.
"Where are you going, and what do you wish?"
   The old moon asked the three.
"We have come to fish for the herring fish
   That live in this beautiful sea;
   Nets of silver and gold have we!"
      Said Wynken,
      Blynken,
      And Nod.

The old moon laughed and sang a song,
   As they rocked in the wooden shoe,
And the wind that sped them all night long
   Ruffled the waves of dew.
The little stars were the herring fish
   That lived in that beautiful sea—
"Now cast your nets wherever you wish—
   Never afeard are we";
   So cried the stars to the fishermen three:
      Wynken,
      Blynken,
      And Nod.

All night long their nets they threw
   To the stars in the twinkling foam—
Then down from the skies came the wooden shoe,
   Bringing the fishermen home;
'T was all so pretty a sail it seemed
   As if it could not be,
And some folks thought 't was a dream they 'd dreamed
   Of sailing that beautiful sea—
   But I shall name you the fishermen three:
      Wynken,
      Blynken,
      And Nod.

Wynken and Blynken are two little eyes,
   And Nod is a little head,
And the wooden shoe that sailed the skies
   Is a wee one's trundle-bed.
So shut your eyes while mother sings
   Of wonderful sights that be,
And you shall see the beautiful things
   As you rock in the misty sea,
   Where the old shoe rocked the fishermen three:
      Wynken,
      Blynken,
      And Nod.

## *Miss Lilywhite's Party*
### by George Cooper

"May I go to Miss Lilywhite's party?"
But Grandmamma shook her head;
"When the birds go to rest,
I think it is best
For mine to go, too," she said.

"Can't I go to Miss Lilywhite's party?"
Still Grandmamma shook her head:
"Dear child, tell me how,
You're half asleep now;
Don't ask such a thing," she said.

Then that little one's laughter grew hearty:
"Why, Grannay," she said,
"Going to Miss Lilywhite's party
Means going to bed!"

## *Two Little Kittens*
### Anonymous

Two little kittens, one stormy night,
Began to quarrel, and then to fight;
One had a mouse, the other had none,
And that's the way the quarrel begun.

"I'll have that mouse," sad the biggest cat;
"You'll have that mouse? We'll see about that!"
"I will have that mouse," said the eldest son;
"You shan't have the mouse," said the little one.

*Notes*

I told you before 'twas a stormy night
When these two little kittens began to fight;
The old woman seized her sweeping broom,
And swept the two kittens right out of the room.

The ground was covered with frost and snow,
And the two little kittens had nowhere to go;
So they laid them down on the mat at the door,
While the old woman finished sweeping the floor.

Then they crept in, as quiet as mice,
All wet with the snow, and cold as ice,
For they found it was better, that stormy night,
To lie down and sleep than to quarrel and fight.

Charlotte also mentioned these three poems for young children (Vol. 1, p. 225).

## Dolly and Dick
### by E. Coxhead

Dolly came into the meadow
    And sat on the grass to cry;
Her tears made the daisies wither,
    And the yellow buttercups die.

The little birds heard her sobbing;
    Their songs broke off in surprise:
What could have happened to Dolly,
    That she had such sorrowful eyes?

"I am unhappy!" cried Dolly,
    Sobbing aloud in despair;
"I fought with Dick in the garden,
    And pulled out a lot of his hair."

Softly there flew down a robin—
    A dear little redbreast bird;
His voice was clear as the ripples
    Of a pool with the wind has stirred:

"After the night comes the morning,
    After the winter the spring:
We can begin again, Dolly,
    And be sorry for everything.

"It is a pity to quarrel;
    I think it never is right:
But if you fight in the day-time,
    You can make it up in the night.

"We love, and so we are happy;
    No beautiful thing ever ends:
'Tis good to cry and be sorry,
    But better to kiss and be friends."

Dolly stopped crying to listen,
    But the robin had flown away.
"I'll go and say I am sorry
    I quarrelled with Dick to-day."

"What made you come back?" asked Dicky,
    As they kissed on the nursery stairs.
"I met," said Dolly, "a robin
    Who, I think, was saying his prayers."


## *Do you ask what the birds say?*
### by Samuel Taylor Coleridge

Do you ask what the birds say? The Sparrow, the Dove,
The Linnet and Thrush say, "I love and I love!"
In the winter they're silent -- the wind is so strong;
What it says, I don't know, but it sings a loud song.
But green leaves, and blossoms, and sunny warm weather,
And singing, and loving -- all come back together.
But the Lark is so brimful of gladness and love,
The green fields below him, the blue sky above,
That he sings, and he sings; and for ever sings he --
"I love my Love, and my Love loves me!"


## *Little lamb, who made thee?*
### by William Blake

Little Lamb, who made thee?
Dost thou know who made thee?
Gave thee life, and bid thee feed,
By the stream and o'er the mead;
Gave thee clothing of delight,
Softest clothing, woolly, bright;
Gave thee such a tender voice,
Making all the vales rejoice?

## Notes

Little Lamb, who made thee?
Dost thou know who made thee?
Little Lamb, I'll tell thee,
Little Lamb, I'll tell thee.
He is called by thy name,
For He calls Himself a Lamb.
He is meek, and He is mild;
He became a little child.
I a child, and thou a lamb,
We are called by His name.
Little Lamb, God bless thee!
Little Lamb, God bless thee!

# Chapter 14
# English Grammar

*English grammar is taught as specific language arts lessons.*

"You mean I don't have to teach English grammar all year long in every grade?" Esther was astonished.

"You're already teaching the correct way to use words every time you have the children read or write or tell or listen. 'Grammar' just means the set of rules for speaking and writing a language." Beth smiled. "Think of it this way: Let's say you wanted to learn how to play chess. Your household was full of chess players already, so you had ample opportunity to watch them play and try your hand at playing too. Would you learn how to play correctly?"

"I would think so. I might need a little coaching now and then, but I would pick up a lot on my own," said Esther.

"Exactly," replied Beth. "Now, if I asked you to recite all the rules of chess, you may not be able to do that right away. You could probably come up with many of the rules just based on your own observations and experience. But if I insisted that you formally study the rules, it wouldn't take you very long to learn them, especially because you were so familiar with chess anyway."

"That's true," Esther agreed.

"It's the same with English. Your children are learning the proper way to use that language every day, by hearing and reading, telling and writing. You have to coach them sometimes on proper use, but they're picking up a lot," Beth explained. "Along the way, you will want them to formally study the rules, but it's not going to take them twelve years. So use the early grades to let them get familiar with the language in all the ways it's used around them, and save the formal studies of grammar for when they're older."

## Charlotte's Thoughts on English Grammar

### *General Guidelines for All Grades*

*1. The success of grammar lessons depends largely on the teacher's skill and the student's habit of attention.*

"The success of the scholars in what may be called disciplinary subjects, such as Mathematics and Grammar, depends largely on the power of the teacher, though the pupils' habit of attention is of use in these too" (Vol. 6, p. 7).

"But these are matters familiar to all teachers and we have nothing new in the teaching of grammar to suggest; but we probably gain in the fact that our scholars pay full attention to grammar, as to all other lessons" (Vol. 6, p. 211).

*2. English grammar helps train your child in the habit of clear and ordered thinking.*

"We divest ourselves of the notion that to develop the faculties is the chief thing;

**"We probably gain in the fact that our scholars pay full attention to grammar, as to all other lessons."**

## Notes

and a 'subject' which does not rise out of some great thought of life we usually reject as not nourishing, not fruitful; while we usually, but not invariably, retain those studies which give exercise in habits of clear and orderly thinking. We have some gymnastics of the mind whose object is to exercise what we call faculties as well as to train in the habit of clear and ordered thinking. Mathematics, grammar, logic, etc., are not purely disciplinary; they do develop, if a bull may be allowed intellectual muscle. We by no means reject the familiar staples of education, in the school sense, but we prize them even more for the record of intellectual habits they leave in the brain tissue than for their distinct value in developing certain 'faculties'" (Vol. 2, pp. 230, 231).

### 3. Few children take pleasure in English grammar, even if they enjoy using their reasoning power to argue about trifles in other areas.

"We find that, while children are tiresome in arguing about trifling things, often for the mere pleasure of employing their reasoning power, a great many of them are averse to those studies which should, we suppose, give free play to a power that is in them, even if they do not strengthen and develop this power. Yet few children take pleasure in Grammar, especially in English Grammar, which depends so little on inflexion" (Vol. 6, p. 151).

### 4. Provide abundant enjoyable material for your child's reason to feed upon.

"Perhaps we should accept this tacit vote of the majority and cease to put undue pressure upon studies which would be invaluable did the reasoning power of a child wait upon our training, but are on a different footing when we perceive that children come endowed to the full as much with reason as with love; that our business is to provide abundant material upon which this supreme power should work; and that whatever development occurs comes with practice in *congenial fields of thought*" (Vol. 6, p. 151).

### 5. Don't allow your child to neglect English grammar, even if he doesn't enjoy it.

"At the same time we may not let children neglect either of these delightful studies [Grammar or Arithmetic]" (Vol. 6, p. 151).

### 6. Eventually, your child will see how valuable precise and well-used words are for conveying truth.

"The time will come when they will delight in words, the beauty and propriety of words; when they will see that words are consecrated as the vehicle of truth and are not to be carelessly tampered with in statement or mutilated in form; and we must prepare them for these later studies" (Vol. 6, p. 151).

## Grades 1–3

### 7. Do not hurry your child into a study of English grammar.

"In the first place, grammar, being a study of *words* and not of *things*, is by no means attractive to the child, nor should he be hurried into it" (Vol. 1, p. 295).

> "The time will come when they will delight in words, the beauty and propriety of word."

*8. English grammar can be hard for a young child (ages 6–8) to grasp, since it is a study of words that depends on position and logical connection.*

"English grammar, again, depending as it does on the position and logical connection of words, is peculiarly hard for him to grasp" (Vol. 1, p. 295).

"One limitation I did discover in the minds of these little people; my friend insisted that they could not understand English Grammar; I maintained that they could and wrote a little Grammar (still waiting to be prepared for publication!) for the two of seven and eight; but she was right; I was allowed to give the lessons myself with what lucidity and freshness I could command; in vain; the Nominative 'Case' baffled them; their minds rejected the abstract conception just as children reject the notion of writing an 'Essay on Happiness' " (Vol. 6, p. 10).

*9. Begin with the parts of a simple sentence—subject and predicate—before tackling the parts of speech.*

"Because English grammar is a logical study, and deals with *sentences* and the positions that words occupy in them, rather than with *words*, and what they are in their own right, it is better that the child should begin with the *sentence*, and not with the parts of speech; that is, that he should learn a little of what is called *analysis* of sentences before he learns to parse; should learn to divide simple sentences into the thing we speak of, and what we say about it—'The cat—sits on the hearth'—before he is lost in the fog of person, mood, and part of speech" (Vol. 1, p. 296).

"Most children can be got to take in the notion of a sentence as, words making sense, especially if they are allowed a few excursions into non-sense, the gibberish of strings of words which do not make sense. Again, by dint of many interesting exercises in which they never lose sight of the *subject*, they get hold of that idea also" (Vol. 6, p. 210).

"*English* is rather a logical study dealing with sentences and the positions that words occupy in them than with words and what they are in their own right. Therefore it is better that a child should begin with a sentence and not with the parts of speech, that is, he should learn a little of what is called analysis before he learns to parse. It requires some effort of abstraction for a child to perceive that when we speak, we speak about something and say something about it; and he has learned nearly all the grammar that is necessary when he knows that when we speak we use sentences and that a sentence makes sense; that we can put words together so as to make utter nonsense, as,—'Tom immediately candlestick uproarious nevertheless'—a string of words making perfect nonsense and therefore not a sentence. If we use words in such a way as to make sense we get a sentence; 'John goes to school' is a sentence. Every sentence has two parts, (1), the thing we speak of, and (2), what we say about it. We speak of John, we say about him that he goes to school. At this stage the children require many exercises in finding out the first and second parts of simple sentences. When they are quite familiar with the fact that the first part of a sentence is what we speak about, they may get a name for it, subject, which will be made simpler to them if they know the word subject means that which we talk about. For instance, we may say, the subject of conversation was parsley, which is another way of saying the thing we were speaking about was

*Notes*

"English grammar, again, depending as it does on the position and logical connection of words, is peculiarly hard for him to grasp."

## Notes

*The scene with the King and Queen is an excerpt from* Palace Tales *by Fielding Hall.*

*You can see the introductory grammar lessons on page 187.*

*Parsing refers to labeling each word in a sentence with its part of speech in that context.*

*Analyzing refers to identifying what jobs various words are performing in a sentence.*

"Perhaps we should postpone parsing, for instance, until a child is accustomed to weigh sentences for their sense."

---

parsley. To sum up such a lesson, the class should learn,—Words put together so as to make sense form a sentence. A sentence has two parts, that which we speak of and what we say about it. That which we speak of is the subject" (Vol. 6, pp. 209, 210).

"Perhaps we should postpone parsing, for instance, until a child is accustomed to weigh sentences for their sense" (Vol. 6, p. 151).

### 10. It is important that your child should not be puzzled with grammar.

" 'So then I took up the next book. It was about grammar. It said extraordinary things about nouns and verbs and particles and pronouns, and past participles and objective cases and subjunctive moods. "What are all these things?" asked the King. "I don't know, your Majesty," and the Queen did not know, but she said it would be very suitable for children to learn. It would keep them quiet.'

"It is so important that children should not be puzzled as were this bewildered King and Queen, that I add a couple of introductory grammar lessons; as a single example is often more useful than many precepts" (Vol. 1, p. 296).

## Grades 4–6

### 11. Allow your child plenty of time to play with figures of speech before you attempt grammatical analysis of sentences.

"Should let them dally with figures of speech before we attempt minute analysis of sentences" (Vol. 6, pp. 151, 152).

### 12. Don't be in a hurry to introduce grammatical terms. Allow your child time to gather particulars and form impressions for himself first.

"And should reduce our grammatical nomenclature to a minimum. The fact is that children do not generalise, they gather particulars with amazing industry, but hold their impressions fluid, as it were; and we may not hurry them to formulate" (Vol. 6, p. 152).

### 13. A young child deals with concrete items, not abstract concepts.

"Children will probably be slow to receive this first lesson in abstract knowledge, and we must remember that knowledge in this sort is difficult and uncongenial. Their minds deal with the concrete and they have the singular faculty of being able to make concrete images out of the merest gossamer of a fairy tale" (Vol. 6, p. 210).

### 14. Do not attempt to personify the parts of speech; such an abstraction will offend a child.

"A seven year old child sings,—
  'I cannot see fairies,
  I dream them.
  There is no fairy that can hide from me;
  I keep on dreaming till I find him.
  There you are, Primrose! I see you, Blackwing!'

"But a child cannot dream parts of speech, and any grown-up twaddle attempting to personify such abstractions offends a small person who with all his love of play and nonsense has a serious mind" (Vol. 6, p. 210).

**15. Two-word sentences are a great way to introduce the concept of verbs.**

"One more initial idea is necessary if children are not to wander blindfold through the mazes of grammar 'as she is' not 'spoke,' but writ in books. They must be familiar with verbs and perhaps the simplest way to approach this idea is to cause them to make sentences with two words, the thing they speak of and what they say about it,—Mary sings, Auntie knits, Henry runs. In each of these examples, the child will see the thing we speak of and what we say about it" (Vol. 6, pp. 210, 211).

**16. By age 12, your child should have a fair knowledge of English grammar.**

"In Language, by twelve, they should have a fair knowledge of English grammar, and should read some literature" (Vol. 3, p. 235).

"The six years' work—from six to twelve—which I suggest, should and does result in the power of the pupils— . . .

"(o) They should have some knowledge of English Grammar" (Vol. 3, p. 301).

**17. Include word studies in your grammar lessons, such as prefixes, suffixes, synonyms, antonyms, and homonyms.**

(An exam question for a 12-year-old) "Give some words with each of the following prefixes :—*eft, hypo, cata, di, syn*" (Vol. 3, p. 310).

## Questions to Ask about English Grammar

### General Guidelines for All Grades

- Am I comfortable with my level of skill in teaching English grammar, or have I found material that will help me teach grammar in a competent and clear way?
- Does my child have the habit of attention that will contribute to his success in grammar lessons?
- Do I understand the value of English grammar to help train my child in the habit of clear and ordered thinking?
- Am I not surprised if my child doesn't seem to take pleasure in English grammar?
- Am I trying to provide an abundance of enjoyable material in grammar lessons for my child's reason to feed upon?
- Am I being careful not to neglect English grammar even if my child doesn't enjoy it?
- Do I trust that my child will eventually see the value in precise and well-used words to convey truth?

### Grades 1–3

- Am I being careful not to hurry my child into studying English grammar?

*Notes*

*See samples of English grammar lessons for older students, including one of the books used in Charlotte's schools, on page 187.*

"But a child cannot dream parts of speech, and any grown-up twaddle attempting to personify such abstractions offends a small person who with all his love of play and nonsense has a serious mind."

- Do I understand how the concepts of English grammar are abstract and difficult for younger children to grasp?
- Am I starting by teaching the parts of a simple sentence—subject and predicate?
- Am I doing my best to make sure my child is not puzzled with English grammar?

## Grades 4–6

- Am I allowing my child plenty of time to play with figures of speech before attempting to analyze sentences for grammar?
- Am I allowing my child time to observe and form his own impressions about words and their use in sentences before introducing grammatical terms?
- Is my child ready to deal with abstract concepts, or is he still focusing on concrete items and should postpone grammar lessons?
- Am I being careful not to try to make the parts of speech seem like little persons or other cute but offensive gimmicks?
- If my child is ready, am I using two-word sentences to introduce the concept of verbs?
- Does my twelve-year-old child have a fair knowledge of English grammar?
- Am I including word studies in our English grammar lessons, such as prefixes, suffixes, synonyms, antonyms, and homonyms?

## More Quotes on English Grammar

"My attitude toward punctuation is that it ought to be as conventional as possible. The game of golf would lose a good deal if croquet mallets and billiard cues were allowed on the putting green. You ought to be able to show that you can do it a good deal better than anyone else with the regular tools before you have a license to bring in your own improvements."—Ernest Hemingway

"English usage is sometimes more than mere taste, judgement, and education. Sometimes it's sheer luck, like getting across the street."—E. B. White

"That punctuation is important all agree; but how few comprehend the extent of its importance! The writer who neglects punctuation, or mis-punctuates, is liable to be misunderstood—this, according to the popular idea, is the sum of the evils arising from heedlessness or ignorance. It does not seem to be known that, even where the sense is perfectly clear, a sentence may be deprived of half its force—its spirit—its point—by improper punctuation. For the want of merely a comma, it often occurs that an axiom appears a paradox, or that a sarcasm is converted into a sermonoid."—Edgar Allan Poe

"They should have some knowledge of English Grammar."

# Appendix

Proofreading and Reference Skills.................................. 137

Written Narration/Composition Samples..................... 139

Poetry Narration Samples............................................ 159

Narration Questions that Charlotte Used..................... 173

Narration Ideas ........................................................... 175

Two Mothers' Conversation about Teaching Reading.. 179

A Beginning Reading Lesson Plan ............................... 183

English Grammar Lessons ........................................... 187

# Proofreading and Reference Skills

Though we do not find specific directions as to how to teach proofreading and reference skills, both were included in Charlotte's language arts program.

## Proofreading

The closest we can find to Charlotte's mentioning anything like proofreading is when she encourages young writers to look over their attempts at drawing a new letter, compare those attempts to a good model, and determine what they might need to re-draw (Vol. 1, pp. 160, 234, 235).

Since Charlotte emphasized looking at correct models for copywork, as well as for spelling and dictation, we would draw the conclusion that we don't want to give students exercises that purposely present sentences incorrectly formatted just so they can proofread and correct them.

Instead, the CM principle seems to be similar to the training a bank teller receives. Study the correct items, the real thing; then if any counterfeit appears, you will recognize it because it doesn't measure up. If we concentrate on teaching our children the correct way to spell, capitalize, and punctuate, mistakes along those lines will become obvious when they arise.

Proofreading will naturally occur when our children get to composition lessons in the older grades. Until then, it seems prudent to focus on keeping correct models before them, rather than intentionally incorrect material.

## Reference Skills

Charlotte must have included reference-book skills in her program. We don't have specifics, but mention is made of 12-year-old students being able to read an easy French book without a dictionary (Vol. 3, p. 301). That description would seem to imply that the students knew how to use a dictionary, in that case a French-English dictionary.

Charlotte also talks about encouraging the habit of thoroughness (not being satisfied with a slipshod grasp of a subject) by referring "to an encyclopedia, to clear up any doubtful point, when it turns up" (Vol. 3, p. 120).

It would seem that the most practical way to teach reference skills is by showing your child how to use a dictionary or encyclopedia as they are needed along the way. When your child asks a question that you don't know the answer to, use that opportunity to look up the answer together. You will be demonstrating a valuable mind-set of a lifetime of learning, as well as teaching your child how to use different reference books.

In the same vein, take opportunity as it is provided to teach your child how to do research on the Internet. Perform some searches together, then gradually turn over the searching tasks to your child while you supervise.

---

*Notes*

*See page 91 for more on Copywork and page 99 for more on Dictation.*

*See page 63 for more on Composition.*

# Written Narration/Composition Samples

(from Vol. 3, pp. 272–299, 312, 318 and Vol. 6, pp. 203–208)

> Notes
>
> See page 173 for a summary of the questions that Charlotte used when asking for narrations/compositions.

"At the end of the term an examination paper is sent out containing one or two questions on each book. Here are a few of the answers. The children in the first two classes narrate their answers, which someone writes from their dictation."

> Any student's incorrect spelling or grammar is included verbatim and acknowledged with a "(sic)", which means "as such."

## Grades 1–3

Q. Tell the story of Naaman.

"Naaman had something the matter with him, and his master sent a letter to the King of Israel, and the king was very unhappy and did not know what to do because he thought that he wanted to come and fight against him, and he rent his clothes. And he said, 'I can't cure him,' so he sent him to Elisha, and he told him to take a lot of presents and a lot of things with him. And when Naaman came to Elisha's door, Elisha sent Gehazi to tell him to dip himself seven times in the waters of Jordan, and he said to himself, 'I surely thought he would have come out, and I thought a lot of people would come out and make a fuss'; and he went back in a rage. And his servant said to him, 'Why didn't you go?' And he said, 'My rivers are much the best.' So his servants said, 'If he had asked you to do some great thing, wouldst thou have done it?' So he went and dipped himself seven times in the water, and when he came out he was quite all right again. And when he was coming home they saw Gehazi coming, so Naaman told them to stop the horses, and so they stopped, and Gehazi said, 'There are some people come to see me, please give me some money and some cloaks,' and they were very heavy, so Naaman sent some of his men to carry them, and when he came near the house he said to his servants, 'You can go now.' Elisha said, 'Because you have done this you shall have the leprosy that Naaman had.'"

> *Dictated by a 6-year-old.*

Q. Tell a fairy story.

"When Ulysses was coming back from Troy he passed the Sirens. He could hear them, but he couldn't get to them, because he was bound. He wanted to get to them so as he could listen to them a long time, because a lot of people had come and listened to them, and they found it so beautiful that they wanted to stay there, and they stayed till they died. His companions couldn't hear them because they stopped up their ears with wax and cotton-wool. And this was the song they sang:—

'Hither, come hither and hearken awhile,
    Odysseus far-famed king,
No sailor has ever passed this way
    But has paused to hear us sing.
Our song is sweeter than honey,
    And he that hears it knows

> *Dictated by a 6-year-old.*

*Appendix*

*Notes*

What he never learnt from another,
 And his joy before he goes.
We know what the heroes bore at Troy
 In the ten long years of strife,
We know what happened in all the world,
 And the secret things of life.'

And then they rowed on till at last the song faded away, and they rowed on and on for a long time, and then when they could not hear them nor see them, the wax was taken out of their ears, and then they unbound Ulysses."

Q. What have you noticed (yourself) about a spider?

"We have found out the name of one spider, and often have seen spiders under the microscope—they were all very hairy. We have often noticed a lot of spiders running about the ground—quantities. Last term we saw a spider's web up in the corner of the window with a spider sucking out the juice of a fly; and we have often touched a web to try and make the spider come out, and we never could, because she saw it wasn't a fly, before she came out.

*Dictated by a 7-year-old.*

"I saw the claw of a spider under the microscope, with its little teeth; we saw her spinnerets and her great eyes. There were the two big eyes in one row, four little ones in the next row, and two little ones in the next row. We have often found eggs of the spiders; we have some now that we have got in a little box, and we want to hatch them out, so we have put them on the mantelpiece to force them.

"Once we saw a spider on a leaf, and we tried to catch it, but we couldn't; he immediately let himself down on to the ground with a thread.

"We saw the circulation in the leg of another spider under the microscope; it looked like a little line going up and down."

Q. Gather three sorts of tree leaf-buds and two sorts of catkin, and tell all you can about them.

(1) "The chestnut bud is brown and sticky, it is a sort of cotton-woolly with the leaves inside. It splits open and sends out two leaves, and the leaves split open.

*Dictated by a 6-year-old.*

(2) "The oak twig has always a lot of buds on the top, and one bud always dies. Where the bud starts there is a little bit of knot-wood. The oak-bud is very tiny.

(3) "The lime bud has a green side and a red side, and then it bursts open and several little leaves come out and all the little things that shut up the leaves die away.

(4) "Golden catkins and silver pussy palms of a willow tree. The golden catkins have stamens with all the pollen on them. They grow upwards, and two never grow opposite to each other. The silver pussy palms have seed boxes, with a little tube growing out, and a little sticky knob on the top. The bees rub the pollen off their backs on to the sticky knob."

"*Beech Twig.*—It has rather a woody stalk, and it is a very light grey-browny stalk, and it is very thin, and the little branches that grow out are light brown and it is thicker where the buds are and it is a lighter brown up at the top than it is at the bottom, and the buds are a light reddy-brown and very pointed, and they are scaly. The bark is rather rough and there is a lot of little kind of brown spots on it.

*Dictated by a 9-year-old.*

"*Lime Twig.*—It is called Ruby-budded Lime because the buds are red, and they are fat rather, and they have got some green in as well, and they come rather to a point at the top, they grow alternately and the little stalk that they grow out of is reddy-green, and the top part of the stalk is green, and it is woody, and it is rough, and it is a reddy-green at the bottom. Where the buds come out it is swelled out, the bark has come off and it has left it white and woody. At the top of one of the stalks the bud has come off.

"*Sycamore Twig.*—Well, the back is *very* woody, and it is a brown stalk and it is rough and there is a little weeny bud growing out of the side, and the buds grow out two and two, and there are a lot of little buds.

"*Willow.*—Well, the stalk is a dark brown, and is very smooth and it will bend very easily, and the buds when they first come on the stalk are little brown ones, and then a silvery-green comes out and there is a scale at the bottom, and then they get greyer and bigger with little green leaves at the bottom, and then it comes yellow, and there is a lot of pollen on it. If you touch it the pollen comes on your finger.

"*Hazel.*—Well, the stalk is a dark brown, something the colour of the willow, and it bends easily, and the buds are green and there is little scales, and then the catkins come and they grow very long, and there is a lot of little flowers in one, and there is pollen in that, and the stalk is rather rough, and there are some big buds at the top just bursting, and the leaves are coming out, and the buds are very soft and glossy, and the scales are at the bottom."

Q. Tell about the North-West Passage. (Book studied, *The World at Home.*)

"People in England are very fond of finding things out, and they wanted to find out the North-West Passage. If people wanted to go to the Pacific Ocean, they had to go round Africa by the Cape of Good Hope, or else round South America by Cape Horn. This was a very long way. They thought they might find out a shorter way by going along the North Coast by America, and they would come out in the Pacific Ocean. They would call this way the North-West Passage. First one man and then another tried to find a way. They found a lot of straits and bays which they called after themselves. The enemy they met which made them turn back was the cold. It was in the frozen zone, and the sea was all ice, and the ice lumps were as big as mountains, and when they came against a ship they crashed it to pieces. Once a man named Captain Franklin tried over and over again to find the North-West Passage, and once he went and never came back again, for he got stuck fast in the ice, and the ice did not break, and he had not much food with him, and what he had was soon eaten up, and he could not get any more, for all the animals in that country had gone away, for it was winter, and he could not wait for the summer, when they would return. A ship went out from England called the *Fox* to look for him, but all they found was a boat, a Bible, a watch, and a pair of slippers near each other. After looking a lot they found the North-West Passage, but because there is so much ice there the ships can't use it."

*Dictated by a 7-year-old.*

Q. Tell all you know about St Patrick. (Book studied, *Old Tales from British History.*)

"St Patrick was the son of a Scotch farming clergyman, and one day some Irish pirates came and took Patrick with them to make him a slave; and they sold him to an Irish nobleman. And the Irish nobleman made him a shepherd to take care of his flocks, and shepherds have a lot of time to think when they are out guarding their flocks by night. And Patrick was very sorry that the poor Irish were heathens. One day he slipped off and got into a boat with some sailors, and after a great

*Dictated by a 7-year-old.*

# Appendix

## Notes

adventure, for their food ran short, they arrived safely in Scotland. And Patrick was still thinking about the Irish, so he went off in a boat of his own, with a few followers, to Ireland. A shepherd saw them coming, and told his master the pirates were coming. So he armed his servants and went down to meet the pirates, but when he heard the errand they were on, he offered them to come into his house. Now Patrick settled in Ireland, but some heathen priests rose up against him, and a wise man said, 'What is the good of killing him? Other Irish people are now Christians, and they will teach too.' So he saved his life. And Patrick gave him the book of Psalms written by his own hand. One day Patrick asked a rich man if he might have a little plot of land on the top of a hill, but the rich man refused him, but gave him a little plot of land at the bottom of the hill. And there Patrick built a church, and a house for himself and servants to live in. Then the rich man got ill, and was just about to die, but got better, but as he thought Patrick was like a wizard, who could foretell his fortune, he thought he'd better try to please him. So he sent him a brass cauldron, enough to hold one whole sheep, and Patrick said 'I thank you, master.' The rich man was angry, and sent for the cauldron back again, and Patrick said, 'I thank you, master.' So the rich man was ashamed, and brought back the cauldron, and said he could have the little plot of land on the top of the hill. So they went up to measure it. Then a roe-deer dashed out of the thicket, but left her fawn behind her, and the men were going to kill the fawn, but Patrick took it up and carried it down the hill; the mother followed, for she saw he was doing no harm to it. On that place he built a fine church, which is still standing. And Patrick died on a journey, and was buried at a place called Downpatrick after him."

Q. Tell what you know about Alfred Tennyson. (Book studied, Mrs Frewen Lord's *Tales from Westminster Abbey*.)

"Alfred Tennyson was born in 1809, and he loved the country very much. One Sunday when they were going out to chapel, except Lord Tennyson as he was very young, his brother Charles gave him his slate to write about birds and flowers, and when they came back he had filled his slate with his first poem. He and his brother used to make up stories that sometimes lasted a month. He was very shortsighted, and when he was looking at anything it looked as if he were smelling it. He had good ears, for he could hear the shriek of a bat. Alfred Tennyson wrote *The Revenge* and *The Siege of Lucknow*, and Sir John Franklin's poem:—

'Not here; the white North hath thy bones,
    And thou, heroic sailor soul,
Art passing on thy happier voyage now,
    Toward no earthly pole.'

And he also wrote the *May Queen* and *Cradle Song*. Because his poetry was so good the Queen gave him a name and knighted him. He says that if you tread on a daisy it will turn up and get red. He was 83 years old when he died—the year he died in was 1892. He was buried in Westminster Abbey, in Poets' Corner."

Q. What is a hero? What heroes have you heard of? Tell about one.

"(1) A hero is a brave man. (2) Count Roland, Huon at Bordeaux, the Horatii and Curatii. (3) Once there was a brave Emperor called Charlemagne, and he was fighting with the heathen King of Saragossa. Just a wee bit of land was left to the heathen king, so he sent a messenger to speak about peace. They pretended that

*Dictated by a 7-year-old.*

# Appendix

they would have peace, so they went back to Charlemagne and asked him to leave Roland behind to take charge of the mountain passes. So Charlemagne said that he would leave Roland behind because there was none so brave as him, so that when Charlemagne had turned his army they should come in great numbers to fight against Roland. And Roland stayed behind with twenty thousand men, and Oliver heard a great noise by the side of Spain, and then Oliver climbed on a pine tree, and he saw the arms glimmering and the spears shining, and then he said to Roland that there were a full hundred thousand, and that they just had so few, and that it was much better to sound his horn and Charlemagne will turn his army. Roland said he would be mad if he did that. Oliver said again to sound his horn, and Roland said he would lose his fame in France if he did it. Then Oliver said again, 'Friend Roland, sound thy horn and Charles will hear it, and turn his army.' Then all the mountain passes were full of the enemies, and when they came nearer they fought, and they fought, and they fought, and at last the Christians were falling too, and when there were only sixty left he blew his horn. Charlemagne heard it and said he must go, and Ganelon said he was just pretending, but then Charlemagne heard it fainter, and knew that it was true that he must go, and then fainter again, but Charlemagne was nearer and so heard it better. And Roland said, 'Ride as fast as you can for many men have been killed, and there are few left.' Then Charlemagne bade his men sound their horns, so that they knew that help was near and then the heathen fled away. There were just the two left, Roland and the Archbishop, and Roland said to the Archbishop that he would try to fetch the dead bodies of the braver soldiers. Then the Archbishop said to Roland, 'Quick, before I die.' Then Roland went and brought them before the Archbishop and laid them down there. Then he went and searched the field again, and under a pine tree he found Oliver's body, then he brought it too and laid it in front of the Archbishop. Then Roland fainted to the ground, then the Archbishop tried to bring some water for Roland, and he fell down and died. Then Roland put the hands over the chest of the Archbishop, then he prayed to God to give him a place in Paradise, and then he said that the field was his. Before he died he put his sword and his ivory horn under him, and laid himself down on the ground, so that Charlemagne, when he came, would know that he was the conqueror. And God sent St Michael and another saint to fetch his soul up to heaven."

Q. What have you noticed about a thrush? Tell all you know about it.
"Thrushes are browny birds. They eat snails, and they take the snail in their mouths and knock it against a stone to break the shell and eat the snail. I found a stone with a lot of bits of shell round it, so knew that a thrush had been there. Where we used to live a thrush used to sing every morning on the same tree. The song of the thrush is like a nightingale. We often see a lot of thrushes on the lawn before breakfast or after a shower. They have yellow beaks and their breasts are specked with lovely yellow and brown. Once we found a thrush asleep on a sponge in a bedroom and we carried it out and put it on a tree. Thrushes eat worms as well as snails, and on the lawn they listen with their heads on one side and go along as the worm gets under the ground, and presently, perhaps, the worm comes up and they gobble it up, or they put their beaks in and get it. Thrushes build their nests with sticks at the bottom and line them with little bits of wool they pick up, or feathers, and they like to get down very much."

## Notes

*Dictated by a 7-year-old.*

*Dictated by an 8-year-old.*

Appendix

Notes

*Dictated by an 11-year-old.*

*Written by a 10-year-old.*

Grades 4–6

Q. "Ah! Pericles, those that have need of a lamp, take care to supply it with oil." Who said this? Tell the story. (Book studied, Plutarch's *Lives: Pericles*.)

"Anaxagoras, the philosopher, said these words to Pericles.

"Pericles was the ruler of Athens, and Anaxagoras had taught him when a boy. Being ruler of Athens, he led a very busy life, attending to the affairs of State, and so was not able to give much time to his household affairs. Once a year he collected his money, and could only manage his income by giving out an allowance to each member of his family and household every day: this was done by Evangelus, his steward. Anaxagoras thought this a very wrong way of arranging matters, and said that Pericles paid too much heed to bodily affairs, because he thought you ought to mind only about philosophy and spiritual doings, and not about the affairs of the world. To give an example to Pericles he gave up all his household and tried to live entirely on philosophy. But he soon found his mistake when he found himself starving and penniless, with no house. So he covered his head up and prepared to die. Pericles, hearing of this, went immediately to his rescue and begged him to live; not because he thought death a misfortune, but that he said, 'What shall I do without your help in the affairs of State?' And then Anaxagoras uttered the words which are above, meaning, of course (though putting it in a clever way), that Pericles was to keep him. On the other hand, he might have meant that he had been mistaken in his philosophy."

Q. Tell the history of 'F.D.' on a penny. (Book studied, Arnold-Forster's *History of England*.)

"The letters 'F.D.' stand for the Latin words *Fidei Defensor*, meaning 'The Defender of the Faith.' Henry VIII. had a little while ago written a book on the Pope (who was Clement VII.) saying that the Pope was the true head of the Church, and everyone ought to obey him. The Pope was so pleased that he made Henry *Fedei Defensor*. It must be remembered that the king had married his brother Arthur's widow, a Spanish princess, namely, Catherine of Aragon *(sic)*, and as they had no son Henry wished to divorce her, but the Pope would not allow him to, as he had given Henry special leaf *(sic)* to marry her. At this Henry was furious, and began to think about the Pope's words, 'Defender of the Faith.' He would not act as he thought till someone suggested it. So two men, called Cromwell and Cranmer, came forward, telling the king to take the Pope's words, not as he meant them, but as they really were, as they stood. The king was delighted, and made Cranmer a bishop and Cromwell his wisest counsellor. In 1534 Parliament was called upon to declare Henry head of the Church. All said he was, except two men, Sir Thomas More and Fisher, bishop of Rochester; these would not agree, and were executed in 1535. If we look on a penny we see the letters 'F.D.,' which shows from the reign of Henry VIII. till now the Pope has not been allowed to interfere with England. In order to spite the Pope, Henry allowed the Lutherans and learned men to come into England."

Q. What did you see in the Seagull sailing up the Firth of Forth? (Book studied, *Geographical Reader, Book II.*)

"In sailing up the Forth we first of all see Leith, which is the seaport town of Edinburgh. Then we come to Edinburgh. The old and new Edinburghs are built on opposite hills, the valley in between is laid out in lovely gardens. One thing very odd about Edinburgh is that the streets look as if they are built one on top of the other. At one end of the town there is a castle which looks so like the rocks and mountains it is built on, one can hardly distinguish it. At the other end of the town there is Holyrood, where the ancient kings used to live. We do not see many merchantmen because there are no good harbours, there are a good many fishing smacks and pleasure boats. As we go along we see women with big baskets with a strap across their foreheads, and they are calling out 'caller herrings.' "

*Dictated by a 9-year-old.*

Q. "And Jonathan loved him as his own soul." Of whom was this said? Tell a story of Jonathan's love.

"This was said of David. Saul's anger was kindled against David; and Jonathan and David were talking together, and Jonathan had been telling David that he would do anything for him, and David said, 'To-morrow is the feast of a new moon, and Saul will expect me to sit with him at the table; therefore say, 'David earnestly asked leave of me to go to Bethlehem, his city, where there is a sacrifice of his family.' If Saul is angry, then I shall know that he would kill me, but if he is not angry, it will be all right.' Jonathan said, 'So shall it be, but it will not be safe for anybody to know anything about it; come into the field, and I will tell you what to do. Thou shalt remain hidden by the stone, and I will bring a lad and my arrows and bow, and I will shoot an arrow as if firing at a target; and if I say "Run," to the lad, "is not the arrow beyond thee? go fetch it," then thou shalt know that thou must flee from Saul.' David's seat was empty at the feast that night, but Saul said nothing. But the next day his seat was empty, and when Saul asked why, Jonathan told him what David had asked him to say. And. Saul's anger was kindled, so much so that Jonathan feasted not that day, for he was grieved; and next morning he went out with his bow and arrows, and the lad, and shot an arrow as if at a mark. Then Jonathan said to the lad, 'Run, is not the arrow beyond thee? haste.' Then Jonathan gave his artillery unto the lad and sent him back to the city ; and David came out of his hiding-place, and they made a covenant together, for Jonathan loved him as his own soul. Then David had to flee to Naioth in Ramah and Jonathan went back to the city."

*Dictated by a 9-year-old.*

Q. What do you know of Richelieu? (Book studied, Mrs Creighton's *First History of France.*)

"Cardinal Richeleu *(sic)* was brought to the French Court by the Queen mother, who thought he would do as she wished, but she was mistaken, for he no sooner was there than he turned against her, for Louse *(sic)* took him into his favour and made him Prime Minister after he had been there a few weeks. Richeleu *(sic)* was a devoted Catholic, and was determined to put down the Hugenots *(sic)*, or Protestants as we call them, so he laid siege to La Rochelle, the chief town of the Hugenots *(sic)*, who applied to the English for help. Charles sent a fleet to La Rochelle under pretence of helping the Hugenots *(sic)* [After this point the answer was dictated] but Admiral Pennington, who was in command of the ships, received orders when half way down the channel to take in French soldiers and sailors at Calais and to go to the French side. When Admiral Pennington ordered the ships to take in the soldiers, his men mutinied and he had to go back. Richeleu had thrown up earthworks across the harbour so that it was impossible to get in. Now Rochelle held out bravely, but at last it had to surrender, and out of 40,000, 140

*Partly written and partly dictated by a 10-year-old.*

# Appendix

## Notes

crawled out, too weak to bury the dead in the streets. La Rochelle was razed to the ground, and never recovered its prosperity. One by one the Huguenot towns surrendered, and thus the Huguenots were destroyed. When Richelieu was made Prime Minister, the nobles did not like him, because they thought he had too much power, and now when Louis was ill, the Queen mother came to him, and in a stormy passion of tears begged Louis to send away his ungrateful servant. Louis promised he would do so, and Richelieu's fall seemed certain. Now all the nobles crowded to the Queen mother to pay their respects to her, as they thought she would now be the most important person in the Government. But one noble, who was wiser than the rest, went to Richelieu and begged to plead his cause before the King. The King promised he would keep him if he would serve him as he had done before. The Queen mother was foiled, and returned to Brussels, where she died."

*Dictated by a 9-year-old.*

Q. What towns, rivers, and castles would you see in travelling about Warwickshire? (Book studied, *Geographical Reader, Book III.*)

"Warwick, Kenilworth, Coventry, Stratford, Leamington, and Birmingham are all towns which you would see if you travelled through Warwick.

"The Avon stretches from north to south of Warwickshire. It has its tributary the Leam, upon which Leamington is situated.

"There is a castle of Warwick and Coventry and Kenilworth.

"Warwick is the capital of the county. It has a famous castle, whose high and lofty towers stand upon the bank of the river Avon.

"Coventry is a very old town. It also has a beautiful castle, where the fair Lady Godiva and her father used to live, about whom I suppose you have read.

"Stratford is called 'The Swan on the Avon,' because that is where Shakespeare, the great poet, was born and died, and this is a little piece of poetry about him;—

'Where his first infant lays, sweet Shakespeare sung,
Where the last accents faltered on his tongue.'

"The river Avon takes its rise in the vale of Evesham, then winds through pleasant fields and meadows till it comes to the south of Warwickshire, and then it becomes broad and stately and flows on up to Coventry, where the Leam branches off from it (!), and then it becomes narrower and narrower until it gets out of Warwickshire and stops altogether at Naseby (!)"

Q. How many kinds of bees are there in a hive? What work does each do? Tell how they build the comb. (Book studied, *Fairyland of Science.*)

"Three kinds. The *drones* or males, the *workers* or females, and the *queen* bee. The drone is fat, the queen is long and thin, the workers are small and slim. The queen bee lays the eggs, the worker bee brings the honey in and makes the cell, and the drones wait to be fed. On a summer's day you see something hanging on a tree like a plum pudding, this is a swarm of bees. You will soon see someone come up with a hive, turn it upside down, shake the bough gently, and they will fall in.

*Dictated by a 10-year-old.*

They will put some clean calico quickly over the bottom of the hive, and turn it back over on a bench. The bees first close up every little hole in the hive with wax, then they hang on to the roof, clinging on to one another by their legs. Then one comes away and scrapes some wax from under its body, and bites it in its mouth until it is pulled out like ribbon, this she plasters on the roof of the hive, then she flies out to get honey, and comes home to digest it, hanging from the roof, and in 24 hours this digested honey turns to wax, then she goes through the same process again. Next, the nursing bees come and poke their heads into this wax, bite the wax away (20 bees do this before one hole is ready to make a cell). Other bees are working on the other side at the same time. Each cell is made six-sided, so as to take up the least wax and the smallest space. When the cells are made the bees come in with honey in their honey-bag or first stomach; they can easily pass the honey back through their mouths into the cells. It takes many bees to fill one cell, so they are hard at work."

Q. Write a composition on 'The Opening of Parliament.'
"The opening of Parliament by King Edward VII and Queen Alexander *(sic)* was rather grand. First, they drove to the Houses of Parliament in a grand state carriage which had been used by George III, and then when they got there they had to robe in a certain room in great big robes, all edged with ermine fur, and with huge trains. Queen Alexandra had an evening dress on, and King Edward a very nice kingly sort of suit (which was nearly covered up by his robes), and then they walked along to the real Houses of Parliament, where the members really sit. Then the king made a speech to open Parliment *(sic)*, and other people made speeches too, and everything was done with grandeur and stateliness such as would befit a king. May Parliament long be his!"

*Written by a 9-year-old.*

## Grades 7–9

Q. Describe the founding of Christ's Kingdom. What are the laws of His Kingdom?
"Christ came to found His kingdom. He preached the laws to His people. He taught them to pray for it: 'Thy kingdom come.' And He told His chosen few to 'go and preach the Gospel of the kingdom.' He founded His kingdom in their hearts, and He reigned there. He will still found His kingdom in our hearts. He will come and reign as King. The kingdom was first founded by the sea of Galilee. 'Follow Me,' said our Lord to Andrew, and from that moment the kingdom was founded in Andrew's heart. Then there were Peter, James, John, Phillip *(sic)*, Nathaniel *(sic)*, and the kingdom grew. From that moment Christ never stopped His work for the kingdom—preaching and teaching, healing and comforting, proclaiming the laws of the kingdom. 'Think not that I am come to destroy the law or the prophets. I am not come to destroy, but to fulfil.' 'One jot or one tittle shall in no wise pass from the law.' ' Whosoever shall break one of these least commandments, and shall teach men so, the same shall be called the least in the kingdom.' No commandment was to pass from the law, but there was a new commandment, a new law, and that was 'love.' 'Love your enemies.' The Pharisees could not understand it. 'Love your friends, and hate your enemies,' was their law. But Jesus said, 'Bless them that curse you, and pray for them that despitefully use you.' 'Give, hoping for nothing in return'; and, 'Whosoever shall smite thee on one cheek turn to him the other also.' Christ's law is the love which 'suffereth long and is kind . . . . seeketh not her own . . . . never faileth . . . . hopeth all things, endureth all things'; and 'now abideth faith, hope, and charity, these three, but the greatest of these is—love.' "

*Written by a 13-year-old.*

Q. Explain 'English Funds, Consols 2 3/4 per cent., 113. And give an account of the South Sea Bubble. (Book studied, Arnold-Forster's *History of England*.)

Appendix

Notes

*Written by a 14-year-old.*

"This means that when the South Sea Company first appeared, the Government gave them £113 on condition that the Company should give 2 ¾ per cent., which means £2 15s. on every £100 lent, for a certain number of years. In the reign of George I. the money matters of the country were in a very bad state. The Government was very much in debt, especially to those people who had purchased annuities, and had a right to receive a certain sum of money from the Government every year as long as they lived. Sir Robert Walpole, who was then Prime Minister, was most anxious to pay off part of this debt. He heard of a Company which had just been started, called the South Sea Company, whose object was to trade in the South Seas. This was what Walpole wished for. He suggested to them that they should pay off the debt due to the people who had bought annuities, and in return the Government would give them some priveleges *(sic)* and charts which would be useful to them. This the Company agreed to do, but instead of paying the people in money they gave them what were called 'shares' in the South Sea Company. These shares were supposed to be very valuable, and it was thought that the South Sea Company was really prosperous, and that those who had shares in it would have most enormous profit in the end. Thousands of people came to buy shares, and some of them were so anxious to get them that they spent enormous sums of money on these worthless pieces of paper. All was well for a time, but at last the people began to wish for their money instead of the shares, and claimed it loudly from the Company. It was then that the bubble burst. It was discovered then that the Company was quite unable to pay what was due, and that all this time they had been deluding the nation by promises and giving them shares, and that they had never been the rich and prosperous Company they made themselves out to be. Naturally, the most dreadful distress prevailed everywhere, and many were absolutely ruined, so that the Government had to help those who were most distressed. At this point Sir Robert Walpole came to the rescue. He made the Bank of England pay some of the debts, and behaved with such cleverness that he saved the country almost from ruin."

Q. What do you know of the States General? (Book studied, Mrs Creighton's *First History of France.)*

"The States General met in May, 1789. The people had long wanted reforms, and been talking about them, and now on the 5th of May, 1789, the States General met again for the first time since 1614. If the nobles sat in one house, and the people in another, as was the custom, they could never get tbe changes made. So the people with their leader, the Marquis of Mirabeau, declared that they would not leave the tennis court on which they were standing till it was agreed that they could sit together with the nobles. When Louis XVI. came down in State, and told them they were to sit apart, they said they would not leave their place except at the bayonets *(sic)* point. When he heard this he said, 'Very well, leave them alone.' So they sat together."

*Written by a 12-year-old.*

Q. Show fully how Aristides acquired the title of 'The Just.' Why was it a strange title for a man in those days? (Book studied, Plutarch's *Lives: Anstitles.*)

"Aristides acquired the title of 'The Just' by his justice, and because he never did anything unjust in order to become rich or powerful. While many of the judges and chief men in Athens took bribes, he alone always refused to do so, and he also never spent the public money on himself. When, after having defeated the Persians,

## Notes

*Written by a 13-year-old.*

at Platae, the Greek States decided to have a standing army, it was Aristides who was sent round to settle how much each town should contribute. And he did this so fairly and well, that all the Greek States blessed and praised his arrangement. It is said that Aristides could not only resiste *(sic)* the unjust claims of those whom he loved, but also those of his enemies. Once when he was judging a quarrel between two men, one of them remarked that the other had often injured Aristides. 'Tell me not that,' was the reply of Aristides, 'but what he has done to thee, for it is thy cause I am judging, not my own.' Another time when he had gone to law himself, and when, after having heard what he had to say, his judges were going to pass sentence on his adversary without having heard him, Aristides rose and entreated his judges to hear what his enemy could say in his own defence. In all that he did Aristides was inflexibly just, and many stories were told of his justice. Though he loved his country well, he would never do anything wrong to gain for Athens some advantage, and in all he did his one aim was justice, and his only ambition to be called 'The Just.' He was so just and good, that he was called the 'most just man in Greece.' In the times in which Aristides lived, men used to care more to be called great, rich, or powerful than just. Themistocles, the great rival of Aristides, used to do all he could to become the first man in Athens, and rich as well as powerful. He did not hesitate to take bribes, and all he did for the Athenians was done with a view to making himself the head of the people, and the first man in the State. He used often to do unjust as well as cruel things in order to get his own ends. It was the same with most other men who lived at this time, they prefered *(sic)* being rich, powerful, or great, to being distinguished by the title of 'The Just.' "

Q, Describe a journey in Northern Italy. (Book studied, *Geographical Reader*, Book IV.)

"I am about to go for a tour round the northern part of Italy, and after I have taken a train to Savoy, which is about the south-east of France, I enter into Italy by the Cenis pass, which is very lofty, about 7,000 feet above sea level.

"On arriving in Italy, I come into the province of Piedmont, which has three mountain torrents or streams running through it. These streams join at Turin, the capital of Piedmont, and form the Po river, which flows out on the east coast of France into the Gulf of Venice. On the banks of the three mountain streams are some Protestants by the name of Waldenses, who say they are followers of the disciples, but if you ask any outsider, they will say, 'Oh! the Waldenses are followers of a good man, by the name of Waldo, who fled out of France in the 12th century.'

*Written by a 12-year-old.*

"We will now go and see Turin, and the first thing we say is, 'What a clean town,' and so it certainly is, for it is quite the cleanest town in Italy, as the people have only to turn on the fountain taps to clean their paved streets. And after we have looked at Alessandria, where Napoleon gained his great victory, we leave Piedmont and follow up the river Po, until we come to its next tributary, the river Ticino, which runs up north into the Lake Maggiore, which is five to six miles wide and about sixty miles in length, This lake has four islands, which are named after Count Borromeo and so called the Borromean Islands, which are cultivated like gardens with terrases *(sic)* for resting places.

"Now let us go to Milan, which is so well known by its beautiful cathedral of white and black marble which have *(sic)* no less than 4000 sculptures of white marble, with pillars of Egyptian granite. Milan is famous for silks and lace to provide for the numerous palaces.

# Appendix

## Notes

*Written by a 13-year-old.*

"We will now go back to the next lake, Lake Como, which is surrounded by mountains, and supposed to be the most beautiful of all lakes. At the south it goes out in a fork, and between the fork is a beautiful piece of land called Bellagia *(sic)*.

"The next lake we come to is the Garda, the largest of all the lakes, and then we go on to the smallest of lakes called Lugano.

"We now having visited all the lakes, take a look at Lodi, the famous cheese market in Italy; after which we visit Verona, where Pliny the naturalist was born, also Paul Veronese. Shakespeare lays the scene of his play 'Romeo and Juliet' in Verona. The short time we have we spend at Venice, the queen of the Italian citys *(sic)* with its wonderful canals and the marvellous cathedral of St Mark's, also the dark, gloomy palace of the Doge."

Q. How are the following seeds dispersed:—Birch, Pine, Dandelion, Balsam, Broom? Give diagrams and observations. (Book studied, Mrs Brightwen's *Glimpses into Plant Life.*)

"The seeds of the Birch are very small, with two wings, one on each side, so that in a high wind numbers of them are blown on to high places, such as crevises *(sic)* on the face of a rock, or crevises *(sic)* on a church tower, or the tower of an old ruin. They are so light that they are carried a long way.

"The seeds of the Pine are very small, and the veins in the seed are wriggly, so that the seed is curly, which makes it whirl rapidly in the air, and the whirling motion carries it along a little way before it rests on the ground. It has two small wings.

"The seeds of the Dandilion *(sic)* are large, with a kind of silky parashute *(sic)* attached, so that when they fall off they do not fall to the ground, but are carried a little way because the wind catches the under part of the parashute *(sic)*. The seed has a little hook at the top of it which prevents it from being pulled out of the ground by the parashute *(sic)* after it is once in.

"The Balsam seed case splits when the seeds are ripe and sends them flying in all directions, so they are far enough dispersed, and need no wings or parashutes *(sic)* to help them.

"The Broom seed case is a carpel, more like that of the sweet pea. When the seeds are ripe the two sides of the carpel split open and curl up like springs and send the seeds flying out, so they are dispersed without needing wings or parachutes."

*Written by a 13-year-old.*

Q. Describe the tissue of a potato and of a piece of rhubarb. (Book studied, Oliver's *Elementary Botany.*)

"The tissue of *Rhubarb* is *very* fibrous indeed. In fact, it is almost entirely made up of vessels. These are cells which have become tubes by the dividing cell-wall being absorbed. These vessels are very beautiful when seen under a microscope, for their walls are all thickened in some way, in order to make them strong enough to bear the weight of the leaf. Some are thickened by a spiral cord, which goes round and round the wall of the vessel. In some vessels this is quite tightly twisted round the wall, that is to say, the rings do not come far apart; in others it is quite loose and far apart. Another kind of thickening is by rings, which just go round the tube and are not joined to each other. Other vessels, again, have little knots in them like what there are in birch bark.

"The *Potato* tissue is mainly made up of starch, as it is one of the plant's storehouses, and starch is one of the plant's principal foods."

Q. Give a diagram of the eye, and explain how we see everything. (Book studied, Dr Schofield's *Physiology for Schools.*)

"The eye can be likened to a camera, and the brain to the man behind the camera. The image enters at the hole, passes through the lens, is reflected on the plate, but the camera does not see, it is the man behind the camera who sees. In the same way, the image passes in at the pupil and through the lens, both sides of which are curved, and can be tightened or slackened according to the distance of the image. Then the image passes along the nerve of sight to the two bulbs in the brain which see. If you hold a rounded glass between a sheet of paper and the image at the right distance (for the glass cannot tighten or slacken like our lens), you will see the image reflected upside-down on the paper. This is the way the lens acts. There is a small yellow spot a little below the middle of the back of the eye; here the sight is more acute, and so, though we can see lots of things at one time, we can only look at one thing at a time. There is a blind spot where the nerve enters the eye (which shows that the nerve of sight itself is blind) so that some part of every image is lost, like a black dot punched in it. But we are so used to it that we cannot see it."

*Written by a 13-year-old.*

Q. Describe your favourite scene in *Waverley*.

"*A Highland Stag Hunt.*—The Highland Cheifs *(sic)* were in various postures: some reclining lazily on their plaids, others stalking up and down conversing with one another, and a few were already seated in position for the sport. MacIvor was talking with another Cheif *(sic)* as to what the sport would be; but as they talked in Gaelic, Edward had no part in the conversation, but sat looking at the scene before him. They were seated on a low hill at the head of a broad valley which narrowed into a small opening or cleft in the hills at the extreme end. It was hemmed in on all sides by hills of various heights. It was through this opening that the beaters were to drive the deer. Already Waverly *(sic)* could hear the distant shouts of the men calling to each other coming nearer and nearer. Soon he could distinguish the antlers of the deer moving towards the opening like a forest of trees stiped *(sic)* of their leaves. The sportsmen prepared themselves to give them a warm reception, and all were ready as the deer entered the valley.

"They looked very ferocious, as they advanced towards where Edward and the cheifs *(sic)* were standing and seemed as if they were determined to fight; the roes and weaker ones in the centre, and the bulls standing as if on defence. As soon as they came within range, some of the cheifs *(sic)* fired, and two or three deer came down. Waverly *(sic)* also had the good fortune (and also the skill) to bring down a couple and gain the aplause *(sic)* of the other sportsmen. But the herd was now charging furiously up the valley towards them. The order was given to lie down, as it was impossible to stem the coming wave of deer; but as it was given in Gaelic it conveyed no meaning to Edward's mind, and he remained standing.

*Written by a 12-year-old.*

"The heard *(sic)* was now not fifty yards from him; and in another minute he would have been trampled to death; but MacIvor at his own risk, jumped up and literaly *(sic)* dragged him to the ground just as the deer reached them. Edward had a sensation as if he was out in a severe hail storm, but this did not last long.

"When they had passed, and Edward attempted to rise, he found that besides a number of bruises he had also severely sprained his ancle *(sic)*, and was unable to walk, or even stand. A shelter was soon made for him out of a plaid in which he was laid; and then MacIvor called the Highland doctor or herbalist, to attend him. The doctor approached Edward with every sign of humilation, but before

# Appendix

## Notes

attending to his ancle *(sic)*, he insisted upon walking slowly round him several times, in the direction in which the sun goes, muttering at the same time a spell over him as he went, and though Waverly *(sic)* was in great pain he had to submit to his foolery. Waverly *(sic)* saw to his great astonishment that MacIvor believed or seemed to believe in the old man's cantations *(sic)*. At last, when he had finished his spells, which he seemed to think more necessary than the dressing, he drew from his pocket a little packet of herbs, some of which he applied to the sprained ancle *(sic)* and after it had been bound up, Edward felt much relieved. He rewarded the doctor with some money, the value of which seemed to exceed his wildest imaginations, for he heaped so many blessings upon the head of Waverly *(sic)* that MacIvor said, ' A hundred thousand curses on you,' whereupon he stopped."

Q. Write some account of (a) Recent events with regard to Korea and Macedonia; or, (b) Scott or Burns and his work.

*Written by a 12-year-old.*

"Sir Walter Scott was a well-known writer in the early part of the 19th century. His novels are read by almost everyone; and though, perhaps, his poetry is not quite so well-known, still, at most places one finds people who have read or heard of the 'Lady of the Lake' or 'Marmion.' The first of his novels was 'Waverly' *(sic)*, and so they are often called the 'Waverley Novels.' The historical tales are very good, giving the reader a splendid idea of life in the 12th or 13th centuries; 'Ivanhoe,' 'Betrothed,' 'The Talisman' and 'Kenilworth' (this latter is about the 16th century, in Queen Elizabeth's reign). 'The Heart of Midlothian' is also very interesting, and 'Peveril of the Peak' tells about the fighting between the Cavaliers and Roundheads in the time of Charles I., and Oliver Cromwell. The 'Lady of the Lake' is about the longest poem Sir Walter Scott ever wrote; it is very beautiful, and many pieces in it are most interesting. 'Marmion' tell *(sic)* of a battle, and how a Lord Marmion was killed there."

## Grades 10–12

Q. For what purpose were priests instituted? (Book studied, Dr Abbot's *Bible Lessons*.)

"The system of the Jewish priesthood was almost entirely symbolical. God ordained it, we believe, to lead the primitive mind of his chosen people onwards and upwards, to the true belief and earthly comprehension of that great sacrifice, by the grace of which we are all now honoured to become 'kings and priests unto God.' In the earliest times of the patriarchs, there was in every holy and honourable Jewish family some voluntary priest to offer up the burnt offerings and yearly sacrifices. We have an example of this in Job the patriarch, who, we read, ministered to his family in the capacity of priest of their offerings. In the wilderness, however, God commanded through Moses the foundation of a separate and holy priesthood to minister in His Tabernacle and offer His appointed sacrifices. The tribe of Levi and the family of Aaron were set apart for this purpose, and in the building of the tabernacle, and the annointing *(sic)* of Aaron and his four sons, the cornerstone was laid to that great building which became a fit dwelling for the presence of God and the heart of Israel, until Christ came to change and lighten the world; and the symbol and the shadow became the truth."

*Written by a 15-year-old.*

Q. "His power was to assert itself in deeds, not words." Write a short sketch of the character of Cromwell, discussing the above statement. (Book studied, Green's *Shorter History of the English People*.)

"Cromwell was no orator. It has been said that if all his speeches were taken and made into a book, it would seem simply a pack of nonsense. In Parliament though, the earnestness with which he spoke attracted attention. His deeds proved his innate power, which could not express itself in words. He may be called the inarticulate man. In his mind, everything was clear, and his various actions proved his purposes and determinations, but in speaking, he simply brought out a hurried volume of words, in the mazes of which one entirely lost the point meant to be implied. Cromwell also was more of an administrator than a statesman, unspeculative and conservative. He was subject to fits of hypocondria *(sic)*, which naturally had some effect on his character. He considered himself a servant of God, and acted accordingly. Undoubtedly he was under the conviction that he was carrying out the Lord's will in all he did. He was not in calm moods a bloody man, but when his anger was kindled he would spare no one. At times he would be filled with remorse for the part he had taken in the martyrdom of the king; then, again he would say it was the just punishment of heaven on Charles. In giving orders his words were curt and to the point, but in making speeches he adopted the phraseology of the Bible, which added to their ambiguity. One would think he was ambitious, for at one time he asked Whitelock: 'What if a man should take upon himself to be king?' evidently having in view the regal power, and yet according to his own assertion he would rather have returned to his occupation as a farmer, than have undertaken the government of Britain. But in this, as in other acts, he recognised the call of God, (as he thought) and obeyed it."

*Written by a 15-year-old.*

Q. What do you know of the Girondins? (Book studied, Lord's *Modern Europe*.)

"The Girondins were the perhaps most tolerant and reasonable of the revolutionary parties. They were a body of men who found the government of France under the king more than they could stand, and who were the first to welcome any changes, but were shocked and horrified at the dreadful riots and massacres which followed the fall of the throne. Such a party, representing justice and reform, could not be popular with the more violent Jacobins and like clubs. The day came when these latter were in power, and all the Girondins were thrown into prison.

"They were all taken from prison before the Court of Justice for trial, and placed before the judge, where they sat quite silently; they were one by one condemned to execution, receiving the sentence of death with perfect calmness. Only their leader was seen to fall down; one of his companions leant over him and said: 'What, are *you* afraid?' 'Non,' was the answer, 'Je mours,' he had stabbed himself with his dagger.

"As the Girondins marched back to their cells, condemned to die the next morning, they all sang the 'Marseillaise,' as they had arranged, to tell their fellow-prisoners what the sentence had been. When they reached the prison a splendid supper was placed for them, and they all sat down with great cheerfulness to eat it, none of them showing the least signs of breaking down. Towards morning priests were sent to them, and very early in the day they all marched to the foot of the guillotine, singing as they went. They kept on singing a solemn chant when the executions commenced, which became fainter and fainter as one by one they were beheaded, until all were gone."

*Written by a 17-year-old.*

# Appendix

## Notes

*Written by a 15-year-old.*

Q. Distinguish between *arrogant* and *presumptuous*, *interference* and *interposition*, *genuine* and *authentic*, *hate* and *detest*, *loathe* and *abhor*, *education* and *instruction*, *apprehend* and *comprehend*, using each word in a sentence. (Book studied, Trench's *Study of Words*.)

"A man who is 'arrogant' is a man who has right to what he wants, but who is harsh and exacting in taking it. A 'presumptuous' man is a man who expects more than is due and takes it. 'Judge Jeffries was an *arrogant* old man.' 'Charles II. was a *presumptuous* king, he thought he could have absolute power.'

" 'Interference,' is not minding your own business, and meddling with other people's when we are not wanted. 'Interposition' is more the 'doing good by interfering' as protecting a little boy from a bully. 'But for the *interference* of James all would have gone well.' 'Thanks to the *interposition* of Mary a quarrel was averted.'

" 'Genuine' means real, true, what it seems to be as—'a real *genuine* ruby.' 'Authentic,' in speaking of a book, means really written by the author to which it is ascribed. 'Dickens' *Oliver Twist* is certainly *authentic*.'

"You would 'hate' a man who killed your father. 'Charles II. hated Cromwell.' You would 'detest' a man who had not done you any personal injury, but who *(sic)* you knew to be a murderer. 'Yeo *detested* the Spaniards.'

"You would 'loathe' a poisonous snake or a hypocrite. 'David Copperfield *loathed* Uriah Heep.' You would abhor a man inferior to you in intellect or principles, as a great king would 'abhor' a cringing coward, leave him behind, go on without him, refuse to listen to him. 'Napoleon *abhorred* the traitor.'

" 'Education' is the lessons you receive as a matter of course, as French, writing, grammar. 'Instruction' is this, but more also, it includes moral teaching, the teaching of honesty, and the teaching of gentleness. 'Henry had a good *education*.' 'No well-*instructed* Britain *(sic)* is a coward.' "

" 'Apprehend' is to see, or hear, and notice. 'Comprehend' is to understand, without seeing or hearing perhaps. 'Phillip *apprehended* that danger was near, but he did not *comprehend* it.' "

*Written by a 17-year-old.*

Q. Give shortly Carlyle's estimate of Burns, showing what he did for Scotland, and what was the cause of his personal failure in life. (Book studied, Carlyle's *Essay on Burns*.)

"Carlyle looked upon Burns as one of the nicest of men and greatest of poets; rather a weak man, perhaps, but covering all his faults with his genius and kindness of heart, clever and persevering, and basely neglected and shunned by his contemporaries. It is quite extraordinary to read the world-famous poems of this poet, and to remember that he was a ploughman, and surrounded only by the most uneducated peasants and fellow-labourers, though, of course, the life of a ploughman in the hills of Scotland is far more likely to encourage poetry and reflection than the life of many a London dentist or hair-dresser far higher in rank; but it is easy to believe in fact, that Burns would have found inspirations for his genius in a flat sandy waste or a grocer's shop, and, as Carlyle says, a man or woman is not a genius unless they are extraordinary, not really inspired if such a person could have been imagined before. Robert Burns has provided Scotland for centuries at least, with plenty of national poetry, his poems are such as can be enjoyed, like flowers and trees and all things really beautiful, by old and young, stupid and clever, fishermen and prime ministers—surely that is a work of which any man would be proud!

"Burns *(sic)* chief fault, if fault it can be called, and the cause of his failure in life, seems to have been a sort of bitterness against people more fortunate than himself without the art of hiding it. This, real or affected, seems very common in poets, and such an inspired man, a man with a mind greater than kings, must have felt very deeply, almost without knowing it, the 'unrefinedness' of the people he loved best, and his own distance from the admirers who clustered round him later in life.

"All his life, it seems, he was in a place by himself, now spending his time with his own family, acting a part all day, trying to make his relations feel him an equal, pretending to take a great interest in what he did not care for—the pigs, and cows, and porridge, seeing his own dearest friends looking at him with awe, and feeling him something above them, thinking of his 'great' friends, and feeling embarrassed when he came, and more at ease without his presence.

"Now, on the other hand, associating with people, high in rank and education, enjoying their friendship and praise, but feeling, be they ever so kind and familiar, that he was not their equal by birth, and that they could not treat him quite as such, however hard they might try, turning familiarity in his mind into slights, and kindness into condescension. This to a proud man must have been misery, and Burns must have been very lonely in a crowd of companions, thronged with admirers, but without a friend.

"Nobody understood Burns; he shared his opinions with no one he knew. When, at the beginning of the French Revolution he expressed his delight and approval, the people who admired him were shocked, refused to speak to him, and regarded him either as mad or terribly wicked. His poems were not admired as much as they deserved to be, he had hardly any money, was never likely to get on in the world, was shunned and disgraced, and began, as a last resource, to drink too much. Ill-health was one of his misfortunes, and this intemperance killed him.

"Thus died at the age of thirty-seven, poor, friendless, despised, the man who has given pleasure to thousands, and an undying collection of poems and songs to his country."

Q. Give some account, as far as you can in the *style* of Carlyle, of the Procession of May 4th. (Book studied, Carlyle's *French Revolution*.)

"See the doors of Notre Dame open wide, the Procession issuing forth, a sea of human faces that are to reform France. First come the nobles in their gayly *(sic)* tinted robes, next the clergy, and then the commons, the Tiers Etats in their slouched hats firm and resolute, and lastly the king, and the Œuil-de-bœuf, these are greeted by a tremendous storm of vivats. Vive le roi! Vive la nation! Let us suppose we can take up some coigne *(sic)* of vantage from which we can watch the procession, but with eyes different from other eyes, namely with prophetic eyes. See a man coming, striding at the head of the Tiers Etats, tall and with thick lips and black hair, whose father and brother walk among the nobles. Close beside walks Doctor Guillotin, learned Doctor Guillotin, who said, 'My friends (*mes amis*), I have a machine that will whisk off your heads in a second, and cause you no pain,' now doomed for two years to see and hear nothing but guillotin, and for more than two centuries after yonder a desolate ghost on this *(sic)* of the Styx. Mark, too, a small mean man, a sea-green man with sea-green eyes, Robespierre by name, a small underhand secretary walking beside one Dantun *(sic)* tall and massive, cruelty

*Notes*

*Written by a 14-year-old.*

# Appendix

## Notes

and vengeance on their faces. We may not linger longer, but one other we must note, one tall and active with a cunning air, namely, Camille Desmouellins *(sic)*, one day to rise to fame and the next to be forgotten.

"Many more walk in that procession one day to become famous, Bailli, future president of a New Republick *(sic)*, and Marat, with Broglie the War-God and others.

"The Tiers Etats with Mayor Bailli march to the rooms where they are to sit, but the doors are shut: there is sound of hammering within.

"Mayor Bailli knocks, and wants to know why they are shut out? It is the king's orders. He wants his papers. He may come in and get them, and with this they must be content.

"They swarm to Versailles, the king steps out on the balconny *(sic)* and speaks. He says the room is being prepared for his own august presence; a platform is being erected, he says he is sorry to inconvience *(sic)* them; but he is afraid they must wait, and with that he retires. Meanwhile patriotism consults as to what had best be done. Shall they meet on the palace steps? or even in the streets? At length they adjourn to the tennis court, and there patriotism swears one by one to be faithful to the New National Assembly, as they now name themselves. This is known as the Oath of the Tennis Court."

Q. Write a letter in the manner of Gray on any Modern Topic.
"Mr. Gray to Mr.—                                                    At Torquay.
My dear—

" 'Savez vous que je vous hais, que je vous deteste—voici des termes un peu forts,' still, I think that they are justified, imagine leaving a friend for two months in this place without once taking up the pen upon his behalf. If this neglect be due only to your low spirits, I will for once pardon you but only upon condition that you should come down here to visit me and at the same time strengthen your constitution. I can promise you but little diversion, but I think that the scenery will repay the journey—not to speak of myself. You will also be able to study many 'venerable vegetables' which are not usually to be found in England. But, I waste your time and my paper with these 'betises' and I know well upon what subject your mind is at present dwelling—which of us indeed is not thinking of Ireland. I would give much to hear your views upon the subject. For my part it seems to me that there can be but one true view, and it surprises me mightily to hear so much discussion upon the subject. Are we not truly a peculiar nation who pass bills of Home Rule etc with much discussion and debate, when neither of the two parties concerned will accept the conditions that we offer them? The one considering they give too little freedom, and the other too much. Accursed be the man who invented a bill which was and will be the cause of so much trouble 'in saecula saeculorum.' Surely we need not have any doubt as to what line of action we should adopt, surely it has not been the habit of England to let her subjects revolt without an attempt to quell them, surely the government will not stand by and see its servants murdered, and the one loyal province oppressed. But alas many things are possible with such a government. Here it is said by people who have been driven from that country by incendiaries that the Government will let things take their course till everything is in such a condition that the Premier will rise in the house and say, 'You see how things stand—it is no use trying to control Ireland, let us leave it to the Seinn Feiners, and live happily ever afterwards, free from such unprofitable cares.'

*Written by a 17-year-old.*

"Such is the talk, but I believe it not. We have as a nation always muddled things but we have muddled through triumphant in the end. It is so obvious that our interests and those of Ireland co-incide, that even to contemplate separation is to me incredible,

"Thus I remain your harassed friend, etc."

Q. Sketch a scene between a "Mr. Woodhouse" of to-day and a neighbour of his.

SCENE: Mr. Woodhouse's private study.

*Persons present*:—Owner of study, and Miss Syms, a very modern young lady.

*Mr. Woodhouse.*—"Oh, good afternoon Miss Syms, I am charmed to see you. Dear, dear, how dark it is. One might almost think it were evening, if the clock opposite did not directly oppose the fact."

*Miss S.*—"Oh, I don't know, it's not so bad out. I'm awfully sorry to blow in like this, but I came to enquire after Miss Woodhouse's cold. Is she better?"

*Mr. W.*—"How very thoughtful of you! No, I am afraid dear Emma is very indisposed. It is so trying having an invalid in the house, it makes me quite miserable when I think of my poor daughter having to stay all alone, in bed. But really, that is almost the best place in this dreadful weather. Do you really mean to say that you have been taking a walk."

*Miss S.*—"Yes, why on earth shouldn't I? It's about the only way to get really warm."

*Mr. W.*—"If the liberty might be allowed me, (dryly) I should say, that it was the one way in which to get a feverish cold, besides making oneself thoroughly miserable; and the ground is so damp under foot!"

*Miss S.*—"Oh, it hasn't been raining much lately. I only got caught in a little shower, (visible start from Mr. W.). (coyly,) Excuse me, but *is* that a box of cigarettes up there on the mantlepiece?"

*Mr. W.*—"Cigarettes? Oh, no! I couldn't think of keeping them near the house. I *never* smoke. It irritates my throat, which is naturally weak."

*Miss S.*—"But don't your visitors ever take the liberty of enjoying something of the sort? Besides, what about Miss Woodhouse?"

*Mr. W.*—(horrified,) "Dear Emma smoke a cigarette!! Why, I never heard of such a thing. What would she say if I told her. Dear Emma smoke, no, no, certainly not."

*Miss S.*—(laughing,) "Oh, I am sure I'm very sorry. I didn't mean to offend. How do you think the old Johnnies in Ireland are behaving themselves?"

*Mr. W.*—(coldly,) "I *beg* your pardon."

*Miss S.*—(sweetly,) "I said, how do you think matters are looking, in Ireland."

*Mr. W.*—"I am sorry, I think I could not have heard aright before.—Matters in Ireland, yes, oh I think the Irish rebels are positively awful. To think of breaking into houses, and turning the poor inhabitants out into the cold streets, (where they probably nearly die of cold), it is too dreadful!"

*Miss S.*—"Oh, I s'pose they are rather brutes sometimes. But in a way I almost sympathise with them. I wouldn't like to have to knuckle under to the English (catching sight of Mr. W.'s expression of horror and pained surprise,) I really think I'd better get a move on. Please don't look at me like that! I really don't mean half I say. Cheerio!"

*Mr. W.*—"Good afternoon Miss Syms, it was so kind of you to come. (aside)

*Notes*

*No age was given for the student who wrote this scene, only the grade level.*

# Notes

Oh, how unfeeling of dear Emma to have a cold, if it means visitors like this every hour. (aloud,) Good afternoon, can you find your way out. I really shall catch cold if I move out of this room!"

# Poetry Narration Samples
(from Vol. 6, pp. 168, 169, 195–209, 243)

Sometimes Charlotte asked the students to write their narrations in poetry. Here are some of their poems.

## Grades 4–6

ARMISTICE DAY
    Soldiers dying, soldiers dead,
    Bullets whizzing overhead.
    Tommies standing cheerily by.
    Waiting for their time to die;
    Soon the lull of firing comes,
    And naught is heard but the roll of drums.

    And now the last shell crashes down,
    A soldier reels in pain
    Too late the glad news comes to him.
    He never moves again,
    He is the Unknown Warrior,
    A man without a name.

    Two years have passed and home he comes,
    To the hearts that loved him well,
    Who is the Unknown Warrior?
    No lips the tale can tell,
    His tomb is in the Abbey,
    Where the souls of Heroes dwell.

    A nations sorrow and a nations tears,
    Have gone with the nameless man,
    Who knows, who can tell, the Warriors name,
    We think that no man can,
    So let our sorrow turn to joy
    On the grave of the Unknown man.

    Q. Write twelve lines on 'Cordelia.'

CORDELIA
    Nobliest lady, doomed to slaughter,
    An unlov'd, unpitied daughter,
    Though Cordelia thou may'st be,
    "Love's" the fittest name for thee;
    If love doth not, maid, bestow
    Scorn for scorn, and "no" for "no,"

---

**Notes**

*These poems are uncorrected, so you may find spelling and grammar errors.*

*No age was given for the student who wrote this poem, only the grade level.*

*Written by a 10-year-old.*

# Appendix

## Notes

If love loves through scorn and spite,
If love clings to truth and right,
If love's pure, maid, as thou art,
If love has a faithful heart,
Thou art then the same as love;
Come from God's own realms above!

### Grades 7–9

Q. Write some lines, in blank verse, that must scan on one of the following: (a), Scylla and Charybdis; (b), The White Lady of Avenel; (c), The Prince of Wales in India.

THE WHITE LADY OF AVENEL
    The sun had set and night was drawing on,
    The hills stood black against the twilight sky.
    A faint young crescent moon shone dimly forth
    Casting a pale and ghostly radiance
    Upon the group of pine trees on the hill,
    And silvering the rivers eddying swirl.
    Now all was silent, not a sound disturbed
    The summer night, and not a breath of wind
    Stirred in the pines. All nature slept in peace.
    But what was that, standing up in the shade?
    A woman, straight, and slim, all clad in white,
    Upon her long soft hair a misty crown,
    And ever and anon she deeply sighed,
    Leaning against the rugged mountain rock,
    Like to a moon beam, or a wisp of smoke.
    And on her shimmering, moonlit, robe she wore
    A golden girdle, in whose links was woven
    The fortunes of the house of Avenel.
    A cloud past o'er the moon, and the slim ghost
    Faded and disappeared into the air.
    A breeze sprang up among the pine trees tall;
    And then the river murmuring on its way
    Whispered a sad lament unto the night.

*Written by a 13-year-old.*

Q. Write in Ballad Metre some lines on "Armistice Day" or "Echo."

ARMISTICE DAY, OR THE UNKNOWN WARRIOR
    Within the ancient Abbey's sacred pyle,
    Which proudly guards the noblest of our dead.
    Where kings and statesmen lie in every aisle,
    And honoured poets, soldiers, priests are laid;

*Written by a 13-year-old.*

Behold a stranger comes. From whence is he?
Is he of noble birth; of rank or fame?
Was he as great as any whom we see
Around, who worked to make themselves a name?

Surely he is a prince, nay, e'en a king?
For see the waiting thousands gathered here;
And hear the streets of ancient London ring
To the slow tramp of men who guard his bier!

And, surely, 'tis the King himself who comes
As chiefest mourner on this solemn day,
And these who walk behind him are his sons—
All here to mourn this man. Who is he? Say!

How long the ranks of men who follow him
To his last resting-place—the House of God.
Our bishops, soldiers, statemen all are here,
Gathered to lay him in his native sod.

You ask "Is he a prince?" I answer "No!
Though none could be interred with greater state!
This man went forth to guard us from a foe,
Which threatened this our land—He did his work!

He raised the flag of Liberty on high
And challenging the powers of Wrong and Might
He gave up all he had without a sigh
And died for the good cause of God and Right.

Q. Write in Ballad Metre some lines on "Echo."

ECHO
Jupiter once went away from his wife
   To flirt with some nymphs in a wood
But Juno, suspecting that he was with them
   Came after as fast as she could.

Now Echo, a nymph, knew that Juno was there
   That the nymphs they would soon be found out,
And so she kept Juno away from the wood
   For if they had gone she did doubt.

But Juno knew all; and her anger was great
   And Echo this dreadful thing heard
"Since you are so fond of talking, from now
   You only shall have the last word!"

---

## Notes

*Written by a 13-year-old.*

# Notes

Now Echo went far from the dwellings of men
    And spent her sad life all alone
And often she'd weep and think of the past
    And over her fate make her moan.

Echo loved a Greek youth, but he could not love her.
    And she watched him all day from her bower
Till she pined away, all but her voice, which lives still,
    And the youth was turned into a flower.

## Grades 10–12

LIVINGSTONE
"The whole of Africa is desert bare,
Except around the coast." So people said,
And thought of that great continent no more.
"The smoke of thousand villages I've seen!"
So cried a man. He knew no more. His words
Sank down into one heart there to remain.
The man who heard rose up and gave his all:
Into the dark unknown he went alone.
What terrors did he face? The native's hate,
The fever, tetse-fly and loneliness.
But to the people there he brought great Light.
Who was this man, the son of some great lord?
Not so. He was a simple Scottish lad
Who learnt to follow duty's path. His name
Was Livingstone, he will not be forgot.

*Written by a 15-year-old.*

Q. Write an essay or a poem on the Bread of Life.

"How came He here," ev'n so the people cried,
Who found Him in the Temple: He had wrought
A miracle, and fed the multitude,
On five small loaves and fish: so now they'd have
Him king; should not they then have ev'ry good,
Food that they toiled not for and clothes and care,
And all the comfort that they could require?—
So thinking sought the king. . . .
    Our Saviour cried:
"Labour ye not for meat that perisheth,
But rather for the everlasting bread,
Which I will give"—Where is this bread, they cry,
They know not 'tis a heavenly bread He gives
But seek for earthly food—"I am the Bread of Life

*Written by a 17-year-old.*

*Appendix*

And all who come to Me I feed with Bread.
Receive ye then the Bread. Your fathers eat
Of manna in the wilderness—and died—
But whoso eats this Bread shall have his part
In everlasting life: I am the Bread,
That cometh down from Heaven; unless ye eat
Of me ye die, but otherwise ye live."
So Jesus taught, in Galilee, long since.

The people murmured when they heard His Word,
How can it be? How can He be our Bread?
They hardened then their hearts against His Word,
They would not hear, and could not understand,
And so they turned back to easier ways,
And many of them walked with Him no more.
May He grant now that we may hear the Word
And harden not our hearts against the Truth
That Jesus came to teach: so that in vain
He may not cry to hearts that will not hear,
"I am the Bread of Life, for all that come,
I have this gift, an everlasting life,
And room within my Heavenly Father's House."

Q. "The people sat in darkness" . . . "I am the Light of the World." Shew as far as you can the meaning of these statements.

The people sat in darkness—all was dim,
No light had yet come unto them from Him,
No hope as yet of Heaven after life,
A peaceful haven far from war and strife.
Some warriors to Valhalla's halls might go
And fight all day, and die. At evening, lo!
They'd wake again, and drink in the great hall.
Some men would sleep for ever at their fall;
Or with their fickle Gods for ever be:
So all was dark and dim. Poor heathens, see!
*The Light ahead*, the clouds that roll away,
The golden, glorious, dawning of the Day;
And in the birds, the flowers, the sunshine, see
The might of Him who calls, "Come unto Me."

*Written by a 13-year-old.*

Q. (on Plutarch's *Life of Pericles*)

Oh! land, whose beauty and unrivalled fame;
Lies dead, obscure in Time's great dusty vault.
Not so in memory, for truly here,
Each and alike look up and do revear

*Written by a 14-year-old.*

*Appendix*

**Notes**

Those heroes of the hidden past. Plato,
Who's understanding reached the wide world's end;
Aristides, that just and noble man.
And last, not least, the great wise Pericles
Who's socialistic views and clever ways
For governing the rich and poor alike
Were to be envied. In his eyes must Greece
Live for ever as the home of beauty.
So to the Gods great marble shrines he made,
Temples and theatres did he erect;
So that the beauty of his beloved Greece
Might live for ever. And now when seeing
What is left of all those wondrous sights
We think not of the works *themselves*
But rather of the man who had them built.

Q. Write some verses on (a) 'Dandie Dinmont,' or, (b) 'Atalanta,' or, (c) Allenby.

*Written by a 15-year-old.*

Atlanta was a huntress,
Who dearly loved the chase.
She out-ran the deer in fleetness,
And possessed a lovely face,

Many eager suiters sought her,
But they sought her all in vain,
For she vowed she'd never marry
And her suiters all were slain.

She had heeded well the warning,
From a witch well skilled in lore,
Who had told her if she married,
Happiness was hers no more.

Then a youth whom Venus favoured,
Came one day to run the race,
And by throwing golden apples,
He out-ran her in the chase.

In their hour of joy and triumph
Venus they forget to thank,
And the goddess sore offended,
Lowered them to the wild beast's rank.

*No age was given for the student who wrote this poem, only the grade level.*

(another response)
Phaëton was a wilful youth who always got his way.
He asked to drive his father's charge upon a certain day.

# Appendix

But Phoebus knowing well what danger lurketh in the sky;
Implored of him to wish again and not that task to try.
But Phaëton determined was to best this dangerous way,
And leaped into the chariot to spite his father's sway.
The horses started forward at a dashing headlong pace,
Phaëton tried to hold them back and modify the race.
With dreadful swiftness on he flew, losing his proper road,
The earth and sky began to smoke in an alarming mode.
At length when all had burst in flames, Jupiter cried aloud,
Phaëton who had lost his head was killed beneath a cloud.

Q. Write thirty lines of blank verse on (a), "A Spring Morning" (following "A Winter Morning Walk"), or, (b), Pegasus, or, (c), Allenby.

A SPRING MORNING.
 'Tis Spring; and now the birds with merry song
 Sing with full-throated voice to the blue sky
 On which small clouds float, soft as a dove's wing.
 Against the blue the pale-green leaflet gleams.
 The darker green of elder, further down,
 Sets off the brilliance of the hawthorn-hedge.
 Close to the ground, the purple violet peeps
 From out its nest of overhanging leaves.
 On yonder bank the daffodils toss their heads
 Under the shady lichen trees so tall.
 Close by a chestnut, bursting into leaf,
 Drops down it's sticky calyx on the ground;
 An early bumble-bee dives headlong in
 To a half-opened flower of early pear.
 O'erhead, in the tall beech trees, busy rooks,
 With great caw-caws and many angry squawks
 Build their great clumsy nests with bits of twig
 And little sticks just laid upon a bough.
 And by the long, straight, path tall fir trees wave
 Their graceful heads in the soft whisp'ring breeze
 And pressed against one ruddy trunk, an owl
 In vain tries to avoid the light of day,
 But blinks his wise old eyes, and shakes himself,
 And nestles close amid the sheltering leaves.
 Now on the rhubarb-bed we see, glad sight,
 Large red buttons, which promise fruit quite soon
 And further down the lettuce shoots up pale
 Next to a row of parsley, getting old.
 But see the peas, their curly tendrils green
 Clinging to their stout pea-sticks for support.

## Notes

*Written by a 15-year-old.*

# Appendix

## Notes

*Written by a 15-year-old.*

A SPRING MORNING
    Soft on the brown woods
    A pale light gleams,
    And slowly spreading seems
To change the brown wood to a land of dreams,
   Where beneath the trees
    The great god Pan,
    Doth pipe, half goat, half man,
   To satyrs dancing in the dawning wan.
   And then comes Phoebus,
    The visions fade
    And down the dewy glade
The rabbits scuttle o'er the rings they made.
    In the fields near-by
      The cattle rise
   And where the river lies
A white mist rises to the welcoming skies.
   Where the downs arise
    And blue sky crowns
    Their heads, fast o'er the mounds
The mist is driv'n to where the ocean sounds.
   White wings against blue sky,
    Gulls from the cliffs rise,
    Watching, with eyes
That see from shore to where the sky line lies,
   Where blue sea fades in bluer skies
     Soft, doth the tide creep
     O'er the golden sands
     With sea-weed strands
   Which, mayhap, knew the dawn of other lands.


Q. Write thirty lines of blank verse on "Pegasus."

*No age was given for the student who wrote this poem, only the grade level.*

   The sky was blue and flecked with tiny clouds
   Like sheep they ran before the driving wind
   The sun was setting like a big red rose
   The clouds that flew by him like rose-buds were
   And as I gaz'd I saw a little cloud
   White as the flower that rises in the spring
   Come nearer, nearer, nearer as I looked
   And as it came it took a diff'rent shape
   It seemed to turn into a fairy steed.
   White as the foam that rides the roaring waves
   Still it flew on until it reached the earth
   And galloping full lightly came to me
   And then I saw it was a wondrous thing
   It leapt about the grass and gently neighed
   I heard its voice sound like a crystal flute

# Appendix

"Oh come" he said "with me ascend the sky
Above the trees, above the hills we'll soar
Until we reach the home of all the gods
There will we stay and feast awhile with them
And dance with Juno and her maidens fair
And hear dear Orpheus and the pipes of Pan
And wander, wander, wander up above"
"Oh fairy steed, oh angel steed" I said
Horse fit for Jupiter himself to ride
What is thy name I pray thee tell me this"
Then came the magic voice of him again
"If thou wilt know my name then come with me."
Yet tell me first I hesitating said
He told me and when I had heard the name
I leapt upon his back and flew with him.

Q. Write some verses, in the metre of Pope's "Essay on Man," on the meeting of the League of Nations.

From each proud kingdom and each petty state
The statesmen meet together to debate
Upon the happy time when wars shall cease
And joy shall reign, and universal peace.
No more shall day with radiance cruelly bright
Glare down upon the carnage of the fight.
No more shall night's dark cloak be rent aside
By flashing shells and searchlight's stealthy glide
No more shall weary watchers wait at home
With straining eyes for thoes that cannot come
The nations shall forget their strife and greed
The strong shall help the weak in time of need
May they succeed in every peaceful plan
If war can cease as long as man is man.

*Written by a 16-year-old.*

Q. Gather up in blank verse the impressions you have received from your reading of Tennyson's poems.

Take up a volume of the poet's works,
Read on, lay it aside, and take thy pen,
Endeavour in a few, poor, worthless lines
To give expression of thy sentiments. . . .
Surely this man loved all the joys of life,
Saw beauty in the smallest and the least,
Put plainer things that hitherto were dim,
And lit a candle in the darkest room.
His thoughts, now sad, now gay, may surely be
The solace sweet for many a weary hour,

*Written by a 16-year-old.*

# Appendix

## Notes

His words, drunk deeply, seem to live and burn
Clear, radiant, gleaming from the printed page,
Nature to him was dear and so has made
Her wiles for other men a treasure vast.
Old Books, his master mind could comprehend
Are shown to us as pictures to a child,
Read on—and when the volume's put away,
Muse on the learnings thou hast found therein;
The time thus spent thou never will repent,
For love of good things all should seek and find.

### ON READING TENNYSON'S POEMS.

*Written by a 15-year-old.*

Oh! Prophet of an era yet to come,
When men shall sing where men were wont to speak
In words which even Englishmen knew not.
And when I read thy songs, at once I felt
The breath of Nature that was lurking there.
And then I knew that all thy life thou dwelt
Amid the changing scenes of Nature's play,
And knew the very language of the birds,
And drank the essence of the honeysuckle.
And when thou wast but young, I knew thy thoughts,
Thy Doubts and struggles, for thou gave them me;
And yet, had I been thee, my thoughts would still
Have rested deep within my heart; but still
T'would be relief to pour out all my woes
In the sweet flow of sympathetic verse.
Thy epithets produce a vivid scene
Of knights in armour or of maiden fair,
And yet, methinks, the fairness of her face
Doth sometimes cover many a fault below.
But to thy genius and thy work for ever
Be owed a debt of thankfulness that we
No longer tread the paths of level Pope
Or read those words that are not English-born.

### A LULLABY SONG

*Written by a 16-year-old.*

The little waves are sighing on the shore,
And the little breezes sobbing in the trees;
But the little stars are shining,
In the sky's blue velvet lining,
And Lady Sleep is tapping at the door.

The little gulls are flying home to shore,
And the little lights are flashing from the ships,
But close your eyes, my sweet,

And be ready then to greet
Dear Lady Sleep who's tapping at the door.

The wind is rising all around the shore,
And the fishing boats speed home before the gale;
But hark not to the rain
That is lashing on the pane,
For Lady Sleep has entered by the door.

The storm has sunk the ships and swept the shore,
But there's weeping in the town and on the quay,
But, sweet, you're dreaming fast
Even though the dawn be past,
And Lady Sleep has gone, and closed the door.

THE CLOUDS
    Among the spirits of the nearer air
    There are three children of the sun and sea—
    The Genii of the clouds; it is their care
    To give the ocean's bounty to the earth:
    Oft they retain it in a time of dearth,
    But they give all, however much it be.

    The youngest of the three is very fair;
    She is a maiden beautiful and sweet,
    Of ever varying mood, changeful as air.
    Now, plunged in merriment, she takes delight
    In all she sees, now tears obscure her sight;
    A breeze-swept lake shows not a change more fleet.

    The fleecy clouds of April own her sway—
    They, golden, lie against the golden sun,
    Or sport across the blue when she is gay;
    But when, anon, her girlish passions rise,
    She marshalls them across the sunny skies
    To flood the earth, then stops ere half begun.

    Her elder brother is of different mien.
    The clouds he governs are of different mould;
    When the earth pants for moisture he is seen
    To spread his clouds across the filmy blue.
    When his rain falls, it steady is and true;
    Persistent, gentle, ceaseless, yet not cold.

    From the grey bowl with which he caps the earth,
    It sweetly falls with earth-renewing force.
    Not April's rapid change from grief to mirth
    Excites its fall, but calm, determined thought

---

**Notes**

*Written by a 16-year-old.*

# Appendix

## Notes

*Written by a 17-year-old.*

Of middle age, of deeds from judgment wrought;
He recks not blame, but still pursues his course.

Aged, yet of awesome beauty is the third,
Of flashing eye and sullen, scornful brow—
With an imperious hand she guides her herd
Of wild, tempestuous mood; quick roused to ire
Is she, slow to forgive, of vengeance dire;
Before her awful glance the tree-tops bow.

And when enraged, she stretches forth a hand—
A long, thin hand—to North, South, East and West,
And draws from thence clouds num'rous as the sand;
They crowd on the horizon, and blot out
The sun's fair light; then, like a giant's shout,
The thunder booms at her dread spear's behest.

Q. Write some lines on "Spring" in the metre of "Allegro."

SPRING

    Begone! for a short space
Ye whistling winds, and fogs, and snowy clouds,
    And frosts that with fair lace
Each window-pane in dainty pattern shrouds,
    Offsprings of Winter, ye!
Begone! find out some icy arctic land.
    Upon that cheerless strand
'Mongst piercing ice, and chilling glaciers dwell
    Such regions suit ye well,
Go, cold Winter, well are we rid of thee!
    Come Spring, thou fairest season come!
    With the bee's enchanting hum,
    And the dainty blossoms swinging
    On the tree, while birds are singing.
    See how they clothe the branches gray
    In dress of freshest pink, all day,
    Then when the dewy evening falls
    They close their flowers till Morning calls.
    Sweet Morn! Spring leads thee by the hand
    And bids thee shine o'er all the land;
    Thou send'st forth beams of purest gold,
    To bid the daffodils unfold,
    While Spring bends down with her fresh lips
    To kiss the daisie's petal tips.
    And as she walks o'er the green sward
    A cheerful mavis, perfect bard
    Breaks into song; his thrilling notes
    Are echoed from a hundred throats

Of eager birds, who love to sing
To their sweet mistress, fairest Spring.
Then as she sits on mossy throne
A scarlet lady-bird, alone,
Bids her good welcome; and above
Is heard the cooing of the dove.
Two butterflies in russet clad
Fly round her head with flutt'rings glad;
While at her side a giddy fly
Buzzes his joy that she is nigh,
Oh! Spring my heart's desire shall be
That thou wilt ever dwell with me!

# Notes

# Narration Questions that Charlotte Used

*(from Vol. 3, pp. 272–299, 312, 318 and Vol. 6, pp. 178, 193, 194, 203–208)*

It is helpful to know what kinds of questions Charlotte used when asking for narrations. This list is a compilation of questions she used for end-of-term written narration/compositions.

## *Grades 1–3*

- Tell the story of . . .
- Tell a *fairy* story.
- What have you noticed (yourself) about *[an object of nature studied]*?
- Gather three sorts of *[nature object studied]* and tell all you can about them.
- Tell about . . .
- Tell all you know about . . .
- Tell what you know about . . .
- What is a *hero*? What *heroes* have you heard of? Tell about one.
- What have you noticed about *[an object of nature studied]*? Tell all you know about it.

## *Grades 4–6*

*[Quote from a book read]* Who said this? Tell the story.
Tell the history of *[a current item or phrase read about]*.
What did you see in *[picture studied]*?
*[Quote from a book read]* Of whom was this said? Tell the story.
What do you know of *[historical person read about]*?
What *towns, rivers, and castles* would you see in traveling about *[geographical area read about]*?
How many kinds of *bees* are there in a hive? What *work* does each do? Tell how they build the *comb*.

## *Grades 7–9*

Describe the *founding of Christ's Kingdom*. What are the *laws of His Kingdom*?
Explain *[key phrase from historical event]* and give an account of *[related historical event read about]*.
What do you know of *[historical event read about]*?
Show fully how *[historical person read about]* acquired *[a certain title or nickname]*. Why was it a strange title for a man in those days?
Describe a journey in *[geographical area read about]*.
How are the following *seeds dispersed*? Give diagrams and observations.
Describe the *[part of two natural objects]*.

---

## Notes

*I have tried to generalize the wording in these questions so as to make them useable in a variety of situations. Generalizations are in italics. In places where generalizations did not come easily, original wording was kept but italicized to show where you could substitute your own wording.*

*Notice how Charlotte incorporated the four main composition types in her narration questions.*
- *Narrative—Telling a story, either fact or fiction.*
- *Expository—Informing, or explaining a subject.*
- *Descriptive – A type of expository writing. Painting a picture by incorporating imagery and specific details.*
- *Persuasive—Stating an opinion and attempting to influence the reader.*

*Charlotte asked for mostly Narrative and Expository compositions in the earlier grades: "Tell the story . . ."; "What do you know . . ."; Tell how . . . ."*

*In the older grades Charlotte added Descriptive and Persuasive compositions: "Describe . . ."; "Discuss . . ."; "Write a letter to a newspaper . . ."*

## Notes

*Also notice the styles of writing that Charlotte asked for.*
- *Story*
- *Poetry*
- *Letter*
- *Script*
- *Essay*
- *Dialogue*
- *Diary*
- *Exposition*
- *Diagram drawing*

Give a diagram of *[body part studied]*, and explain how *[it works]*.

Describe your favorite scene in *[literature book read]*.

Write twelve lines on *[historical person read about]*.

Discuss *[modern political person's]* scheme. How is it working?

Write an essay on *[current event]*, showing what some of the difficulties have been and what has been achieved.

## Grades 10–12

For what purpose were *[historical group]* instituted?

*[Quote from historical person read about]* Write a short sketch of the character of *[historical person]*, discussing the above statement.

What do you know of the *[historical group or political party studied]*?

Distinguish between *[pairs of related words with subtle differences of meaning]*, using each word in a sentence.

Give shortly *[author's]* estimate of *[historical person read about]*, showing what *[historical person]* did for *[cause or country]* and what was the cause of his personal *failure* in life.

Give some account, as far as you can in the style of *[author]*, of *[historical event read about]*.

Write a letter in the manner of *[historical person read about]* on any Modern Topic.

Sketch a scene between a *[famous character in literature book read]* of today and a neighbor of his.

Describe the condition of *(a) the clergy, (b) the army, (c) the navy, (d) the general public* in and about *[time period studied]*.

Trace the rise of *[country]* before *[famous leader of that country]*.

What theories of government were held by *[historical person read about]*? Give some account of his great ministers.

Describe the rise of *[country read about]* and its condition at *[specific time period]*.

Suppose *[historical or modern-day person in a related event]*, write his diary for three days.

Sketch the character and manners of *[character in literature book]*. How does he appear in *[historical novel]*?

Write a letter to *[a newspaper]* on *[a current event or topic studied]*.

Write a dialogue between *[characters in a literature or history book read]*.

Write a ballad on *[current event studied]*.

Write a *[style of poetry]* on the *[current event studied]*.

Write an essay, dated *[year in the future]*, on the imagined work of *[a current group or movement studied]*.

Write a woeful ballad touching the condition of *[a country studied]*, or, a poem on *[a current event read about]*.

Write an essay on the present condition of *[own country]*, or, on *[leader of another country]*.

*Appendix*

# Narration Ideas

A key component of Charlotte Mason's method is narration. In simple terms, narration is telling back in your own words what you just read or heard. It's a wonderful evaluation tool that requires much thinking and assimilating on the student's part. Narration can be done in many ways; here is a list of suggestions.

## Speaking

1. Compose and tape a radio show that dramatizes the events read about.
2. Compare and contrast a practice in the account you read with a similar practice in modern society (for example, the feudal system vs. free enterprise; or infanticide in Rome vs. abortion today).
3. Compare and contrast two or three rulers read about who lived during the same time period or in the same country. Which one would you rather live under and why?
4. Play the part of the person you read about as he or she is being interviewed.
5. Explain what this story tells you about the character of the person you read about.
6. Name three things the person you read about is remembered for.
7. Tell all you know about . . . (for example, the habits of a bluejay or the founding of Rome).
8. Describe our . . . (for example, trip to the ocean or lighthouse experience).
9. Tell five things you learned from what you read.
10. Tell back the story in your own words.
11. Ask five questions covering the material you read.
12. (For Picture Study) Describe the picture you just saw.
13. (For Picture Study) Which picture did you like best of all you studied? Describe it.
14. Describe your favorite scene in the story you read.
15. Tell what happened into a tape recorder.
16. Tell how the scene reminds you of another story.
17. Say three questions you would ask if you were writing a test about what you just read.
18. Tell me anything new you learned from the passage.
19. Tell what may happen next and why.
20. Describe the problem and how it was solved or how it could be solved.
21. Tell what you think this means: ". . ."
22. Tell how you might have done things differently as a character.
23. Compare how people did things back in those days to how we do them today.
24. Describe any clues left by the author in previous readings pointing to the plot twist.
25. Describe a character's worldview. Compare it to a Christian worldview.

*Notes*

## Notes

26. Compare kindred spirits from this book with those who might be good friends from another book.

27. Compare yourself to a kindred spirit of yours from this book.

28. Tell what you have learned about history, geography, or science from this book.

29. Describe any golden deeds from this book.

## Writing

Any of the Speaking ideas listed above, done in written form, plus . . .

1. Write and perform a play that depicts the event read about.

2. Create a newspaper article about the event or person read. Put the article in a time-appropriate newspaper that you create; just the front page will do. Include ads, weather, and any other elements that would give the feel of the time period.

3. Write an obituary for a person you read about.

4. Write an interview with a person you read about.

5. Write journal or diary entries from the person's point of view whom you read about.

6. Write a letter to a younger sibling, explaining what you learned.

7. Write a poem that retells the story you read about.

8. Write five interview questions you'd like to ask the person you read about.

9. Write five questions covering the material you read.

10. Write five sentences about the passage.

11. Make a fill-in-the-blank quiz (oral or written) about the story for someone.

12. Write a letter (or e-mail) to someone about the passage.

13. Write a letter from one character to another.

14. Write a one-act play of a scene.

15. Write a letter from the author to the publisher about key scenes.

16. Write an imaginary conversation between two characters from two different books.

17. Write a review of the book for Amazon.com.

## Drawing

1. Draw a diagram of a machine or series of events you read about and explain it.

2. Draw a picture of the event or one particular scene in the event you read about.

3. Draw a map of the place you just read about.

4. (For Music Study) Draw a picture of what you hear in this composer's music.

5. (For Picture Study) Draw the basic components of this artist's work, putting each in its proper place.

6. Describe and/or draw a theme park based upon this book (adventure stories).

## Drama

1. Write and perform a play that depicts the event read about.
2. Dramatize and videotape a news broadcast that summarizes the events read about.
3. Spend 10 minutes planning a short skit based on what you read.
4. Describe how you would adapt the scene to a movie.
5. Describe special features for a DVD made from this book.

## Building

1. Make a model of a machine you read about and explain how it works (for example, the Trojan horse or Archimedes' stone-throwing machine).
2. Set up the scene you just read about with blocks, toys, Legos, etc.
3. Model something from the scene with clay.

# Two Mothers' Conversation about Teaching Reading

*(Vol. 1, pp. 207–214)*

"You don't mean to say you would go plump into words of three or four syllables before a child knows his letters?"

"It is possible to read words without knowing the alphabet, as you know a face without singling out its features; but we learn not only the names but the *sounds* of the letters before we begin to read words."

"Our children learn their letters without any teaching. We always keep by us a shallow table drawer, the bottom covered half an inch deep with sand. Before they are two, the babies make round *O* and crooked *S*, and *T* for Tommy, and so on, with dumpy, uncertain little fingers. The elder children teach the little ones by way of a game."

"The sand is capital! We have various devices, but none so good as that. Children love to be doing. The funny, shaky lines the little finger makes in the sand will be ten times as interesting as the shapes the eye sees."

"But the reading! I can't get over three syllables for the first lesson. Why, it's like teaching a twelve-months old child to waltz!"

"You say that because we forget that a group of letters is no more than the *sign* of a word, while a word is only the vocal sign of a thing or an act. This is how the child learns. First, he gets the notion of the table; he sees several tables; he finds they have legs, by which you can scramble up; very often covers which you may pull off; and on them many things lie, good and pleasant for a baby to enjoy; sometimes, too, you can pull these things off the table, and they go down with a bang, which is nice. The grown-up people call this pleasant thing, full of many interests, 'table,' and, by-and-by, baby says 'table' too; and the word 'table' comes to mean, in a vague way, all this to him. 'A round table,' 'on the table,' and so on, form part of the idea of 'table' to him. In the same way baby chimes in when his mother sings. She says, 'Baby, sing,' and, by-and-by, notions of 'sing,' 'kiss,' 'love,' dawn on his brain."

"Yes, the darlings! and it's surprising how many words a child knows even before he can speak them; 'pussy,' 'dolly,' 'carriage,' soon convey interesting ideas to him."

"That's just it. Interest the child in the thing, and he soon learns the *sound-sign* for it—that is, its name. Now, I maintain that, when he is a little older, he should learn the *form-sign*—that is, the printed word—on the same principle. It is far easier for a child to read plum-pudding than to read 'to, to,' because 'plum-pudding' conveys a far more interesting idea."

"That may be, when he gets into words of three or four syllables; but what would you do while he's in words of one syllable—indeed, of two or three letters?"

"I should never put him into words of one syllable at all. The bigger the word, the more striking the look of it, and, therefore, the easier it is to read, provided always that the idea it conveys is interesting to a child. It is sad to see an intelligent child toiling over a reading-lesson infinitely below his capacity—*ath, eth, ith, oth, uth*—or, at the very best, 'The cat sat on the mat.' How should we like to begin to read German, for example, by toiling over all conceivable combinations of letters, arranged on no principle but similarity of sound; or, worse still, that our readings

# Notes

should be graduated according to the number of letters each word contains? We should be lost in a hopeless fog before a page of words of three letters, all drearily like one another, with no distinctive features for the eye to seize upon; but the child? 'Oh, well—children are different; no doubt it is good for the child to grind in this mill!' But this is only one of many ways in which children are needlessly and cruelly oppressed!"

"You are taking high moral ground! All the same, I don't think I am convinced. It is far easier for a child to spell c a t, cat, than to spell p l u m - p u d d i n g, plum-pudding."

"But spelling and reading are *two* things. You must learn to spell in order to *write* words, not to *read* them. A child is droning over a reading-lesson, spells c o u g h; you say 'cough,' and she repeats. By dint of repetition, she learns at last to associate the look of the word with the sound, and says 'cough' without spelling it; and you think she has arrived at 'cough' through c o u g h. Not a bit of it; c o f spells cough!"

"Yes; but 'cough' has a silent *u*, and a *gh* with the sound of *f*. There, I grant, is a great difficulty. If only there were no silent letters, and if all letters had always the same sound, we should, indeed, have reading made easy. The phonetic people have something to say for themselves."

"You would agree with the writer of an article in a number of a leading review: 'Plough ought to be written and printed *plow*; through, *thru*; enough, *enuf*; ought, *aut* or *ort*'; and so on. All this goes on the mistaken idea that in reading we look at the letters which compose a word, think of their sounds, combine these, and form the word. We do nothing of the kind; we accept a word, written or printed, simply as the *symbol* of a word we are accustomed to say. If the word is new to us we may try to make something of the letters, but we know so well that this is a shot in the dark, that we are careful not to *say* the new word until we have heard someone else say it."

"Yes, but children are different."

"Children are the same, 'only more so.' *We* could, if we liked, break up a word into its sounds, or put certain sounds together to make a word. But these are efforts beyond the range of children. First, as last, they learn to know a word by the look of it, and the more striking it looks the easier it is to recognise; provided always that the printed word is one which they already know very well by sound and by sense."

"It is not clear yet; suppose you tell me, step by step, how you would give your first reading lesson. An illustration helps one so much."

"Very well: Bobbie had his first lesson yesterday—on his sixth birthday. The lesson was part of the celebration. By the way, I think it's rather a good idea to begin a new study with a child on his birthday, or some great day; he *begins* by thinking the new study a privilege."

"That is a hint. But go on; did Bobbie know his letters?"

"Yes, he had picked them up, as you say; but I had been careful not to allow any small readings. You know how Susanna Wesley used to retire to her room with the child who was to have his first reading-lesson, and not to appear again for some hours, when the boy came out able to read a good part of the first chapter of Genesis? Well, Bobbie's first reading-lesson was a solemn occasion, too, for which we had been preparing for a week or two. First, I bought a dozen penny copies of the 'History of Cock Robin'—good bold type, bad pictures, that we cut out.

"Then we had a nursery pasting day—pasting the sheets on common drawing-paper, six one side down, and six the other; so that now we had six complete copies, and not twelve.

"Then we cut up the *first page only*, of all six copies, line by line, and word by word. We gathered up the words and put them in a box, and our preparations were complete.

"Now for the lesson. Bobbie and I are shut in by ourselves in the morning-room. I always use a black-board in teaching the children. I write up, in good clear 'print' hand,

C o c k   R o b i n

Bobbie watches with more interest because he knows his letters. I say, pointing to the word, 'cock robin,' which he repeats.

"Then the words in the box are scattered on the table, and he finds half a dozen 'cock robins' with great ease.

"We do the same thing with 'sparrow,' 'arrow,' 'said,' 'killed,' 'who,' and so on, till all the words in the verse have been learned. The words on the black-board grow into a column, which Bob reads backwards and forwards, and every way, except as the words run in the verse.

"Then Bobbie arranges the loose words into columns like that on the board.

"Then into columns of his own devising, which he reads off.

"Lastly, culminating joy (the whole lesson has been a delight!), he finds among the loose words, at my dictation,

'Who killed Cock Robin
I said the sparrow
With my bow and arrow
I killed Cock Robin,'

arranging the words in verse form.

"Then I had still one unmutilated copy, out of which Bob had the pleasure of reading the verse, and he read it forwards and *backwards*. So long as he lives he will know those twelve words."

"No doubt it was a pleasant lesson; but, think of all the pasting and cutting!"

"Yes, that is troublesome. I wish some publisher would provide us with what we want—nursery rhymes, in good bold type, with boxes of loose words to match,—a separate box, or division, for each page, so that the child may not be confused by having too many words to hunt amongst. The point is that he should *see*, and *look at*, the new word many times, so that its shape becomes impressed on his brain."

"I see; but he is only able to read 'Cock Robin'; he has no general power of reading."

"On the contrary, he will read those twelve words wherever he meets with them. Suppose he learns ten words a day, in half a year he will have at least six hundred words; he will know how to read a little."

"Excellent, supposing your children *remember* all they learn. At the end of a week, mine would remember 'Cock Robin,' perhaps, but the rest would be gone!"

"Oh, but we keep what we get! When we have mastered the words of the second verse, Bob runs through the first in the book, naming words here and there as I point to them. It takes less than a minute, and the ground is secured."

"The first lesson must have been long?"

"I'm sorry to say it lasted half an hour. The child's interest tempted me to do more than I should."

"It all sounds very attractive—a sort of game—but I cannot be satisfied that a

Notes

child should learn to read without knowing the powers of the letters. You constantly see a child spell a word over to himself, and then pronounce it; the more so, if he has been carefully taught the sounds of the letters—not merely their names."

"Naturally; for though many of our English words are each a law unto itself, others offer a key to a whole group, as arrow gives us sp arrow, m arrow, h arrow; but we have alternate days—one for reading, the other for word-building—and that is one way to secure variety, and, so, the joyous interest which is the real secret of success."

Appendix

# A Beginning Reading Lesson Plan
*(from Vol. 1 pp. 217–222)*

## Day 1

**Background**: The child knows his letters by name and sound, but he knows no more.

**Objective**: To-day he is to be launched into the very middle of reading, without any "steps" at all, because reading is neither an art nor a science, and has, probably, no beginning. Your child is to learn to read to-day—
"I like little pussy,
Her coat is so warm"—
and he is to know those nine words so well that he will be able to read them wherever they may occur henceforth and for evermore.

### Materials Needed
- Box of loose letters
- First two lines of the poem "Little Pussy" typed in large print on seven sheets of paper; six of the sheets should be cut into separate words
- Chalkboard and chalk, paper and pencil, or whiteboard and dry-erase marker

### Lesson

Step 1: Write "Pussy" on the chalkboard, paper, or whiteboard in a large print and tell your child this word is "pussy."

Step 2: Tell your child to look at the word until he is sure he would know it again.

Step 3: Have your child make "pussy" from memory with his own loose letters.

Step 4: Scatter the individual word slips on the table and have your child find all that say "pussy."

Step 5: Show him the printed sheet with the first two lines of the poem, and have him find "pussy." (Don't tell him the rhyme yet.)

Step 6: Teach each of the remaining words, out of order, following the same steps. As each new word is added, have your child make a column of the already-learned word slips. He may rearrange this column as often as he likes and read the words. Also review your list on the chalkboard, paper, or whiteboard in random order as new words are added.

Step 7: Once all the words have been learned individually, ask your child to find the correct word strips in order as you say them. Make a short sentence using the words he knows. For example, "Pussy—is—warm." Have your child place the word strips in "reading" order and read the sentence.

Step 8: Continue making new sentences with the words he knows. For example, "her—little—coat—is—warm," "Pussy—is—so—little," "I—like—pussy," "Pussy—is—little—like—her—coat." If the rhyme can be kept secret until the end, so much the better.

*Notes*

*Your child should not begin to read until he is equal to the effort required by these lessons. Even then, it may be well to break up one lesson into two, or half a dozen, as he is able to take it.*

*Appendix*

Notes

## Day 2

**Background**: The child knows the nine words from yesterday's poem lines.

**Objective**: Introduce new words by using word families.
 Coat, boat, goat, float, moat, stoat
 Little, brittle, tittle, skittle
 Like, Mike, pike
 So, no, do (the musical "do"), lo
 Warm, arm, harm, charm, barm, alarm

**Materials Needed**
- Box of loose letters
- Word slips from the first two lines of the poem "Little Pussy" (used on Day 1)
- Chalkboard and chalk, paper and pencil, or whiteboard and dry-erase marker
- Tokens or pennies

**Lesson**

Step 1: Have your child make the word "coat" with his letters—from memory if he can; if not, looking at the word slip for a pattern.

Step 2: Pronounce the word slowly, then give the initial consonant sound *C*.

Step 3: Say, "Take away *C*, and what do we have left?" With a little help, he will figure out "oat."

Step 4: Ask, How would you make boat?" (saying the word slowly and emphasizing the sound of *B)*. Write "boat" on the chalkboard or whiteboard and have your child make it with his letters.

Step 5: Continue making new words in that word family by changing the initial consonant. Give brief explanations of any words that are unfamiliar to him.

Step 6: Review the new words in random order as you proceed.

Step 7: Dictate short sentences that use the already-learned words and the new words, and have your child locate and place the words in the correct "reading" order. Use the word slips for the old words and have your child make the new words with his loose letters. For example, "I—like—her—goat," "Her—little—stoat—is—warm."

Step 8: Give a sentence that contains a word or two that your child hasn't learned yet. For example, "Pussy—is—in—the—boat." Have your child put tokens or pennies where the unknown words belong in the sentence with the promise that "they may soon come up in our lessons."

Step 9: Deal with the remaining word families in the same way. Sample sentences: "Her skittle is little," "Her charm is brittle," "Her arm is warm." Take care that the sentences make sense.

Step 10: Have your child write his new words in a notebook.

## Day 3

Do the next two lines of the poem in the same manner as Day 1.

*If your child suggests a word that sounds like the word family you're working on but is spelled differently, simply explain that that word is spelled another way and move on.*

*Pronounce warm as arm. Your child will probably perceive that such a pronunciation is wrong and notice that all these words are sounded like 'arm,' but not one of them like 'warm'—that is, he will see that the same group of letters need not always have the same sound. But do not ask him to make a note of this new piece of knowledge; let it grow into him gradually, after many experiences.*

## Day 4

Learn new words by word families (as on Day 2) based on the words learned on Day 3. Or, if the words learned on the previous day do not offer much in the way of word families, use this day to move on to the next two lines of the poem.

"Our stock of words is growing; we are able, as we go on, to make an almost unlimited number of little sentences. If we have to use counters now and then, why, that only whets our appetite for knowledge. By the time Tommy has worked 'Little Pussy' through he has quite a large stock of words; has considerable power to attack new words with familiar combinations; what is more, he has achieved; he has courage to attack all 'learning,' and has a sense that delightful results are quite within reach. Moreover, he learns to read in a way that affords him some moral training. There is no stumbling, no hesitation from the first, but bright attention and perfect achievement. His reading lesson is a delight, of which he is deprived when he comes to his lesson in a lazy, drawling mood. Perfect enunciation and precision are insisted on, and when he comes to arrange the whole of the little rhyme in his loose words and read it off (most delightful of all the lessons) his reading must be a perfect and finished recitation" (Vol. 1, pp. 221, 222).

## Notes

**I Like Little Pussy**
**Jane Taylor**

I like little Pussy,
Her coat is so warm;
And if I don't hurt her
She'll do me no harm.
So I'll not pull her tail,
Nor drive her away,
But Pussy and I
Very gently will play.
She shall sit by my side,
And I'll give her some food;
And she'll love me because
I am gentle and good.

I'll pat little Pussy,
And then she will purr;
And thus show her thanks
For my kindness to her.
I'll not pinch her ears,
Nor tread on her paw,
Lest I should provoke her
To use her sharp claw;
I never will vex her,
Nor make her displeased,
For Pussy can't bear
To be worried or teased.

# English Grammar Lessons

## Sample Beginning Lessons on a Simple Sentence's Parts

*for ages 8 and 9*
*(from Vol. 1, pp. 296–300)*

## Lesson 1

Words put together so as to make sense form what is called a sentence.
"Barley oats chair really good and cherry" is not a sentence, because it makes no(n)sense.
"Tom has said his lesson" is a sentence.
It is a sentence because it tells us something about Tom.

Every sentence speaks of someone or of something, and tells us something about that of which it speaks.

So a sentence has two parts:
(1) The thing we speak of;
(2) What we say about it.

In our sentence we speak of "Tom."
We say about him that he "has learned his lesson."

The thing we speak of is often called the Subject, which just means that which we talk about.
People sometimes say "the *subject* of conversation was so and so," which is another way of saying "the thing we were speaking about was so and so."

*To be learnt—*
Words put together so as to make sense form a sentence.
A sentence has two parts: that which we speak of, and what we say about it.
That which we speak of is the Subject.

## Exercises on Lesson 1

1. Put the first part to—
   —has a long mane.
   —is broken.
   —cannot do his sums.
   —played for an hour; etc., etc.

2. Put the second part to—
   That poor boy—.
   My brother Tom—.
   The broken flowerpot—.

---

**Notes**

*These lessons, along with the others Charlotte wrote as First Grammar Lessons, are collected in a book called* **Simply Grammar,** *edited by Karen Andreola.*

> Bread and jam—.
> Brown's tool-basket—; etc., etc.

3. Put six different subjects to each half sentence in 1.

4. Make six different sentences with each subject in 2.

5. Say which part of the sentence is wanting, and supply it in—
> Has been mended
> Tom's knife
> That little dog
> Cut his finger
> Ate too much fruit
> My new book
> The snowdrops in our garden, etc., etc.

Draw a line under the subject of each sentence in all the exercises.

## Lesson 2

We may make a sentence with only two words—the name of the thing we speak of and what we say about it:—
> John writes.
> Birds sing.
> Mary sews.

We speak about "John."
We say about him that he "writes."
We speak about "birds."
We say about them that they "sing."

These words, *writes, sing, sews*, all come out of the same group of words, and the words in that group are the chief words of all, for this reason—we cannot make sense, and therefore cannot make a sentence, without using at least one of them.

They are called Verbs, which means *words*, because they are the chief *words* of all.

A verb always tells one of two things about the subject. Either it tells what the subject *is*, as—
> I *am* hungry.
> The chair *is* broken.
> The birds *are* merry;

or it tells what the subject does, as—
> Alice *writes*.
> The cat *mews*.
> He *calls*.

*Appendix*

**Notes**

*To be learnt—*
We cannot make a sentence without a verb.
*Verb* means *word*.
Verbs are the chief words.
Verbs show that the subject is something—
    He is sleepy;
or does something—
    He runs.

## Exercises on Lesson 2

1. Put in a verb of being:—
    Mary—sleepy.
    Boys—rough.
    Girls— —quiet.
    He—first yesterday.
    I—a little boy.
    Tom and George—swinging before dinner.
    We— —busy to-morrow.
    He— —punished; etc., etc.

2. Make three sentences with each of the following verbs:—
    *Is, are, should be, was, am, were, shall be, will be.*

3. Make six sentences with verbs of being in each.

4. Put a verb of doing to—
    Tigers—.
    The boy with the pony—.
    My cousins—; etc., etc.

5. Make twenty sentences about—
    That boy in kilts,
with verbs showing what he *does*.

6. Find the verbs, and say whether of *being* or *doing*, in—
    The bright sun rises over the hill.
    We went away.
    You are my cousin.
    George goes to school.
    He took his slate.
    We are seven.

7. Count how many verbs you use in your talk for the next ten minutes.

8. Write every verb you can find in these exercises, and draw a line under it.

*Appendix*

## Notes

*You can find the entire book of Morris's* **English Grammar** *on Google Books at books.google.com.*

### Sample of English Grammar Book for Older Students

One of the books Charlotte used for older students was Morris's *English Grammar*. On the adjoining page you can see a sample of that book. Notice that it is not a living book; it does not try to make English grammar "come alive" in its lessons.

However, the students would practice what they learned with various literary passages from their living books. For example, an exam question for a twelve-year-old (Vol. 3, p. 310) asked the student to analyze and parse the italicized words in this verse from Christina Rossetti's poem "Twilight Calm":

*One by* one the flowers *close*,
Lily and dewy rose
*Shutting their* tender petals *from* the moon.
The grasshoppers are *still*; but not *so soon*
Are still the *noisy* crows.

### § 119. The Subject.

As the Subject names something that is spoken of, it must be:—

1. A Noun. (See p. 17 for the various *kinds of nouns*.)
2. Some word or words that may take the place and do the duty of a noun, as a Pronoun or a Sentence.

Examples:—

| SUBJECT. | PREDICATE. |
|---|---|
| Man | is mortal. |
| He | is erring. |
| He | is in error. |
| Erring | is human. |
| To err | is human. |
| That he erred | is certain. |

An adjective with the definitive article is equivalent to a noun; as, "*the dead*" = "dead man;" cp., "*the wise* are respected."

### § 120. The Enlarged subject.

The simple subject is a word in the *Nominative* case. We may call this the *grammatical subject*.

Every noun, however, may have an adjective joined to it to qualify it. The noun with its adjective is called the enlarged subject; as,

(1) *Sharp words* give offence.
(2) *A virtuous man* will be rewarded.

| SIMPLE SUBJECT. | ENLARGEMENT. | PREDICATE. |
|---|---|---|
| (1) Words | sharp | give offence. |
| (2) Man | a, virtuous | will be rewarded. |

| ENLARGED SUBJECT. | PREDICATE. |
|---|---|
| (1) *Sharp words* | give offence. |
| (2) *A virtuous man* | will be rewarded. |

§ 121. Instead of adjectives we may use words, phrases, or sentences, to qualify or enlarge the subject. These are called Attributes, and may be:—

(1) A noun or pronoun in the possessive case; as, "*John's* hat is lost;" "*his* coat is torn."
(2) An adjective phrase; as, "A man of *wisdom* is respected;" "A walk *in the fields* is pleasant;" "A desire *to learn* is to be encouraged."
(3) An adjective sentence; as, "John, *who is a carpenter*, made this box."
(4) A shortened adjective clause, called a *noun in apposition*; as, "John, *the carpenter*, made this box."

Participles, whether they come before or after the noun, are adjectives; as, "*rolling* stones gather no moss," or "stones, *rolling continually*, gather no moss."

### § 122. The Predicate.

The Predicate is that part of the sentence that makes a statement about the subject. It must therefore contain the chief verb of the sentence. When the predicate is a single word it is a verb; as, "Dogs *bark*."

The verb "to be," when it does not mean *to live*, or *exist*, cannot form a predicate. We must therefore join some word to it to make the predicate; as, "the earth *is round*."

Here we predicate of the earth, *roundness*, not existence; cp., "The lion *is a noble animal*."

Other verbs, like *become*, *seem*, &c., require another word after them to form the predicate.

§ 123. When the Predicate consists of more than a finite verb it may be called the *Enlarged predicate;* as, "The village master *taught his little school*."

When the simple predicate is a transitive verb an object must of course be added (see § 59, p. 42).

| SUBJECT. | PREDICATE. | OBJECT. |
|---|---|---|
| The village master | taught | his little school. |

(1) The object must be a noun, or some word doing duty for a noun. See Subject, p. 102.

Some verbs have two objects, (1) direct, (2) indirect; as,

| SUBJECT. | PREDICATE. | OBJECT. |
|---|---|---|
| They | gave | him (indirect) a book (direct). |

Others have two direct objects:

| SUBJECT. | PREDICATE. | OBJECT. |
|---|---|---|
| They | made | him a king. |

Some writers on grammar call the object the *Completion of the Predicate, or the Complement of the Predicate*.

§ 124. The verb may be qualified by an Adverb, or some word or words doing duty for an adverb. This addition to the predicate is called the Extension of the Predicate *or* Adverbial qualification of the Predicate; as,

| SUBJECT. | PREDICATE. | EXTENSION. |
|---|---|---|
| He | acted | *wisely*. |
| He | acted | *in a wise manner*. |
| He | acted | *as a wise man should act*. |

§ 125. The Extensions are nothing else than adverbial adjuncts or qualifications of the Predicate, and they may be put into the same classes as Adverbs (see p. 74), according as they mark the *when, where, how*, and *why* of the Predicate.

Examples:—

| Subject. | Predicate. | Object. | Adverbial Adjuncts. |
|---|---|---|---|
| The village-preacher's modest mansion | rose | | near yonder copse (place). |
| All | met | | here (place) on a Sunday-eve (time). |
| I | knew | him | well (manner). |
| He | gave | me a book | yesterday (time). |
| Swallows | appear | | spring coming (time). |
| He | came | | to see me (cause). |

### § 126. The Compound Sentence.

When a sentence contains only one subject and one finite verb it is called a Simple sentence. Two